# Long-Range Effects of Child and Adolescent Sexual Experiences

## Myths, Mores, and Menaces

# Long-Range Effects of Child and Adolescent Sexual Experiences

## Myths, Mores, and Menaces

Allie C. Kilpatrick
*University of Georgia*

**LEA** LAWRENCE ERLBAUM ASSOCIATES, PUBLISHERS
1992   Hillsdale, New Jersey          Hove and London

Lawrence Erlbaum Associates, Inc., Publishers
365 Broadway
Hillsdale, New Jersey 07642


**Library of Congress Cataloging-in-Publication Data**


Kilpatrick, Allie C.
    Long-range effects of child and adolescent sexual experiences:
myths, mores, and menaces / by Allie C. Kilpatrick.
        p.    cm.
    ISBN 0-8058-0913-9 (c). — ISBN 0-8058-0914-7 (p)
    1. Child molesting—United States.    2. Sexually abused children—
Mental health—United States.    3. Sexually abused teenagers—Mental
health—United States.    4. Children and sex—United States.
I. Title.
    [DNLM:    1. Child Abuse, Sexual.    2. Child Abuse. Sexual—
complications.    3. Child Abuse, Sexual—United States—statistics.
4. Social Environment—United States.    WA 320 K48L]
RJ506.C48K56  1992
618.92'8583—dc20
    DNLM/DLC
    for Library of Congress                    NOV   5 1992    91-28233
                                                                CIP

Printed in the United States of America
10  9  8  7  6  5  4  3  2  1

*This book is lovingly dedicated to my parents who taught me mores and morals, my husband who helps me identify myths, and my children who provide merriment (and are definitely not menaces).*

# CONTENTS

# FOREWORD

Most of us harbor strong beliefs and convictions about the long-range effects of sexual experiences encountered during childhood and adolescence. Few of us ever have the opportunity to obtain or examine credible evidence about the long-range consequences of the sexual encounters that most of us have experienced during our early years. This book provides an opportunity to learn a great deal about the effects of early sexuality on adult functioning. It does a great deal more.

Many will be shocked and dismayed over the legally sanctioned sexual treatment of children that the author describes. She begins with the writings of our earliest civilizations and brings us up to date so that we can see how beliefs, attitudes, and legal protections have changed over the centuries. The comprehensiveness of her historical review of legal protections from sexual abuse is outstanding in light of its brevity. More importantly, it lays the foundation for addressing a number of agonizing issues throughout the remainder of the book.

Early on the reader will discover that one aim of this book is to debunk some of the myths about the sexual abuse of children. Such an effort is filled with peril because there is always the grave risk of being misunderstood or misinterpreted. Considerable intellectual courage is required when one sets out to collect factual evidence concerning matters that are believed to have been long since settled. This is especially true if the facts tend to refute passionately held beliefs about so sensitive and important a topic as childhood sexual experiences.

In this regard it is difficult to judge wherein a book such as this makes its largest contribution. On the one hand, it is full of sound evidence that will be useful in a great many ways and to a great many who are concerned about human sexuality and the protection of our children from abuse and harm. On the other hand, one of the greatest merits of the book is its effort to examine the equally serious matters of values and definitions with respect to such terms as abuse, neglect, and harm. Nowhere does the author pretend to offer final answers on such matters. However, few can read this book without being challenged to review once more their long held positions and beliefs about such topics.

An important consequence of this effort is that it helps all of us to better understand how the facts that emerge from an investigation are inextricably connected to the values and beliefs of those who shape the research questions and the design of data collection instruments. This is not to suggest that the influence of beliefs and values is a "bad" thing. To the contrary, they are essential and cannot be eliminated. Nor should they be. Yet, if beliefs and values do, and must, shape the nature of our investigative questions it is imperative that we understand them and the influence they have on shaping the "facts" that are obtained. This book presses these issues forward with such great clarity that it should be regarded as essential reading for any who will conduct research in human sexuality. It is equally essential reading for those who would be the consumers of published research in this and related areas of human endeavor.

Beliefs and values are central to the purposes for conducting research of this kind but they play a far greater role in shaping such vital tools as the assumptions and definitions that must be in place for the conduct of such studies. In this regard, the author has made an outstanding contribution in challenging blind adherence to beliefs, values, and definitions that may have served more to confuse than to clarify. Worse yet, they may have led to early "findings" that have been as misleading as they have been informative.

In this regard, the reader is treated to a brief but excellent review of previous research that has been conducted on the long-range consequences of early sexual experiences. One leaves that review with a better understanding of the strengths and weaknesses of prior efforts to understand a vital but surprisingly ignored topic. And there are many other contributions that should not be ignored. The book has much to say about continuing issues for future research and it addresses important methodological problems that many will want to consider for the design of future studies of human sexuality. The book concludes with an excellent discussion of the relevance of findings to treatment, service delivery, and future research and scholarship.

Always discursive and illustrative, rather than being accusatory, the author has performed an outstanding service by identifying the terrible consequences that can come to children when researchers, scholars, and practitioners allow themselves to be guided by theories that have never been validated. Among those consequences are the punishment of victims and the failure to help those who are in great need of assistance and protection. In confronting these examinations the reader is struck by the relevance of theory to the affairs and concerns of real children with real instances of abuse. One sees how grave can be the consequences of flawed and invalidated theory and how useful can be a simple theory that is well grounded in strong evidence. In these portions of the book the author presents her strongest case for the support and conduct of research into the matters of child and adolescent welfare.

The messages and findings of this book will be many things to many people. Some will be disheartening, disturbing, and outrageous. Others will be informative, hopeful, and enlightening. Few will be dispassionate in meaning or consequence for those who are concerned about the welfare of our children. Yet, in considering the materials contained in this book it may be useful to keep in mind the perpetual unwillingness of our culture to deal openly and honestly with matters related to the sexuality of our children.

Finally, there is a considerable and frightening irony that we dare not ignore. In a country that annually spends billions of dollars on the education of children, the future parents of future children, our school systems rarely bother to teach even the simplest rules for becoming a successful parent or how to protect our children from sexual abuse by us or by others. Perhaps we just don't know enough and perhaps this book will help with that.

*Walter W. Hudson*
*Arizona State University*

# PREFACE

*Children are the least articulate and most exploited population suffering from society's failure to confront realistically the phenomenon of human sexuality.*

—Swift (1978)

Historically, our society has had persistent problems concerning sexuality. Preadult and especially child sexuality are sensitive and emotionally charged subjects. Many people, including researchers, have preferred to ignore what goes on sexually in the lives of children (and the effects of those experiences), to interpret what goes on in terms that are made so palatable as to shed little light on the subject, or to confuse scientific inquiry with the perpetuation of pervading moral standards or social norms.

Statistics on the extent of sexual abuse are confounding and ambiguous. A detailed review of 19 studies concerned with the prevalence of sexual abuse shows widespread disparity in results ranging from a low of 6% to a high of 62% of all females who report having suffered childhood sexual abuse (Peters, Wyatt, & Finkelhor, 1986, Table 1.2, pp. 20–21). This disparity comes from varied definitions of terms, sampling problems, and other methodological concerns, which are discussed in chapter 3.

The first National Incidence Study, conducted by the National Center on Child Abuse and Neglect (1980), attempted to determine systematically and comprehensively the incidence of various kinds of abuse. The study used a national probability sample of 29 counties throughout the United States. As noted by agencies and community professionals using standardized definitional criteria, sexual abuse represented 7% of the total number of maltreatment cases reported, resulting in an estimate of 44,700 cases of sexual abuse known to professionals during 1980. This is clearly lower than the national estimates of sexual child abuse if extrapolated from reports by Kinsey, Pomeroy, Martin, and Gebhard (1953), Finkelhor (1979), or Russell (1983). The 1985 report of the national statistics of child sexual abuse from the American Humane Association (1987) notes that with 62 million children in the United States, the 113,000 reported as sexually abused represented an estimated rate of 17.9 sexually abused children per 10,000 U.S. child population. In terms of reporting statistics, sexual abuse continued, in the early 1980s, to be the fastest growing subset of the various kinds of abuse and neglect reports according to Kadushin & Martin (1988). However, many incidence studies are based on special populations, such as college undergraduates, or on one region of the country, such as San Francisco. The greatest problem with figures describing the incidence of sexual abuse is that they are so large that they tend to create disbelief in the public and among many professionals (Conte, 1987).

More recent national incidence studies reflect some changes in incidence reporting. The second National Incidence Study (1988) compared its findings with the findings of the first study that reflected the numbers of children and adolescents who experienced demonstrable harm as a result of maltreatment. These findings provided minimum estimates of the overall incidence. The second study was conducted in response to a specific congressional mandate given in the Child Abuse Amendments of 1984 (P.L. 98-457) and reflected the incidence of children and adolescents who were placed at risk for harm, but not necessarily harmed yet. Thus, the second revised set of definitional standards was broader and more inclusive. By the first standards (minimum estimate) the incidence rate for sexual abuse was 2.2 children per 1,000, which was more than triple its 1980 rate. By the revised standards (broader) the rate was 2.5 children per 1,000. The American Humane Association (1988), using compatible maltreatment data from 14 states that constitutes 35% of the U.S. child population, gives a profile of officially reported child and adolescent maltreatment in the United States for 1986. Their findings show that the rate for sexual maltreatment was 2.1 children/adolescents per 1,000 or 132,000 children and adolescents.

It is necessary, however, to place the sexual abuse of children and adolescents in perspective as it relates to other forms of child and adolescent maltreatment. The second National Incidence Study (using revised and broader standards) reports that 63% of reported cases were for neglect and less than 43% were for all forms of abuse: 5.7 children and adolescents per 1,000 were physically abused; 3.4 were emotionally abused; and 2.5 were sexually abused. These statistics are reversed from the findings of the first study using the original definitions (minimal) that found that the larger percentage of reported cases (56%) were for abuse and 48% were for neglect. The American Humane Association (1988) reported the incidence of child and adolescent maltreatment cases as follows: neglect (55%), physical injury (28%), sexual maltreatment (16%), emotional maltreatment (8%), and other maltreatment (8%). A caveat to keep in mind when placing these figures in perspective is that these statistics are for *reported* cases. Of these reports, only 37%–40% were substantiated in 1987. In fact, the percentage of children and adolescents who were associated with investigations resulting in substantiated findings decreased in 1987 (American Humane Association, 1989). The substantiation report must, however, be balanced by keeping in mind the cases that are unreported.

These statistics do show that many more children and adolescents are in life-threatening situations through neglect and physical abuse than are sexually abused. In fact, many more children die from neglect than from physical abuse or from sexual abuse, which reports zero fatalities (Kadushin & Martin, 1988). Not only is neglect less dramatic than physical abuse and certainly less titillating than sexual abuse, but it is also more difficult to deal with. Neglect situations, according to Polansky (1972), are likely to be long term, diffuse, and unresponsive, whereas there have been better responses to treatment of sexual abuse as discussed in chapter 10.

This book was written in an effort to provide information—and to dispel some myths—that may be helpful to a society that hopes to confront realistically the phenomenon of human sexuality. It is addressed to both clinicians and researchers. Some of the chapters would be especially useful for clinicians, whereas others would appeal more to researchers. I have been interested in the problems related to human sexuality and the long-range consequences of early sexual experiences for a long time. However, I have found much of the research in this area to be flawed and many popular beliefs to be myths. One goal of this book is to debunk some of these myths.

Previous researchers studying child and adolescent sexual experiences have reported conflicting findings regarding the consequences of these experiences. Some report harmful consequences. Clinicians cite case after case where adult functioning, especially in regard to sexual adjustment, is moderately to severely impaired due to abusive sexual experiences during childhood and/or adolescence. Other researchers state that it is society's reactions to the sexual experience that are harmful. Still others report few, if any, harmful consequences of preadult sexual activity. There are also those who believe that early sexual experiences may be beneficial to the child or adolescent. However, despite the continuing debate in professional, lay, and legal circles over the consequences of child and adolescent sexual experiences for functioning in adult life, few empirical studies had been

done until recently concerning the long-range correlates, let alone the consequences of these experiences.

The phenomenon of sexual abuse of children has been met with denial and
repression by our society. Although the existence of sexual abuse has been
recognized by professionals three previous times during the past 130 years, it was
resuppressed each time by the formidable denial and backlash it illicited (Corwin,
1988). Many of the most heated, fascinating, and unresolvable debates about
sexual abuse represent attempts to declare a single extreme position ultimately
true and right by rejecting as illegitimate the interests represented by the opposi-
tion (Goodwin, 1988). This book represents an attempt to present varying views
as they are found both in the literature and in an original research study in an
open, unbiased, and scientific approach.

When I have discussed my study with individuals and groups, my experience
thus far has been that many people do not want to hear what my findings are
saying. They do not want to hear about positive reactions to early sexual experiences. They do not want their preconceived notions that all early sexual experiences are harmful to be challenged. They especially do not want to hear that
incestuous experiences do not always cause irreparable harm. This is particularly
true of those who work with the clinical population of survivors of child or
adolescent sexual abuse. They see the harm that certain types of experiences can
cause. As a clinician, I was somewhat surprised and apologetic myself when I first
analyzed my data as the findings were not always as I had predicted. I had to come
to terms with my own reactions so that I could present my findings in a scientific
and unbiased way. It is my hope that the readers of this book will seriously consider
what the 501 women who participated in this study are saying, and that they will
try to separate myths from facts, mores from scientific evidence and actual
menaces to healthy development from preconceived notions.

Part I of this book focuses on the contexts and issues in studying child and
adolescent sexual experiences. Chapter 1 presents a history of the folklore, informal sanctions, religious, and legal contexts of sexuality including Jewish, Christian, English, and American law. Furthermore, the positive and negative roles of
social scientists (i.e., both Freud and Kinsey and the more recent findings of
Finkelhor) are discussed.

Chapter 2 addresses the substantive issues confronting helping professionals as
they deal with the phenomenon and consequences of child and adolescent sexual
experiences. Specific issues are the varying dimensions of sexual abuse, the quality
of the family environments that provide fertile ground for sexual abuse, and
societal responses to the abuse that is sometimes harmful to victims also.

In chapter 3 some considerations for researchers in studying long-range effects
are presented. These issues include collecting data and studying sensitive areas,
studying different age groups, defining relevant behaviors and partners, what

constitutes harmful experiences, and measuring consequences. Special attention is given to the issue of defining what has been harmed—the child or the moral code of society. Strengths and weaknesses in previous research studies are analyzed using scientific criteria. Findings from research studies are used to test three hypotheses that relate to the long-range effects of child and adolescent sexual experiences. These effects are long-range harmful effects, long-range neutral effects, or long-range beneficial effects. The need for research in the area of long-range effects, as it is pointed out in the literature, is summarized and related to the original study that is presented in Part II.

In Part II the findings of an original research study on the nature and long-range consequences of child/adolescent sexual experiences that was conducted by the author are presented. Chapter 4 gives a description of the retrospective study of 501 women in the southeastern part of the United States. The methodology used, including the measures of present adult functioning, is discussed. Background characteristics of the women in the study are presented.

The nature of the sexual experiences is described in chapter 5. Incidence rates, the types of behaviors experienced, sexual partners, and who initiated the experiences are discussed. Findings from analyzing differences in experiences of the women over the past 60 years serve to debunk some prevailing myths.

Differences in sexual experiences by ethnicity are explored in chapter 6. Primary groups sampled were Black and White.[1] Some surprising findings are reported in this chapter in regard to incidence, behaviors, and partners. Here again some popular myths are dispelled in relation to these two primary ethnic groups.

Chapter 7 gives the various conditions present at the time of the sexual experiences and the respondents' responses to the experiences. The conditions studied were whether the experiences were voluntary or forced, the type of pressure used, if any, whether the partner was at least 5 years older, the size of the community the women lived in as children and as adolescents, and the differences in the sample groups. The findings from the reactions studied are somewhat surprising also, especially those related to the reaction of pleasure and the help wanted by the women when they had the experience.

The primary findings of the study are the consequences of the experiences for adult functioning that are presented in chapter 8. Hierarchical multiple regression analyses were conducted in order to find the relationship between current adult functioning and background variables, sexual experiences as children and adolescents, and long-range consequences. From these findings we are able to see the real menaces of early sexual experiences.

---

[1]The terms *Black* and *White* are considered proper nouns by the American Psychological Association. In this book I follow their ruling made in November 1986 that these terms be capitalized.

A discussion of the findings and their implications follows in chapter 9. Primary implications were found in all the areas studied, and areas of concern are identified. Recommendations resulting from this study are given for clinicians and clinical researchers.

The closing chapter of the book looks at future directions for treatment. Chapter 10 summarizes current treatment programs and presents a composite treatment program for those harmed by early sexual experiences. Prevention measures, including challenging the concept of patriarchy in our culture, are considered.

## ACKNOWLEDGMENTS

I would like, first, to offer my appreciation to all the women who participated in this study of early sexual experiences. Their willingness to share their experiences in this sensitive area and their retrospective observations about them provide the basis for the research presented in this book.

Without the encouragement, support, and assistance that I have received from colleagues, friends, and family, this volume would have remained unwritten. My appreciation is extended to the University of Georgia School of Social Work for the provision of graduate assistants and for funds from the Research Center for computer runs and to the Center for Family Research of the Institute for Behavioral Research for two grants used in the analyses of my data. Thanks go to Walter Hudson who, along with my husband, nudged me into undertaking this needed research in such a sensitive area in the first place. To Clive Davis who, as Editor of *The Journal of Sex Research*, provided helpful editorial suggestions on earlier manuscripts, Ben Saunders for his interest in this project over the past decade, Tom Holland for his on-going support, encouragement, and insights, Martha Cook for her poignant editorial comments, Ken Gauger for the complicated computer runs with over 700 variables, Kay Pitts for her knowledge of APA style, Wynelle Ruark for proofreading and Gray Kilpatrick and Pam Ingle who completed the name and subject indices, I extend my heartfelt gratitude.

Finally, and most importantly, I want to thank Hammond and Lena Callaway for instilling in me early on the thirst for knowledge; Ebb for his love, understanding, and support during all the nights and weekends I agonized over this book; and Gray, Pam, Galen, and Doug for the delightful diversions they provided to an otherwise arduous task. Without them I would not have had the energy nor the incentive to complete this book.

*Allie Callaway Kilpatrick*

# I

# CONTEXTS AND ISSUES IN STUDYING CHILD AND ADOLESCENT SEXUAL EXPERIENCES

# 1

## CHILDHOOD/ADOLESCENT SEXUAL EXPERIENCES IN HISTORICAL CONTEXT

Folklore, informal sanctions, religious laws, legal controls, and scientific research concerning childhood and adolescence provide the historical context within which to place the current debate on effects of these experiences. Folklore and informal sanctions serve as helpful beacons guiding us to the humanistic center of debates. Religious laws and legal controls reveal much about our taboos, and, although incest is an ancient and widespread taboo, the taboo against using children as sex objects is only a few hundred years old (Schultz, 1980). Professionals and social scientists have chosen to buttress existing norms or mores, to challenge them, or to provide new ways of viewing them.

### FOLKLORE

Folktales often incorporate historical data, and some may be the product of centuries of revision and embroidery in the telling of an actual clinical case history (Goodwin, 1988). Thompson's (1955–1958) *Motif Index of Folk Literature* lists more than 20 categories of incest folktales including incest punished, misshapen child from brother–sister incest, child of incest exposed, flight of a maiden to escape marriage to father, suicide to prevent brother–sister marriage, loss of magic powers after incest, God born from incestuous union, incest unwittingly committed, girl got with child by intoxicated father, lustful stepmother, and aunt seduces nephew.

Some incest myths suggest that formal rules against incest are necessary primarily because incest is such a tempting solution to universal conflicts. An example of this is the Navajo Moth-Way Chant (Goodwin, 1988). In this story:

> the Moth-People are delighted when they realize that if they marry their daughters to their sons, families will never have to part or change and they can be together forever. The Moth-People become so excited at this discovery that they all fly into the flames and perish. (p. 26)

Goodwin observed how economically this story describes the intolerance of separation, change, and aging that characterizes some incest families as well as associated tendencies toward immaturity and impulsive self-destructiveness.

Some folklore data provide numerous illustrations of extreme symptoms in incest victims and support the concept that the incest taboo developed because of the interpersonal stresses that surround the incestuous act. Runaways, hysterical symptoms, and suicidal acts are still major clinical problems among incest victims. Clinicians who are treating families that are entangled in intrafamilial child or adolescent sexual abuse may find much in these incest motifs that they recognize. Also, when anthropologists witness incest, the problems of family isolation and deviance are described in terms remarkably similar to those used by clinical observers (Wilson, 1961).

## INFORMAL SANCTIONS

A millennium before the Hebrews wrote their first Bible and the Greeks their *Iliad and Odyssey*, a rich literature existed in the cuneiform system of writing, which was inscribed on clay tablets. These tablets give us the myths, lamentations, epic tales, proverbs, and laws of the ancient civilizations of Sumer, ancestor to our own modern culture. One table relates the story of a Sumerian who, vehemently disapproving of child marriage, declared, "I will not marry a wife who is only three years old as a donkey does!" (Rush, 1980, p. 17).

Each culture's system of informal sanctions may serve to enforce legal or formal sanctions regarding incest and other sexual behavior or to divert them to more workable solutions. Goodwin (1988, 1982) gave several examples of these. The Navajo maintain their very strict prohibition of incest through a series of informal sanctions. Incest participants are said to fall into fires (a common accident in hogans), to have seizures, and to become witches. Even today these sanctions are powerful enough to create serious difficulties for Navajo epileptics, who are automatically assumed to have committed incest and to be a risk for becoming a witch. English Puritans affixed to the offending father a sign describing his sexual misbehavior, a practice similar to the punishment for adultery described in *The Scarlet Letter*. In Africa, such an offense was reported to the woman's society that then gathered at the man's hut and sang loudly all night about the details of his misbehavior. The story of Manekine, Princess of Hungary, illustrates the healing potential of informal sanctions for the victim that emphasizes public confession and apology by the offender. Upon hearing both her father and her husband express remorse for having abused her, the battered heroine miraculously regains both her severed arm and her dead child that their abuse had caused.

In other cultures where the extreme severity of formal rules—usually death and exile—punished both partners without regard for power differentials between partners, there has been a tendency for informal patterns to develop that divert the majority of cases into more workable pathways. For example, in India where the formal punishment for incest is exile, reinforced by folkloric predictions of earthquakes, leprosy, blindness, and sterility, what actually happens is that the accused father "eats his way back" into the community by giving a feast (Elwin, 1939).

In current clinical practice, conflict between professionals attached to formal sanctions such as the criminal justice system and professionals attached to more informal treatment centers often occurs. The problem with the informal system is that it requires unified action by a functioning community, and it requires an offender capable first of feeling shame or guilt and second of using that feeling to modify aggressive and sexual behavior. It is difficult for communities to meet these two requirements and to also protect and provide healing potential for abused children and adolescents.

## RELIGIOUS LAWS

The religious laws most relevant to our culture are those in the Judeo-Christian tradition. These laws are particularly relevant to the current debate regarding sex abuse of children and adolescents.

### Jewish Law

The history as recorded in the Bible and the Talmud leads us to believe that sex between men and very young girls was encouraged in ancient times through marriage, concubinage, and slavery. The Talmud held that a female child of "three years and one day," with her father's permission, could be betrothed by sexual intercourse. Intercourse with a younger child was not a crime but was invalid. If a prospective groom would penetrate the child just once more after her third birthday, he could legitimately claim her as his promised bride (Rush, 1980). The law as translated by Epstein, read "Mishna [the law]: a girl of the age of three years and one day may be betrothed subject to her father's permission by sexual intercourse" (Nezikin, 1935, p. 376). The age of 3 years and 1 day for betrothal or marriage grew out of an old Semitic tradition and cannot be dismissed as myth, nor is it simply a Talmudic academic exercise (Rush, 1980).

Moses Maimonides, the sophisticated 12th-century physician, philosopher, and Talmudist, reaffirmed that the age given was the correct translation of the law (Maimonides, 1972). By the 12th century, age was certainly reckoned as it is today. Rush (1980) stated that this striking lack of concern for the female child could be better understood if one remembers that the Biblical female, no matter what her age, was a property and was stripped of all human attributes. When God commanded, "Thou shalt not covet thy neighbor's house; thou shalt not covet thy neighbor's wife, not his ox, not his maidservant nor anything that is thy neighbor's," he categorized a man's wife with his house and ox. Because the female was a sexual property, all heterosexual relationships were defined as financial transactions. Marriage was the purchase of a daughter from her father, prostitution was a selling and reselling of a female by her master for sexual service, and rape was the theft of a girl's virginity that could be compensated for by payment to her father. Where the Bible was vague regarding the age of the females involved in these transactions, the Talmud was explicit.

Hebrew law is not unique in its treatment of females. Judaic codes were derived from those of earlier nations. The Bible and the Talmud are very similar to the Assyrian and Babylonian codes. Although many other Judiac laws were altered, basic sexual decrees and customs remained unchanged under Christianity and related primarily to female sexuality (Rush, 1980).

Christian Law

Whereas in the Hebrew tradition, sex with a child under 3 was invalid, in the Christian tradition sex with a child under 7 was invalid (Fulton, 1883). Sex between men and children was debated not out of concern for a child but out of regard for the technical violation of the impediment of affinity (or incest) to all her kin. No reference is made to male children because they were not implicated in affinity. Hence, if a man had sexual relations with a child 7 years of age or older, he was in a state of "affinity" to all her kin, and marriage to her mother or sister, for example, was forbidden. If a man had copulated with the child before the child was 7, he did not violate the impediment of affinity and was therefore free to marry her mother or sister. This was true because, as in the Hebrew tradition where sex with a child under 3 was invalid, so under Christianity was sex with a child under

7 invalid. In fact, sex with a child under 7 was inconsequential (Ayrinhac, 1919). This canon law was based on the "one flesh" principle of the New Testament: "A man shall leave his father and mother and shall cleave to his wife, and the twain shall be one flesh" (Matthew 19:5).

Therefore, we see that early Christian law did not focus on whether a man *did* copulate with a child but rather *when* he copulated with her. An example is the Prince of Norway in the 12th century as given by Rush (1980).

> He became the subject of legal discussion when the woman he was to marry was known to have had carnal relations with the Prince's uncle. The uncle was betrothed to this woman when she was under age seven and he had, by common knowledge and a deposition of witnesses, slept with her. Since all this took place before the child's seventh birthday, the Pope declared both betrothal and sexual relations null and void and the Prince was permitted to marry the woman in question. But soon after this decision, the Pope received additional information. The uncle, now dead, had traveled during the time of his betrothal, but when he returned he married the child after her seventh birthday. Since the uncle had had full marital relations with her after she was seven, the Pope was compelled to revoke his earlier decision. If the Prince married her, he would violate the "impediment of affinity." The marriage did not take place. (p. 34)

The clergy enjoyed even greater sexual privileges than ordinary citizens. Even the most humble cleric had the power necessary to exact sexual submission. Women, children, others' wives, daughters, and penitents on a pilgrimage or in the confessional were all violated by their spiritual fathers. In fact, the confessional was so conducive to lechery that Rome issued edicts calling for the punishment of sexual solicitors. However, the church had little enthusiasm for imperiling its own authority (Rush, 1980). Convents controlled by ministers and prelates became the dumping grounds for unmarried, unwanted female children. In the early 18th century the prioress of the convent of St. Caterian di Pisola openly declared that monks and confessors alike treated nuns and young novitiates as wives, but their victim's mouths were sealed by the dread of excommunication threatened by their spiritual fathers (Rush, 1980).


## ENGLISH LAW

Civil law was separated from church law in England under the statutes of Westminster in the 13th century. The need for some form of child protection law was felt in the early 1500s. A law was passed in 1548 protecting boys from sodomy and in 1576 protecting girls under 10 from forcible rape, with both offenses carrying the death penalty (Radzinowicz, 1948). So, although Christianity may have recognized childhood innocence and the need to protect and preserve it in earlier times, secular law did not reflect this as a state interest until the 1500 to 1600 period.

The delineation between childhood and adulthood was raised from age 7 to age 10 in 1576. Sex with a child below age 10 was considered invalid, but it was not illegal. Ten became the legal age at which a female child could consent to sex, and 12 remained the legal age at which she could consent to marriage. Carnal knowledge of a nonconsenting woman child below age 10 became a felony, whereas carnal knowledge of a consenting woman child between the ages of 10 and 12 was a misdemeanor (Hale, 1847). Thus, the crime of statutory rape evolved. However, proof of a child's age had to be offered for the charge of felonious rape to be upheld. This was during a time when few records were kept (Rush, 1980). As late as 1832, a man was freed of the charge of felonious rape in England because the child's baptismal certificate indicated that on the day the rape took place, she was 2 days beyond her 10th birthday (Hale, 1847). Although the new law recognized the act of child rape, child welfare was still being sacrificed to a legal technicality.

The book of Gerson in 1706 indicated that children should be responsible for protecting themselves from sexual abuse and parents should induce guilt when discovering children masturbating. About the same time, Pascal, the prominent educator, offered parents advice for controlling sexual molestation (deMause, 1974). He warned parents to supervise children at all times, to prevent their nudity near adults, to never let them be alone with servants, and to enforce sexual modesty in the home. Schultz (1980) observed that these simple rules may be the first concrete help parents received in controlling sexual abuse. However, children's innocence was to be enforced not just where adults were involved but where the child showed any sexual precocity. For example, parents were instructed to keep candles burning in children's sleeping areas at night so the parents could check for masturbation or self-stimulation (Aries, 1962). Children could experience up to 1,000 enemas during their early years to assist in the removal of "evil" from their bodies (deMause, 1974). Schultz (1980) observed that children were now considered sexually dangerous, with innocence and asexuality to be enforced, which foretold of the coming attacks on children's sexual integrity by a "well-meaning" society.

Schultz (1980) stated that the period up to about 1800 was characterized as a dark time period in which it was normal that children and minors were indiscriminantly used as sexual objects by various adults in a child's social space. The period after 1800 marked the beginning of society's efforts to protect children from their own sexual instincts "for their own good." During these two phases, the basic legal structure was built with the passage of criminal law designed to sexually protect children from adults and from themselves.

Under English law, the age of consent moved from age 10 to 12 in 1861, to age 13 in 1875, and to age 16 in 1885, although a girl could legally marry at age 12. In 1861, a law was passed to protect children from homosexual attack, and in 1968, another law was passed to protect children from exhibitionism (Schultz, 1980).

## LAW IN THE UNITED STATES

In the United States, the early colonies insisted on strict enforcement of Puritan ethics and scriptural law. Special laws were enacted to punish all nonmarital sexual activities. Parents in the 18th and 19th centuries were advised by physicians, teachers, and clergy that sexual feelings in children and sexual precocity led to self-abuse and self-pollution and were etiologically responsible for almost every pediatric ailment known at that time (Schultz, 1980). Children were seen as undisciplined animals who needed protection from their own sexual instincts. "The spirit of children must at all costs be broken—not out of spite, but for their own good" (Schultz, 1980, p. 9).

What innocence there was in children must be preserved until marriage. There was a fear of parental loss of control of minors during the increasing length of the period from puberty to marriage that was the only approved sexual outlet. The necessity of employment and career before marriage for the male and the increasingly earlier age of menstruation for the female due to increased nutrition and health were factors in this longer period from puberty to marriage (Newman, 1975). The family was to be "God's reformatory," and there was a frenzy of antimasturbation efforts by physicians and parents. The fear was that masturbation in boys caused insanity and early death and that girls would become nymphomaniacs or prostitutes. The "unnatural" acts of children were to be suppressed. The emergence of the idea that childhood is based on weakness and the consequent need for protection demanded that parents deny that children had sexual feelings, drives, and any means of gratification (Newman, 1975). This form of sexual suppression of children "for their own good" was marked by periods of sexual brutality that included surgery (such as cauterizations of clitoris or penis, removal of the clitoris without anesthesia, or cutting out nerves) from 1850 to 1879, and physical and psychological constraints (using chastity belts to prevent touching, placing bells on the hands, dressing the child caught masturbating in uniforms that told the community about it, or strapping hands to bedsides) from 1875 to 1925 (Schultz, 1980).

By 1874 the sexual and physical abuse of children was sufficiently recognized as a social problem, and consequently the first Society for the Prevention of Cruelty to Children (SPCC) was formed in New York. Although there were laws to protect children prior to this time, they were not enforced systematically nor did they mandate a responsibility to search out children at risk. The catalyst that initiated the child protection movement in the United States was the case of Mary Ellen in 1878. A church worker learned of the abuse of a child named Mary Ellen and as a last resort approached Mr. Henry Bergh, President of the New York Society for the Prevention of Cruelty to Animals, requesting his intervention. According to Watkins (1990) Bergh had the situation investigated, and the following day Mary Ellen was forcibly removed from her home by a special warrant issued by the New York Supreme Court. Mr. Bergh called this case to the attention of *The New York Times* which publicized the case widely. *The New York Times* quoted him as stating "that in no sense has he acted in his official capacity as President of the Society for Prevention of Cruelty to Animals" ("Mary Ellen," April 10, 1878, p. 8). Although Mr. Bergh made it clear to the court that his actions were that of a humane citizen, he emphasized that he was determined to prevent the frequent cruelties practiced on children within the framework of the law. By 1922 there were 57 SPCCs and 307 humane societies advocating for both children and animals (Fallow, 1987).

Community responsibility for protecting children from sexual abuse took several forms. One was the use of criminal law to protect children sexually from adults, and another consisted of the juvenile code that was used to protect children from themselves. A third consisted of society's informal conflicting messages regarding sex that came from our Puritan heritage. The form the conflicting messages sometimes took was typically: Sex is dirty—save it for marriage; sex is evil—share it with someone you love; sex is sinful—it's a gift from God. Although these messages may have protected some children from sexual abuse, one wonders what harm they did for future marital relationships. Nonetheless, Schultz (1980) stated that from 1890 to 1960 the "child saving movement" (such as the Society for the Prevention of Cruelty to Children) appointed itself as the guardian of children's sexual morality.

With the passage of the Social Security Act of 1935, the responsibility of private agencies for sexually abused and exploited children began to decline as the public sector assumed a greater role. Today all 50 states have well-established and well-accepted laws designed to protect the sexual integrity of children and adolescents. Among those are laws to protect children from sexual molestation, rape, exhibitionism, sodomy, incest, prostitution, and exploitation in films and magazines. Added protection is also given by age-of-consent laws (although ages range from 12 to 18 years depending on the state) and by laws that require various professionals to report sexual abuse when it is brought to their attention (Schultz, 1980).

In addition to this legal protection, a federal Child Abuse Prevention and Treatment Act was first passed in January 1974 and was extended in 1978. In order for states to qualify for federal assistance under the Act, the state statutes on abuse must protect all children under age 18: cover mental injury, physical injury, and sexual abuse; include neglect and abuse reports; guarantee confidentiality of records; guarantee legal immunity for reporters; and provide for a guardian *ad litem* for children whose cases come to court (Kadushin & Martin, 1988).

Some of the more recent trends in the United States have been to move from a punitive approach with an emphasis on punishing the offender to a more cooperative team approach with emphasis on the treatment of the victim and rehabilitation of the family. However, as a result of decreases in funding and in the face of increasing numbers of reports of abuse that must be investigated, protective service agencies during the 1980s began to assign priorities to the kinds of situations that would receive protective services. Sexual abuse was given high priority, but a 1986 national survey of agencies by the Child Welfare League of America found that because of a lack of resources, many state agencies could not comply with laws requiring immediate or early investigation of reports. Children over age 13, unless actually sexually abused, were given lower priority (Kadushin & Martin, 1988).

A recent development in the United Nations that has implications for child and adolescent sexual experiences comes from the adaption by consensus of the Convention on the Rights of the Child in November 1989. By March 1990, 74 countries in the United Nations had signed the Convention. Although signing does not legally bind governments to the Convention, it is seen as an indication that a government accepts the principles in the treaty and intends to seek ratification in its own country. In the United States, the Convention was reviewed by federal agencies prior to being submitted to President Bush. The Convention was voted down in the United States in the fall of 1990.

In 1954, Bender stated that "The seduction of children by adults is a recognized social problem. It has received attention by legislative bodies in all civilized countries" (p. 132). This historical legal review gives examples of the kinds of attention the seduction of children by adults has received over time. Only in the past century has society begun to intervene in family life for the protection of the child. Only in the past two decades has society begun to focus actively on the welfare and rights of children. This movement has recently suffered a setback, however, by the failure of the United States to sign the United Nations Convention on the Rights of the Child.

## THE ROLE OF SCIENTISTS

Where were the professionals, intellectuals, and scientists during the period that seduction of children by adults emerged as a social problem? Two primary figures, one the founder of psychoanalysis and the other a well-known researcher, played prominent roles in this history. A third, also a researcher, provided a more recent study of the problem.

## Freud's Role

Sigmund Freud presented to the world his theory of infant sexuality in 1905. He informed a strongly Victorian society that very small children have strong erotic drives (Rush, 1980). Child sexual experiences played a key role in Freud's ideas about neurosis. In the early 1890s he theorized that the origin of hysterical neurosis lay in the early sexual traumas experienced by young girls. His seduction theory was that these early sexual traumas, often perpetrated by the father, were real and resulted in a variety of neurotic symptoms and adult psychological problems. In his letters to Fliess, which were published in 1954, he wrote, "I have come to the opinion that anxiety is to be connected, not with a mental, but with a physical consequence of sexual abuse" (Freud, 1954, p. 78). Freud pinpointed vulnerability to sexual trauma as occurring during "primary sexual experiences (before puberty) accompanied by revulsion and fright" (Freud, 1954, p. 126).

However, by 1897, Freud changed his mind and renounced the seduction theory—his belief that neurotics were the victims of child sexual abuse, usually by their fathers—for his theory of innate eroticism. The idea that many fathers were guilty of seducing their daughters was distressing to Freud. In public writings and lectures he did not identify fathers as perpetrators but rather named distant relatives, maids, nurses, and governesses as the seducers. Freud became aware of hysterical symptoms in his sisters that cast suspicion on his own father. In another letter to Fliess, he confided that because he detected hysterical symptoms in his brothers and sisters, his own theory meant even his father was implicated as a sexual abuser of children (Gelman, 1981). In his self-analysis he also became aware of his incestuous fantasies regarding his own daughter, his early sexual feelings toward his mother, and his hatred toward his father. Therefore, he hypothesized that girls have sexual feelings toward their fathers and hatred for their mothers (his Oedipal complex theory) and concluded that memories of sexual trauma were based on sexual wish-fulfillment of the child (Asher, 1988). In other words, he decided that the stories he had heard from his patients were fantasies and not fact-based experiences. Thus, fathers were exonerated and were no longer viewed as responsible for causing the symptoms Freud saw in his young female patients. Rush (1980) noted that Freud seemed unable to point the finger in public at his parent or any male parent, but he later admitted in letters to Fliess (Masson, 1985) to having concealed the guilt of fathers in case studies. Clinical practice in evaluating and treating child and adolescent sexual assault victims today has been directly influenced by what now appears to be theoretical and case distortions that were due to the intrusion of Freud's own personal issues and biases (Lerman, 1988).

Bowlby (1984) argued that Freud underestimated the importance of real-life trauma in the etiology of psychological problems. But the seed of doubt had been planted and taken root. Freud's conclusion that child seduction was mainly fantasy may have helped to cover the guilt of fathers for a few additional decades. Finkelhor (1979) believes that Freud's revised theory helped to rationalize two very negative developments in the study and treatment of sexually abused children. The first consisted of discounting the patient's reports of child sexual experiences, and the second consisted of blaming the victim. Even today children are often brutally questioned concerning the reality of their experiences. Many psychoanalysts still interpret women's child experiences as fantasies arising from Oedipal conflicts. Freud's inability to stay with his original theoretical position, which many are viewing as more accurate, may be seen as typical of society's general inability to accept the empirical reality of the sexual abuse of children (Lerman, 1988).

## Kinsey's Role

The Kinsey studies of sexual behavior in the human male and female assembled large samples of carefully taken sexual histories that were reasonably representative of the general population, although only Caucasians were sampled. In their random study of over 4,000 American women, 25% reported a sexual experience with an adult before age 13. (Kinsey, Pomeroy, Martin, & Gebhard, 1953). This study established that child sexual experiences were virtually universal. However, in spite of their survey evidence that incest, sexual abuse, and child molesting were far more widespread than anyone had known, they de-emphasized these findings, stating that incest "occurs more frequently in the thinking of clinicians and social workers than it does in actual performance" (Kinsey, Pomeroy, & Martin, 1948, p. 558). This was in spite of the fact that their study of sex offenders reported that 9% of their sample admitted to researchers that they had had sexual relations with their sisters, aunts, or mothers (Gebhard and others, 1965), and 1 in 23 adult females reported some kind of incestuous experience to researchers (Kinsey et al., 1953). Kinsey also downplayed the effects of these sexual experiences on children, saying, "It is difficult to understand why a child, except for its cultural conditioning, should be disturbed at seeing the genitals of other persons or disturbed at even more specific sexual contact," or "Why any child should be so distraught at having its genitals fondled by a stranger" (Kinsey et al., 1953, p. 121).

By the mid-1960s the Kinsey team, in comparing human sexual behavior with that of animals, stated, "The horror with which society views the adult who has sexual relations with young children is lessened when one examines the behavior of other mammals." They also said that "sexual behavior between adults and immature animals is common and appears to be biologically normal (Gebhard et al., 1965, p. 54). They then added that "disregard for age, sex, and species need not be regarded as biologically pathological; it is precisely what we see in various animals, particularly monkeys" (Gebhard et al., 1965, p. 276).

The Kinsey studies provided the best information available at that time on the real incidence of incest and other child and adolescent sexual experiences in the United States. However, their de-emphasizing of their findings and down-playing of the effects of these sexual experiences served to suppress the truth for several more decades. Despite their study, the common assumptions continued to be that child and adolescent sexual abuse occurred rarely and that when it did occur, it usually involved chance encounters with strangers or mentally disturbed adults. Haugaard and Reppucci (1988) believe that these assumptions were based at least partially on the widespread belief in Freud's theory of development and his rejection of the tenet that fathers could be sexually interested in their daughters. More resent systematic research has shown both these assumptions to be false.

## Finkelhor's Findings

A landmark study, both in terms of his remarkably thorough coverage of the literature and in terms of his findings, was conducted by Finkelhor (1979) in New England. Finkelhor surveyed 796 college students in introductory and upper level courses in six colleges and universities. In that sample 75% were 21 years of age or under, and the vast majority were single. He found that 19% of the women and almost 9% of the men had been sexually "victimized" as children. Finkelhor's definition of victimization was based on age discrepancy between the child and the sexual partner. Victimization included the three categories of: (a) sexual experiences between a child aged 12 years or younger and an adult aged 18 or over, (b) a child aged 12 years or younger and a person under 18 but at least 5 years older than the child, and (c) adolescents aged 13 to 16 and legally defined adults at least 10 years or more older than the adolescent. Finkelhor also found that 66% of the women reported a sexual experience during childhood as compared to 48% in the Kinsey study.

With the kinds of evidence supplied by Freud (in spite of his cover-up), Kinsey (in spite of his de-emphasis and down-playing), Finkelhor, and more recently many others, it is no longer possible to deny the widespread occurrence of child and adolescent sexual experiences, including abuse and incest.

## CONCLUSION

This first chapter places the study of child and adolescent sexual experiences in its historical context. A historical review of ancient and current laws relating to child and adolescent sexuality demonstrates that society is just now moving from a denial of sexual exploitation of children to at least a partial recognition of children's rights. Social scientists have played various roles in both the development of and the understanding of the problem of confronting realistically the phenomenon of human sexuality.

# 2

# THE HELPING PROFESSIONS AND PROBLEMS OF PREVENTION AND TREATMENT

Professionals who work with abused children and adolescents and their perpetrators and who are involved in a tangled web of myths, mores, and menaces are concerned with several problems. The substantive problems with which they are concerned include the dimensions of child sexual abuse, the quality of the family environment, and the societal response to sexual abuse.

## DIMENSIONS OF SEXUAL ABUSE

Although legal definitions of child/adolescent sexual abuse vary, there is increasing agreement among social workers and other helping professionals that sexual abuse of children involves coercive or nonconsenting sexual acts (Berliner & Stevens, 1982). An age difference between partners, the presence of force or coercion, and the developmental appropriateness of the behavior itself are some concepts that have been used to define the parameters of child sexual abuse.

An age difference between sexual partners of 5 years or more when one partner is a child or adolescent has been considered by Finkelhor (1979) to be child victimization. Berliner and Stevens (1982) referred to this form of sexual abuse as sexual exploitation, which involves an inequality between the sexual partners (e.g., when an older person uses superior knowledge, resources, or skills to manipulate the younger person into a sexual relationship). Thus, there are three terms to describe the results of age discrepancy in sexual relationships involving a minor,

all with somewhat different connotations: *abuse, victimization,* and *exploitation.*
The issue raised here is whether age discrepancy in itself is the most relevant
criterion for defining sexual abuse.

Force or coercion is sometimes present in sexual abuse situations. Although the
degree of physical force varies considerably, there is an increasing recognition that
sexual abuse of children is not as nonviolent as was previously thought (Conte,
1987). For example, in the Seattle sample described by Conte and Berliner
(1981), the use of force was threatened or used in 38% of the cases. Rogers and
Thomas (1984) reported a 50% rate in a Washington, DC sample.

However, even without the presence or the threat of force, some professionals
consider any sexual experience between a child and an adult to involve coercion.
This belief is based on the reasoning that much abuse begins at an age when the
child does not fully understand the nature of the act taking place and when the
child lacks the cognitive, emotional, and physical power to say no to the behavior
(Conte, 1987). Finkelhor (1979) suggested that because these conditions make it
impossible for a child to give informed consent, all sexual contact between
children and adults is abusive or, in his terms, victimization. Although this
dimension is couched in terms of force or coercion and informed consent, the age
differential is still at the heart of his argument. There is then the question of
whether age discrepancy in and of itself constitutes an abusive situation.

The developmental appropriateness, or whether the sexual behavior is appropriate for minors at their specific stage of life-cycle development, is the third
dimension that is considered in sexual abuse. Professional concern for children
involved in sexual behavior rests on the debate about whether children have the
physical, intellectual, and emotional capacity to deal with and understand their
own behavior (Conte, 1987). There have been few, if any, studies conducted or
guidelines formulated that assist in determining such developmental appropriateness of specific sexual behaviors, however. Nor have there been studies that
determine when children have the physical, intellectual, and emotional capacities
to deal with and understand the specific sexual behaviors. The concept of life-
cycle developmental appropriateness could provide important guidelines for what
is abuse. However, in order for the concept to be useful to professionals, it is
necessary that what is developmental and what is appropriate be operationalized
in more specific behavioral terms.

## THE QUALITY OF THE FAMILY ENVIRONMENT

Researchers have repeatedly turned to the family environment and the quality of
relationships provided therein when studying sexually abusing families. Low

self-esteem, guilt, depression, problems with sex and relationships, distrust, and self-destructive behavior all grow out of the kind of parenting that prevails in the incestuous family (Justice & Justice, 1979). Because many children take the position of being responsible for their parents (instead of having parents who are responsible for them), they never learned the social skills or received the kind of love and nurturing that are necessary for healthy growth and development. A lack of maternal warmth while growing up was found by Peters (1988) to be the strongest predictor of the risk of sexual abuse.

The greater the family pathology, the greater the tendency for the offender to be more closely related to the family (De Francis, 1969). This means that experiences such as father–daughter incest would be found in the more pathological families. De Francis also found that in 11% of the cases mothers were found to have been child sex-abuse victims. Professionals who treat incestuous families write of a complex web of interpersonal relationships that often involve three generations of a family in complicated interpersonal dynamics (Kaufman, Peck, & Tagiori, 1954). Others have found that incest occurs in two types of families. The first is an ingrown family where members are not able to form meaningful relationships outside the home. The second is a loosely organized family in which sexual relationships of all types are permitted with few restrictions (Weinberg, 1955).

Additional findings are that the severity of complaints of incestuous actions are related to the degree of family disorganization (Herman & Hirschman, 1977); that abuse in families can be attributed to loose and chaotic organization within the family and solid boundaries between the family and the outside world as well as to other personal, interpersonal, and contextual factors (Bardill, 1977); and that more severe adult symptoms are the result of a more negative family environment (Conte, Briere, & Sexton, 1989). Other characteristics of incestuous families that have been reported are social isolation (Brooks, 1982; Finkelhor, 1984; Johnson, 1983), negative enmeshment (Brooks, 1982), and a high degree of internal disorganization and skewed family structure (Johnson, 1983). Lewis, Beavers, Gossett, and Phillips (1975) found that healthy families (by contrast with dysfunctional ones) have closeness but with distinct personal and generational boundaries.

Thus, the theme of the family environment is an important one. Research findings indicate that the kind of parenting a child receives can be quite abusive. Research findings have provided family assessment tools for dysfunctional families as well as guidelines for healthy family functioning (Achenbach & Edelbrock, 1985; Bardill, 1977; Hudson, 1982; Lewis et al., 1975; Moos & Moos, 1976; Olson et al., 1982; Olson, Sprenkle, & Russell, 1979). Saunders, McClure, and Murphy (1987) have developed a multilevel, multirespondent empirical assessment protocol for sexually abusing families. By using such assessment tools, guidelines, and protocols, it may be possible to develop more functional social norms for family environments.

Some theoreticians have different notions, however, concerning the contribution of the family environment to child sexual abuse. Although preventive measures such as privacy, no overstimulation of the child by the parents, changes in family affection patterns as the child grows older (Rosenfeld, 1977), and the avoidance of nudity with pubertal and near-pubertal children are advocated by some, some feminists do not agree. They see child or adolescent sexual abuse as a result of a patriarchal society. Among some feminists there is a clear recognition that incest taboos or aversions are, at best, weak and easily overcome (Brownmiller, 1975; Janeway, 1981; Rush, 1980). According to Vander Mey and Neff (1987), the key questions then become: "What are the effective external barriers to child and adolescent sexual abuse and incest?" "How can we strengthen those barriers, add to them, and insure that they are in place throughout all segments of our society?" This orientation to the problem challenges the fundamental assumptions of most traditional taboo and aversion theoretical orientations. It is congruent, however, with ecological as well as with feminist orientations because it focuses on the larger societal problem.

From a feminist perspective, consciousness raising may prevent some incest, but father–daughter incest can be eradicated only with the disappearance of male supremacy. Some believe that the greater the degree of male supremacy in any culture, the greater the likelihood of child sexual abuse (Herman & Hirschman, 1977; Rush, 1980). Thus, a patriarchal society could in itself promote abuse of children. The argument is that incest occurs in patriarchal systems where fathers exercise their power and thereby initiate such prohibited relationships. The father has the power and ability to exploit the daughter due to the structure of both the family and society. McIntyre (1981) stated that male supremacy is the cornerstone of the pathological family system.

It can be argued that both society's patriarchal norms and dysfunctional family patterns are major contributing factors to sexual abuse of both males and females. In any prevention or treatment program, both must be addressed. Society's role is discussed further in the following section.

## SOCIETAL RESPONSE TO SEXUAL ABUSE

A third issue is that the helping process involved in child sexual abuse and the helpers themselves are sometimes harmful to children. The National Center of Child Abuse and Neglect (1978) has reported that in the sexual abuse of children "there is often as much harm done to the child by the system's handling of the case as the trauma associated with the abuse" (p. 3244). Schultz (1973) stated that:

> By far the greatest potential damage to the child's personality is caused by society and the victim's parents as a result of (a) the need to use the victim to prosecute the offender, and (b) the need of parents to prove to themselves, family, neighborhood, and society that the victim was free of voluntary participation and that they were not failures as parents. (p. 150)

Schultz added that in most instances sexual trauma, unless reinforced by court testimony or parental overreaction, produced few permanent consequences. He further concluded that it "is clear from studies of child sexual victims that it is not the sexual assault that usually creates trauma, but the parent's behavior upon its discovery, and the effect of this on the child" (p. 150).

There are at least four factors resulting from institutional and societal responses that could be harmful to children and adolescents. These include the imposed secrecy during the abuse, the effects of disclosure, the climate of the environmental response, and the emphasis on prosecution of the offender, all of which are intricately intertwined.

The secrecy imposed upon victims of child sexual abuse usually carries with it threats of harm of some type if the secret is divulged. Professionals who work with these victims see the fear and anxiety manifested when the secret is revealed. A cluster of symptoms in abused children and adolescents resulting from the child's sense of pressure to keep the sexual abuse a secret has been identified by several researchers (Burgess & Holstrom, 1974; Gagnon & Simon, 1969). These symptoms are also in reaction to the disclosure of the secret. More severe adult symptoms have been found to be the result of the child's perceptions of what would happen if he or she revealed the abuse, that is, the child would not be believed or would die (Conte et al., 1989).

The effects of disclosure can be quite traumatic for the victim. For example, blame and disbelief by other family members may be devastating. Many times the way reports are handled by the helping professions contributes to the blaming of the victim and the invalidation of the child's disclosure, even though clinical experience suggests that few children falsely report victimization (Conte, 1987). An excellent illustration of this was given by a judge in Wisconsin who made the following statement in regard to a sexual assault on a 5-year-old girl by a 24-year-old man with whom her mother was living: "I am satisfied we have an unusually sexually promiscuous young lady (5 years old) and that this man (24 years old) just did not know enough to knock off her advances. No way do I believe he initiated the sexual contact that did take place" (Judge, 1982, p. 9A). The child was placed in a foster home. The tendencies to blame the victim and to discount the child's own reports were promoted by Freud and is still prevalent today. However, our society is also guilty of acting in the opposite extreme in the effort to handle what is seen as potentially dangerous situations. For example, in the wake of scandals of sexual abuse in residential centers for children who were not treated responsibly by professionals in a timely fashion, one such center reacted to reports of sex play among latency age boys by calling in the police, sending some of the boys to correctional institutions, and notifying families. One wonders what damage these types of overreactions may be responsible for in terms of normal sexual development. Other effects of disclosure are sexual advances by other men who see the child or adolescent as "fair game," removal from the home, and stressful legal involvement (Justice & Justice, 1979). In their study of the reaction of the child's social system to the disclosure of incest, Summit and Kryso (1978) concluded that the harm observed from incestuous encounters correlates not so much with the forcefulness or the perversity of the encounter as with the climate of environmental response. An illustration of the potential harmfulness of the environmental response is provided by a KNY wire article in March 1982 (Herhold, 1982). A 16-year-old girl was placed in Juvenile Hall behind bars in San Jose, California, for refusing to testify against a former police officer (her Girl Scout adviser) who was facing felony charges for having sex with her. A girlfriend's mother had found her diary describing the encounter and turned it over to the police. Both the girl and policeman admitted their mutual affair, and the girl did not press charges. In this case, it seems that society's response may have caused more harm than the sexual experience itself.

The age of the child or adolescent at the time of the disclosure is a factor in the response of the victim as well as in the response of other persons in the child's social environment. The finding that incest is least harmful psychologically for the younger child, with the risk increasing as the child approaches adolescence, has been documented by several researchers (Sloane & Karpinski, 1942; Summit & Kryso, 1978). Their research maintains that harm resulted from the perception by the child that sexuality is socially inappropriate and that the relationship is exploitative. The various aspects of guilt and betrayal are potentiates both by increasing sophistication in the child and by guilt and ambivalence perceived in the parents. Thus, if the active agent (father) and especially the nonparticipating adult (mother) are comfortable with the incestuous relationship, harm to the child is decreased, according to Sloane and Karpinski.

Parental reactions are a crucial ingredient in the societal response to sexual abuse. In a study of 70 sexually abused children and adolescents and their parents who were treated at the Sex Abuse Center for Children in Honolulu, Mann and Gaynor (1980) specifically studied parental reactions. In this study, 90% of the subjects were female. The subjects were from all social classes and ethnic backgrounds with no predominance of any group. Mann and Gaynor reported that the parental reaction to the assault (including single or multiple, short-term, nonfamily-related sex-abuse incidents), which was usually severe, was the decisive factor in the child's recovery from the assault. Six common parental coping patterns were identified: supportive, overreactive, overprotective, rejecting, overstressed, and problem-child oriented. Only the first two groups benefited from crisis intervention. The rest required more intensive psychosocial support. Their findings—that the severity of symptoms in children and adolescents increased with age—support similar previously discussed findings by Sloane and Karpinski (1942) and Summit and Kryso (1978).

The fourth source of potential harm to children and adolescents who are involved in sexual abuse is the emphasis on the prosecution of the offender rather than on treatment of the victim. As early as 1964, Brunold found that for some of the women he studied, the investigation by the police or the court procedure had a more negative impact than did the offense. In 1969, De Francis reported that the impact of the sexual offense for children was magnified and heightened by the procedures invoked by the prosecution of the offender.

This emphasis on the prosecution of the offender rather than on the well-being of the child has its roots in the early years of the Society for the Prevention of Cruelty to Children (SPCC). The New York SPCC stated its central aim to be "the relentless prosecution of those who have made helpless childhood their victim" (Forty-Second Annual Report, 1916, p. 35). Their approach was to remove children from dangerous situations, which could be interpreted by the victims as punishing them for the offense, and to prosecute maltreating adults, for which victims have the tendency to assume the blame. Many authorities agree that the emotional damage resulting from the intervention of helping agents in our society may equal or far exceed the harm caused by the abusive incident itself (De Francis, 1969; Giarretto, 1976; McKerrow, 1973; Miner, 1966; Schultz, 1973; Sgroi, 1978). From this review it seems that reactions and interventions of the helping agents (social agencies, police, courts, parents and other social systems) may, indeed, promote the possibility of harmful consequences to the child.

## CONCLUSION

Various aspects that confront helping professionals who work with child and adolescent victims of sexual abuse have been identified. One aspect is the varying dimensions in sexual abuse such as age discrepancy between partners, the presence of force or coercion, and the life-cycle developmental appropriateness of the sexual behavior itself. A second aspect is the quality of the family environment in which sexual abuse takes place. This includes dysfunctional family patterns as well as society's patriarchal norms. A third aspect consists of society's response to sexual abuse that includes four sources of potential harm to children and adolescents: the imposed secrecy during the abuse, the effects of the disclosure, the climate of the environmental response, and the emphasis on prosecution of the offender instead of the well-being of the victim.

These are all issues with which professionals must deal when working in the difficult area of child and adolescent sexual abuse. It is not an easy task to carry out society's mandate for protection and treatment of the victims when the issues are not clear or when there are several opposing issues or forces at work. Despite the existence of theories of sexual abuse, helping professionals lack practical standards to guide their work, and with the paucity of program evaluations to determine effectiveness, it is likely that some services will be misdirected, based on weak theory or delivered by poorly trained workers.

# 3

# CONSIDERATIONS FOR RESEARCHERS

There is currently a high level of societal interest in incest and sexual abuse of children and adolescents. It is, therefore, important that more attention be given to researching the implications of various child and adolescent sexual experiences. Until fairly recently, however, little emphasis has been placed on the study of long-range effects of such experiences.

In order to identify issues, problems, and gaps in the study of long-range effects of child and adolescent sexual experiences, I reviewed 39 major research studies that report or attempt to account for long-range effects. These studies do not constitute a comprehensive review of all studies on child and adolescent sexual experiences. The review is selective in that it only deals with research concerned primarily with the long-range outcomes of these experiences. Single case reports and studies that dealt primarily with offenders, epidemiology, treatment, or short-term effects are not included. Studies published through 1987 are included with the exceptions of Jackson, Calhoun, Amick, Maddever, and Habif (1990) and Okami (1989) whose works were shared with me while they were in process and have since been published.

PRIMARY ISSUES

In my analysis of these 39 major research studies, I identified specific issues that researchers must confront if they are to examine long-range effects of child and adolescent sexual experiences. This set of issues and methodological problems is not exhaustive, but it does call attention to crucial components. As specific issues are discussed, attention is given to how the various studies addressed the issues. Table 3.1 provides definitive information concerning each study. A more detailed analysis of each study is given in Appendix A.

Collecting Data on Sensitive Areas

Most researchers agree that the study of phenomena when they occur is more desirable than studying them in retrospect. However, researchers who have attempted to study the sexual abuse of children and adolescents at the time of the abuse have encountered difficulties. One difficulty is the moral dilemma of asking children and adolescents very sensitive questions about their sexual behavior or about the sexual behavior of family members and other acquaintances; the researcher is faced with the potential of upsetting them by asking such sensitive and personal questions. This is especially true when the offending adult has made threats to the child about what will happen if the child tells anyone about the behavior. If a child does tell, by law the researcher must report the situation to the proper authorities. If the offending adult is a parent, then often the result of the investigation is that either the child or the parent is removed from the home. It is not unusual for the child to assume the blame for this disruption of the family (Kilpatrick & Lockhart, in press).

One major constraint in studying such sensitive issues is that the family is considered to be a private institution (Gelles, 1974, 1980; Pagelow, 1981; Straus, Gelles, & Steinmetz, 1980). Therefore, most family interactions take place behind closed doors, out of sight of neighbors, friends, and social researchers. In order to study the family, some researchers have made use of methods and research instruments that allow them to penetrate the walls of the family without actually going into the homes of the families. The difficulty of invading the privacy of the family in order to obtain parents' permission to interview a minor and gain accessibility for research purposes is evident. The situation is complicated further by the fact that the federal government and college and university human subjects committees impose guidelines for studies of sensitive topics under their sponsorship. The typical guidelines contain provisions that call for subjects to give their informed consent. This informed consent assures that the participants have been provided with a full explanation of the research being conducted and that they

TABLE 3.1
Long-Range Effects of Childhood/Adolescent Sexual Experiences

| Researcher, Data, Location | Type of Experience and Age | $N^a$ | Sample Source | Ages & Population Studied[b] | Method/Measures Used | Long-Range Effects Reported[c] |
|---|---|---|---|---|---|---|
| Rasmussen (1934) Norway | Assault, including incest (children) | 54 | Court records | Adults (F, LC) | Interviews, 3rd person reports | 0 to – |
| Sloane & Karpinski (1942) U.S. (PA) | Parental, sibling incest (teen-age) | 5 | Family welfare agency | 18–26 (F, LC) | Interviews (psychotherapy) | – to 0 |
| Bender & Grugett (1952) U.S. (NY) | Various, prolonged (5–13) | 14 | Psychiatric hospital | 21–27 (M&F) | Social & Psychiatric follow-up | 0 to – – |
| Weinberg (1955) U.S. (IL) | Parental, sibling incest (15 av.) | 203 | Criminal cases | Adults (F, LC) | Structured interviews in home | – to – – |
| Landis (1956) U.S. (CA) | Sex with adults (children) | 500* | University students | Adults (M&F, MC-UC) | Questionnaires | 0 to – |
| Greenland (1958) Great Britain | Parental, other incest (uk) | 7 | Advice column | 15–32 (F) | Analysis of letters | – to 0 |
| Kubo (1959) Japan | Parental, other incest (7–23) | 36 | Clinic & agency records | Adults (M&F, LC) | Records and interviews | – to 0 |
| Vestergaard (1960) Copenhagen | Parental incest (8–17) | 13 | Court records | 23–32 (F, LC) | Personal interviews | – – to – |
| Weiner (1962) U.S. (NY) | Parental incest (10–13) | 5 | Psychotherapy with father | 10–23 (F, MC) | Interviews with father | – to 0 |
| Brunold (1964) Netherlands | Assault (5–15) | 62 | Court records | 23 av. (M&F, LC) | Personal and 3rd person interviews | 0, + to – – |
| Gagnon (1965) U.S. | Various, with adults (prepuber.) | 333* | Kinsey study | Adults (F, MC) | Structured interviews | 0 to – |
| Chaneles (1967) U.S. | Assault, paternal incest (children) | 159 | Agency case records | Children (M&F, LC) | Conjecture | – |
| Medlicott (1967) New Zealand | Parental incest (children) | 27* | Psychotherapy cases | 18 up (M&F) | Interviews (psychotherapy) | –, – – to 0 |

27

TABLE 3.1 (continued)

| Researcher, Data, Location | Type of Experience and Age | N[a] | Sample Source | Ages & Population Studied[b] | Method/Measures Used | Long-Range Effects Reported[c] |
|---|---|---|---|---|---|---|
| De Francis (1969) U.S. (NY) | Sex offense by adults (0–15) | 263 | Child protection agencies | Children (M&F, LC) | Objective & subjective measures | – – to 0 |
| Lukianowicz (1972) Northern Ireland | Parental, other incest (5–14) | 55 | Gen. hospital patients | 11–33 (M&F, LC) | Interviews (psychotherapy) | 0 to – |
| Katan (1973) U.S. (OH) | Rape (1–5) | 6 | Private practice | 20–40 (F, MC–UC) | Interviews (psychoanalysis) | – – |
| Benward & Densen-Gerber (1975) U.S. | Parental, sibling incest (under 15) | 52* | Drug treatment center | Adol.-adults (F, LC) | Structured interviews | – to – – |
| Molnar & Cameron (1975) Canada | Parental incest (14–17) | 18 | Hospital psychiatric dept. | 14–37 (F, LC) | Interviews (psychotherapy) | – to – – |
| Herman & Hirschman (1977) U.S. | Parental incest (4–14) | 15 | Psychotherapy cases | 15–55 (F) | Interviews (psychotherapy) | 0 to – |
| James & Meyerding (1977) Western U.S. | Older partner (children) | 228 | Prostitutes | Adol.-adults (F, LC) | Questionnaires, interviews | – to – – |
| Meiselman (1978) U.S. (CA) | Parental, other incest (3–11) | 58* | Psychiatric clinic | 11–43 (F, LC–MC) | Interviews, charts, MMPI | – – to 0 |
| Justice & Justice (1979) U.S. (TX) | Parental, sibling incest (children) | 112 | Clinical | Families (M, F) | Interviews, records (psychotherapy) | – to – – |
| Gross (1979) U.S. (OH) | Parental incest (13–15) | 4 | Hospital psychiatric clinic | 15–16 (F) | Hysterical seizures | – – |
| Goodwin et al. (1979) U.S. (NM) | Parental, other incest (0–10) | 6 | Hospital psychiatric dept. | 14–18 (F) | Hysterical seizures | 0 to – – |
| Tsai et al. (1979) U.S. | Incest and other (6–12 av.) | 60* | Clinical, non/clinical | 18–65 (F, MC) | MMPI, scales, self-report | – to 0 |

TABLE 3.1 (continued)

| Researcher, Data, Location | Type of Experience and Age | $N^a$ | Sample Source | Ages & Population Studied[b] | Method/Measures Used | Long-Range Effects Reported[c] |
|---|---|---|---|---|---|---|
| Bernard (1981) Netherlands | "With pedophile" (7–15) | 30 | Convenience sample | 20–60 (M&F, LC–MC) | Self-report | +, 0 to – |
| Symonds et al. (1981) U.S. (CA) | Sibling, other incest | 109 | Ads in newspapers | 26–45 (M&F, MC) | Phone interviews | 0,+ to – |
| Nelson (1981) U.S. (CA) | Parental, other incest (3 up) | 100 | Ads in periodicals | 19–73 (M&F, MC) | Questionnaires (mailed) | 0,+ to – |
| Finkelhor (1981) U.S. (New England) | Sex with sibling (0–13+) | 7968 | College students | Adults (M&F, MC–UC) | Questionnaires | 0,+ to – |
| Fritz et al. (1981) U.S. (WA) | Various (Prepubertal) | 952* | College students | 18 up | Questionnaires | 0 to – |
| Emslie & Rosenfeld (1983) U.S. (CA) | Incest (4–14) | 268 | Psychiatric hospital | 9–17 (F) | Personal interviews | 0 to – |
| Sedney & Brooks (1984) U.S. | Various (children) | 301* | College students | 18–58 (F, MC–UC) | Questionnaires | – |
| Cleveland (1986) U.S. | Parental incest (5–8) | 3 | Mixed | 26–28 (F) | Life history interviews | – to 0 |
| Kilpatrick (1986) U.S. (GA & FL) | Various (0–14) | 501* | Deliberate sample | 18–66 (F, MC) | Questionnaires scales | 0,– to + |
| Herman et al. (1986) U.S. (CA) | Incest (0–18) | 205* | Clinical, nonclinical | 24–53 (F, MC) | Interviews, clinical records | –,–,0 |
| Bryer et al. (1987) U.S. (?) | Sexual abuse | 66* | Hospital inpatients | 18–64 (F, MC) | Questionnaires records | –,–,- |
| Saunders et al. (1987) U.S. (SC) | Crime Victims | 391* | Self-selected from representative sample | 18 up (F, MC) | Structured interviews | –,–,0 |

29

TABLE 3.1 (continued)

| Researcher, Data, Location | Type of Experience and Age | $N^a$ | Sample Source | Ages & Population Studied[b] | Method/Measures Used | Long-Range Effects Reported[c] |
|---|---|---|---|---|---|---|
| Jackson et al. (1990) U.S. (GA) | Incest (0–18) | 40 | Newspaper & radio ads, Uni. students | 18–33 (F, UC) | Battery of instruments | –,–,– |
| Okami (1989) U.S. | Various (3–15) | 70* | Media advertisements | 16–69 (M&F, MC) | Battery of instruments, interviews | +,–,0 |

[a]An * indicates the study included a control population.

[b]F=female, M=Male, LC=lower class, MC=middle class, UP=upper class.

[c]Indicates reported outcomes from very negative(– –), negative (–), neutral (0), to positive (+). The first symbol indicates most frequent outcome reported.

have been informed that they can withdraw at any time. If legal minors (under 18 years of age) are participants, a problem with informed consent arises because it must be obtained from parents or guardians prior to meeting with the minor. This restriction virtually guarantees that children will seldom be subjects of research on sensitive topics (Gelles, 1978).

A problem also exists in studying sexual abuse retrospectively. This problem concerns questions about the reliability of this retrospective data. The accuracy of recall of details must be considered, and other threats to validity of recall data must be recognized. There is the possibility of memory loss or impression management. Minor incidents related to the experience may be forgotten or distorted. There is no way to verify the data with the reported partner or abuser. It is also impossible to trace the current condition in a direct causal line from the previous conditions associated with the sexual abuse (Kilpatrick, 1987).

Thus, there is no easy answer to the issue of when to collect such sensitive data. It would be ideal if data were collected at the time of the abuse, and then the victims were followed developmentally into adulthood in order to study long-range effects. Of the 39 studies reviewed, 64% were retrospective studies of adults.

## Studying Sensitive Areas

First, the size of the sample is becoming increasingly important. Research on sexual abuse has moved beyond the stage of descriptive studies. Larger samples are needed that are theory-driven, methodologically advanced, and that lend themselves to more sophisticated analytic procedures. Of the studies listed in Table 3.1, 7 based their findings on fewer than 10 cases, 16 used fewer than 50 cases, 24 used fewer than 100 cases, and 33 used fewer than 300 cases. Three studies used between 300–500 cases (Gagnon, 1965; Saunders et al., 1987; Sedney & Brooks, 1984), and 3 studies based their findings on over 500 cases (Fritz, Stoll & Wagner, 1981; Kilpatrick, 1986; Landis, 1956). The majority (64%) of the studies published since 1981 and shown in Table 3.1 used over 100 cases. This is an indication of a trend away from small descriptive case studies toward studies of larger samples.

Second, the use of control or comparison groups is just as necessary in the study of sensitive areas as in any other subject. Without such groups it is impossible to determine causal effects or isolate contributing factors. However, only 16 of the 39 studies reviewed (41%) utilized control groups, 10 of which have been published since 1981.

Third, the use of clinical and offender populations should be considered when collecting data on sensitive areas. An example of the problems involved in using samples from these types of populations is found in Meiselman (1978). She found a higher incidence of sexual problems of all types among patients with father–

daughter incestuous experiences than among patients without incestuous experiences. If a woman seeks help because she has problems in social functioning, and she is then selected for study because she has a history of certain childhood sexual experiences, it is impossible to determine whether the problems in social and personal functioning are due to the childhood sexual experiences or to all the other things that may lead to the problem being treated. Another problem with this type of study is that it is not known how these cases differ from a nonclinical population. The same points can be made for offender populations. Primarily, the use of these populations tends to create bias and to limit the generalizability to other populations. Of the studies reviewed, 64% utilized clinical or offender populations.

Fourth, combining socioeconomic groups should also be questioned. Combining the findings across the range of socioeconomic groups tends to obscure differences in long-range effects. Background variables that include socioeconomic variables explain more variance in adult functioning than do types of sexual experiences women had as children (Kilpatrick, 1986). Controlling for socioeconomic class and using comparison groups provide more definitive data on effects that can be attributed to child sexual experiences and not the socioeconomic class of the subject. In this review, most of the studies sampled many classes. Nine studies did not specify the socioeconomic group used. There were 12 studies in which primarily lower-class samples were used, 11 used primarily middle-class samples, 4 used middle- to upper-class samples, 2 used a lower to middle-class sample, and 1 used an upper-class sample.

Other considerations for researchers when collecting data on the long-range effects of early sexual experiences are the specificity of which outcomes are for males and which are for females and the separation of racial and ethnic groups in order to determine if racial/ethnic differences exist. Research on long-range outcomes for both males and minority groups has been neglected.

## Studying Different Age Groups

Another issue for researchers is the combining of different age groups in the study. Problems occur when ages of the sample groups vary but are combined, and general conclusions are drawn. The studies reviewed included samples from ages 1 to 77. Also, the interval between when the child or adolescent experiences occurred and when the effects were studied varied from a few years to 50 years. Of particular concern is the combining of data on effects in prepubertal children with postpubertal children. Early researchers found that prepubertal experiences are more critical (Bender & Blau, 1937; Rasmussen, 1934). Later findings are in marked contrast to these earlier results. More recent researchers have found that effects are much more critical after puberty (Mann & Gaynor, 1980; Murphy et al., 1988; Peters, 1984; Sloane, & Karpinski, 1942). The findings are that sexual abuse in the postpubertal period leads to serious repercussions. This contrast may be explained by the increased strength of the superego in the postpubertal years. In the teenage years adolescents realize that sexual experiences with family members are not socially acceptable. As children they believed whatever they were told by their parents and trusted them to know what was best for them. When children realize that a discrepancy exists between what their parents and society say is acceptable, somehow they begin to blame themselves. Guilt and self-blame are important factors in the reactions to incestuous experiences especially by the postpubertal female. In other words, older victims may suffer more negative consequences because they are more aware of the sexual meaning of the abusive experience and more likely to feel responsible for its occurrence. The point is that the two age groups of prepubertal and postpubertal females should be studied separately and compared for similarities and differences. When generalizations are made across these groups, important data may be lost, and findings may be misleading.

## Defining Relevant Behaviors

Whatever behaviors are included, researchers must be specific about which ones they are studying and how they are defined and ensure that they are separated for analysis. Specific behavioral definitions should be given for each behavior. For example, the definitions of *incest* in the studies reviewed range from the dictionary definition of *incest* (*Webster's*, 1978) as "sexual intercourse between persons too closely related to marry legally" (Kilpatrick, 1986) to a definition of *incest* that includes the behavior of sexual propositioning (Finkelhor, 1979) to a definition that includes various behaviors with relatives by marriage as well as by blood (Meiselman, 1978). In the 47 studies cited by Meiselman, 22 used *intercourse* as the incest criterion, 14 used *sexual contact*, 7 used *sexual approach*, and 4 defined incest as either *advances, attempts at incest, abnormal sexual interest,* or *strong incestuous wishes*. The studies reviewed in this chapter used *intercourse, fondling, exposure, attempted seduction,* and vague, nonspecific terms such as *seduced, had relations,* or *a wider range of comportments which may or may not include intercourse.*

Thus, terms describing sexual behaviors are used differently by different researchers, and the same terms are often used to describe different behaviors. The concern is that researchers are making generalizations about behaviors that may be too varied for such general conclusions to be valid. It is necessary to determine that outcomes are consistent across types of behaviors before such generalizations are appropriate.

## Defining Relevant Partners

Definitions vary, also, with respect to the partner involved. An elaboration of this confusion is seen in the Meiselman review. Of the 47 studies cited in that review, 36 used *blood relative* as the incest partner criterion, whereas 11 used both blood relative and *relative by marriage*. Of the more than 21 studies involving incest that are reviewed in this chapter, partners are described as *parental, paternal, sibling,* or *other*.

Researchers focusing on *child–adult contacts* have also varied in their definitions of *adult* and *child*. For example, some researchers referred to *parent–child relations,* and some of these were so vague that the reader is unable to determine their definitions of child and adult. The majority of these researchers did not specifically deal with this concern. Gagnon (1965) defined *adult* as a male at least 5 years older and postpubertal, whereas the female was prepubertal. A *child* was a female before age 13. Finkelhor (1979) used three categories: (a) a child 12 or under with an adult 18 or over, (b) a child 12 or under and another person under 18 but at least 5 years older than the child, and (c) adolescents 13 to 16 and legally defined adults at least 10 or more years older than the adolescent. Kilpatrick (1986) studied children ages birth through 14 years and defined *older partner* as a person at least 5 years older than the child.

The concern is the lack of specificity about the ages of both partners. Researchers often generalize about effects of partners without specifying if partners are older, younger, or of the same age. In their conclusions, researchers need to discriminate between partners of different ages who had sexual experiences with children of various ages.

## Defining Harmful Experiences

*Abuse* has been the catch-all term for almost any type of child–adult contact. However, other terms are used by researchers to refer to similar partners. Finkelhor (1979) referred to child–adult contact in all three of his previously mentioned categories as *victimization*. This term is based, however, not on effects on the child but on age discrepancy and community standards regarding exploitative sexual relationships. Fritz et al. (1981) used the term *molested* in much the same way Finkelhor used *victimized* and as Gagnon used *child–adult contact*. *Molested children* were those who reported at least one sexual encounter with a postpubertal individual before the child reached puberty. Kempe and Kempe (1978), in a review of child abuse, defined *sexually exploited children* as those children and adolescents who are robbed by sexual abuse of "their developmentally determined control over their own bodies and of their own preference, with increasing maturity, for sexual partners on an equal basis" (p. 43). In their view, all sexually exploited children are categorized as *harmed* although no specific measure of harm was used.

Of primary importance is whether the researcher defines *abuse* as some type of harm (a consequence of sexual activity that can be quantitatively measured) or whether *abuse* is defined in relation to violation of social norms or mores. When the two issues of scientific objectivity and maintenance of moral standards are not separated, problems arise in tying to determine what it is that has been harmed, abused or violated: Is it a child or an adolescent, or is it society's expectations? This tension between science and the real world is important. On the one hand, science is a pursuit to understand the world as it is. On the other hand, social norms are rules by which people choose to live. Failure to make a distinction between the two has caused many researchers to buttress existing social norms or morals rather than to conduct scientific investigations. Both Freud and Kinsey were guilty of this to some extent as was reported in chapter 1. In spite of survey evidence that incest, sexual abuse, and child molesting are far more widespread than anyone had known, Kinsey et al. (1953) de-emphasized these findings. Another researcher, Finkelhor (1979), built his victimization theme around social norms, as previously discussed. Also, as Renshaw (1982) has observed: "An article on incest may alter its perspective from a legal to a moral or psychosocial frame of reference without explanatory transition, seemingly without an author's awareness of a switch, leaving assumptions of forced coitus and crime" (p. ix).

In researching the effects of child and adolescent sexual experiences, this confusion between violations of the moral code and actual harm done is problematic. To assume that violations of social norms lead to harm for the child or adolescent without data with which to confirm the assumption is not scientifically sound. The fundamental question concerning the definition of abuse, therefore, becomes "What has been harmed—the child or the moral code?" Only after the issues involved in defining sexual abuse are clarified can the remaining problems involved in studying the long-range effects of child and adolescent sexual experiences be resolved.[1]

## Measuring Effects

Specific measures of effects or consequences must be used in order to determine which findings are important. Many of the studies shown in Table 3.1 did not utilize such specificity. Column 6 in the table lists the methods or measures used in each study to determine long-range effects. For example, Bender and Grugett (1952) judged adult functioning in terms of whether the person married, had

---

[1]Studies in which it was assumed that harm was done without any scientifically obtained data to support this assumption are not included in the studies reviewed in Table 3.1.

children, or held a job. As indicated in Table 3.1, Column 6, the method they utilized to determine consequences was available follow-up information on social and psychiatric adjustment. How this information was collected, when, and from whom was not stated. More specificity is needed. Likewise, there is a vagueness of meaning in the terms *character disorder* and *neurosis* used by Lukianowicz (1972) in describing consequences. Behavioral indicators of the terms used would provide a clearer understanding of consequences.

Another example of specific measures is shown by Rasmussen (1934) who questioned the role of sexual trauma as a decisive factor in causing mental disturbance and abnormalities of deportment in 8 of the 54 cases she studied. She stated that the role was doubtful because in most of them she found evidence of an independent constitutional predisposition to mental unbalance. However, it is not known what specific measures or behavioral indicators she used in coming to that conclusion. Nor is it possible to understand just what her conclusion meant. Chaneles (1967) admitted that he could only conjecture about the long-range effects on sexual offense victims. The lack of specificity in these studies is problematic when measuring effects.

A further drawback of some of the studies is the lack of specific data regarding the length of time between the experience itself and the measures of the so-called long-range effect. This information should be available by comparing Columns 2 and 5 in Table 3.1. However, the information given in some studies is too vague (e.g., Greenland, 1958; James & Meyerding, 1977; Justice & Justice, 1979; Medlicott, 1967). Other researchers were very specific regarding the time span between the experiences and the study. For example, in the Bender and Grugett (1952) study there were 11–16 years; in Brunold's (1964) there was a minimum of 15 years; in De Francis' (1969) the span was up to 3 years; and in Vestergaard's (1960) the span was from 11 to 19 years. Immediate effects are sometimes quite different from long-range effects, and it is important to distinguish between the two.

In the more recent studies reviewed here, some researchers were more specific regarding the measures of long-range effects. There are several examples of this. First, Finkelhor (1981) used well-defined terms, data on specific behaviors, and a comparison group. Although he stated that his study was not well equipped to grapple with the question of outcome, he did have three indicators of adult behavior: the frequency of current heterosexual activity, frequency of current homosexual activity, and a scale designed to evaluate the level of respondents' sexual self-esteem. These indicators were used to measure consequences. A second example is Fritz et al. (1981) who studied adult sexual adjustment. Their terms were operationally defined, and behaviors were specified. They used both objective and subjective measures of adult sexuality. A third example is Sedney and Brooks (1984) who studied factors associated with a history of childhood sexual experiences. They looked at specific sexual behaviors and 18 adult symptoms such as depression, obesity, or trouble sleeping. Kilpatrick (1986) also used well-defined terms, data on specific sexual behaviors, and a comparison group. Her measures of consequences included five standardized scales that measured current adult functioning in the areas of self-esteem, family relationships, depression, marital satisfaction, and sexual satisfaction.

The use of terms like *consequences* and *effects* is also problematic. These terms imply causal relationships between childhood sexual experiences and adult functioning. Such causal inferences are usually inappropriate given the retrospective and/or correlational nature of many of the studies. For example, there have been many reports that the social system's handling of incidents regarding sexual abuse of children caused as much or more harm as the sexual experience itself (Brunold, 1964; De Francis, 1969; Justice & Justice, 1979; Mann & Gaynor, 1980; Schultz, 1973; Summit & Kryso, 1978). Effects or consequences attributed to the sexual experience itself may have actually been caused by the way the report of the experience was handled and responded to by the police, social agencies, family members, and others, or, for that matter, by any number of other factors. Extreme caution must be exercised in claiming causal relationships.

## FINDINGS FROM PREVIOUS STUDIES

The 39 studies that are shown in Table 3.1 were also analyzed considering the issues for researchers. I then determined if the data presented were relevant to three hypotheses and if they met enough of the scientific criteria to be given serious consideration in accepting or rejecting the hypotheses. The studies are summarized and analyzed in the order of appearance in Table 3.1 and according to the hypothesis to which they relate. They are presented in Appendix A. The findings of the studies that meet the scientific criteria sufficiently support the hypothesis and contribute to the state of our knowledge are given in this chapter. The three hypotheses relate to findings regarding long-range effects of child and adolescent sexual experiences.

### Hypothesis 1: Child/Adolescent Sexual Experiences Inevitably Lead to Long-Term Harmful Effects

Twenty-four studies reported negative outcomes as the more frequently reported effect, with 9 of these reporting very negative outcomes. However, only 9 of the 24 studies met enough of the scientific criteria to be given serious consideration in accepting or rejecting Hypothesis 1 (see Appendix A for the analysis of each and for the summary in Table A-1). All 9 studies went beyond using a few descriptive cases in regard to numbers, all utilized control groups, all clearly defined their terms, and all used specific measures of consequences. The state of our knowledge regarding Hypothesis 1 according to their findings is summarized as follows:

1. Childhood incest experiences in lower-class families where the perpetrator has been prosecuted are associated with harmful effects (Weinberg, 1955).

2. Occurrence of incest may predispose the individual to certain kinds of problems (Meiselman, 1978; Sedney & Brooks, 1984).

3. Child victims of various reported sex crimes, in addition to incest, in lower-class families are likely to experience harmful effects (De Francis, 1969).

4. Older age at cessation of molestation, stronger negative feelings, higher frequency, and longer duration seem to contribute to adult maladjustment (Sedney & Brooks, 1984; Tsai, Feldman-Summers, & Edgar, 1979).

5. Victims of child sexual assault have a greater risk for developing many psychiatric disorders, especially anxiety disorders, than do nonvictims (Saunders, Villeponteaux, Kilpatrick, & Veronen, 1987).

6. Incest victims evidence poorer functioning with regard to sexuality, emotional responses, social adjustment, and self-esteem than do nonvictims (Jackson et al., 1990).

7. Incest victims who have experienced forceful or repeated, prolonged abuse or severe physical violation by much older men, especially fathers or stepfathers, are likely to report difficulties in their adult lives (Herman, Russell, & Trocki, 1986).

8. A correlation exists between the severity of adult psychiatric symptoms and a combination of child physical and sexual abuse in a clinical population (Bryer, Nelson, Miller, & Krol, 1987).

9. No differences in adult symptomology were found between women who experienced incest and those who experienced other child sexual abuse (Bryer et al., 1987).

## Hypothesis 2: Child/Adolescent Sexual Experiences Inevitably Lead to Long-Term Neutral Effects

Primarily neutral effects were found in 14 of the 39 studies that were reviewed and analyzed (see Appendix A for the analysis of each and the summary of the analysis in Table A-2). Only 5 of these studies met the scientific criteria sufficiently for their findings to be considered for the state of our knowledge regarding Hypothesis 2:

10. College students from middle-class families show few permanently harmful effects from child sexual experiences with adults (Landis, 1956).

11. Only a small number of middle-class women show severe damage from prepubertal sexual experiences with adults (Gagnon, 1965).

12. Sibling sexual experiences in middle-class families have little influence on adult sexual functioning (Finkelhor, 1981).

13. A small percentage of middle-class females and a significantly smaller percentage of males who have experienced prepubertal molestation have problems with adult sexual adjustment (Fritz et al., 1981).

14. The adult functioning of middle-class females who have or have not had child sexual experiences does not differ significantly. However, the interactions of negative child sexual experiences with the identity of the partner were found to be statistically significant for four measures of adult functioning (Kilpatrick, 1986).

## Hypothesis 3: Child/Adolescent Sexual Experiences Inevitably Lead to Long-Term Beneficial Effects

Only 2 studies found the long-term effects to be primarily beneficial. Sampling problems and the lack of any conclusive evidence led to the rejection of the findings in one study. The findings of the second study are included as this is one of the few studies that allowed for positive responses, and although the sample was self-selected, the methodology was rigorous. There is no claim here, however, that beneficial effects are inevitable, only that some exist and under special circumstances that are quite different from the experiences of those children and adolescents who experienced abuse:

15. Persons reporting positive child or adolescent sexual experiences with persons at least 5 years older appear to have different experiences from the ones with negative experiences. They are predominantly male, a high percentage of female partners are involved, no force or violence is present, and partners are primarily adult friends, not family members (Okami, 1989). See Appendix A, Table A-3, and p. 145.

It is recognized that much controversy exists concerning any positive or beneficial effects that may be experienced by children and adolescents with an older partner. These are circumstances that have been defined in the literature as victimization, abuse, and exploitation due to the absence of true informed consent. However, in the interest of scientific endeavor, these results must be reported. Researchers and professionals may then analyze the methods, process the findings, come to their own conclusions, and then, more importantly, effect methods of treatment and understanding.

## THE NEED FOR RESEARCH

Much of the literature on the consequences of child and adolescent sexual experiences for adult functioning is impressionistic, anecdotal, or summarizing. Other studies are characterized by a small number of cases and/or the lack of control groups. Some studies that utilized large numbers and comparison groups used no reliable measures of long-term consequences. There are few empirical studies of long-term consequences of childhood sexual experiences that used reliable measures of adult functioning until fairly recently.

A generally acceptable summary of the findings to date is that the sexual abuse of a child is potentially damaging, but not necessarily so. However, many studies are marred by a lack of adherence to scientific procedures. Therefore, many findings are questionable. Researchers, clinicians, and others have consistently pointed out the need for studies that meet accepted scientific criteria on long-range effects of child and adolescent sexual experiences (Burgess, Groth, Holmstrom, & Sgroi, 1978; Elwell, 1979; Finkelhor, 1979; Meiselman, 1978), on 18-year-olds that give a more accurate picture of the sexual abuse experience of children for the last decade (Finkelhor, 1984), on victims from various socioeconomic backgrounds and ethnic/cultural groups (Powell, 1988), on a broad range of risk factors including demographic variables, on family constellation variables, and on nonclinical populations (Finkelhor, 1984).

## CONCLUSION

The analysis of 39 major research studies on the long-range effects of child and adolescent sexual experiences points out issues, problems, gaps, and strengths in previous research. Primary issues raised for researchers are:

1. problems in collecting data at the time of the abuse and in retrospect;

2. methodological concerns such as the use of large samples, control groups, offender and clinical populations, and the combining of socioeconomic, racial/ethnic, and male and female groups for analyses;

3. differences in reactions of prepubertal and postpubertal samples;

4. the importance of specificity and clear definitions in regard to both sexual behaviors and sexual partners;

5. the confusion between the violations of mores or moral codes and actual harm done; and

6. problems in the measurement of consequences and the assumption of causal relationships.

Major research studies on the long-range effects of child and adolescent sexual experiences were analyzed according to scientific criteria and their contribution to the state of our knowledge. Findings were then utilized to accept or reject three hypotheses concerning long-range effects. Of the 24 studies reporting harmful effects, 9 studies met the scientific criteria to support long-term harmful effects. Of the 14 studies that reported primarily neutral effects, 5 met the scientific criteria and, therefore, supported the hypothesis regarding neutral effects. There were only 2 studies where long-term effects were found to be primarily beneficial. Only 1 met the scientific criteria for inclusion in supporting the claim for positive effects. The 15 findings that were considered as the state of our knowledge provide the bases for future research.

The need for research in specific areas of long-term effects has been advocated by various researchers. Many previous findings are questionable due to flawed methodology and biased conclusions. The potentially damaging effect of sexual abuse on a child or adolescent is generally accepted. However, there is not always a detrimental effect on adult functioning. Specificity regarding the elements that cause the greatest harm or that are the greatest menaces and the interactions of such elements are much needed.

# II

## NATURE AND CONSEQUENCES OF CHILD AND ADOLESCENT SEXUAL EXPERIENCES— A RESEARCH STUDY

# 4

# ORIGINAL RESEARCH STUDY

This original study has significance both in terms of broad contemporary relevance and in terms of its specific implications for the helping professions. The debate continues in professional, lay, and legal circles over the long-range consequences of child and adolescent sexual experiences for functioning in adult life. Many clinicians cite case after case where adult functioning, especially in regard to sexual relationships, is moderately to severely impaired due to abusive sexual experiences during childhood or adolescence. Others state that it is society's reactions to the sexual experience that is harmful, and yet other researchers have found relatively minor effects on adult adjustment. Still another group finds the effects to be beneficial.

There are also implications for the helping professionals. The social work profession is partially entrusted by society with the function of protecting its children and adolescents from abuse. This mandate includes sexual abuse. Professionals must base their practice upon what is known about sexual abuse and its causes, dynamics, consequences, and treatment. There is less known about the consequences of child and adolescent sexual abuse then any other area of abuse. The purpose of the research reported in the following section is to obtain information that describes the strength of the relationship between child and adolescent sexual experiences and long-range consequences. The findings regarding the strength of this relationship may suggest to the helping professions avenues of prevention, social program development, and treatment.

This research is a retrospective study of the sexual experiences that women had as children and adolescents. There are several reasons for studying this population. Agency reports (Mann & Gaynor, 1980) and research surveys (De Francis, 1969; Finkelhor, 1979) indicate that women have a much higher incidence rate than men for childhood sexual abuse. Girls are reported as abused from 2 to 10 times as often as boys. Finkelhor (1979) found a ratio of over 2 females to 1 male who were sexually victimized, Mann and Gaynor (1980) found a ratio of 9 females to 1 male who were sexually abused, and De Francis (1969) found a ratio of 10 females to 1 male who were sexually abused as children. This incidence rate is a primary reason for studying females.

The reasons for studying women instead of children are twofold: One reason grows out of the moral dilemma of asking young children very sensitive questions about sexual behaviors and the risk of upsetting them, especially if silence has been enforced by threats; a second reason is that the study is to be retrospective, that is, sexual experiences from birth to 18 years of age were studied as they were remembered by adult women. Certain limitations of retrospective data such as accuracy of recall and inability to verify information are recognized.

For purposes of this study, a *sexual experience* is defined as any experience of a sexual nature that occurred during childhood or adolescence to the age of 18. This definition includes kissing and hugging in a sexual way, exhibition, fondling, masturbation, oral sex, anal sex, attempted intercourse, and intercourse. The decision as to whether or not the kissing and hugging experiences were sexual was left to the judgment of the respondent. Instructions to the respondents were: "In this section you will be asked to remember various types of sexual experiences that you engaged in at various ages," and different age groups were indicated. Surprisingly, few respondents had difficulty defining what was sexual. The primary difficulty was in trying to remember just how many times the experiences happened with a particular partner. The observation in this study regarding the recognition of a sexual experience by children parallels that of Finkelhor (1979) who reported, "We were impressed at how accurately children perceived sexual experiences as sexual" (p. 47).

The two definitions of abuse discussed previously must be kept in mind. These two definitions of creating measurable harm and violating social norms or mores are carefully separated in this study of the long-range effects of child and adolescent sexual experiences.

I conducted this research in order to provide some enlightening and definitive information concerning the long-range consequences of child and adolescent sexual experiences for adult functioning. Although this research may not end the on-going debate regarding long-range effects, it may help to destroy some myths regarding the consequences of child and adolescent sexual experiences, separate scientific inquiry from social mores and political ideology, and identify the menaces in our society that actually do cause harm.

## DESCRIPTION

The purpose of this research is to present both a description of the sexual experiences of the women studied and the consequences for their adult functioning. The nature of the experiences are presented including incidence rates, who initiated the experience, what type of behaviors were most prevalent, and who were the partners. The relationship of the nature of the sexual experiences to other variables such as age, ethnic groups, community size, and sample groups are discussed.

Women described what they felt were abusive or harmful experiences. Because some researchers equate harmful/abusive experiences with an older partner, women were asked about older partners (at least 5 years older) and the characteristics of experiences with them. Specific questions were asked regarding respondents' reactions of pleasure, participation, guilt, reactions, and conditions such as pressure or force. Respondents rated their responses on a continuum. Other questions asked concerned whom respondents told about the experiences and whether or not they found these people to be helpful.

The primary question of interest in this study concerns the consequences of child and adolescent sexual experiences for adult functioning and what type of sexual experiences have an effect on the present functioning of respondents. Thus, this study looks at the correlation between the measures of adult functioning and background variables, the effects of sexual experiences with different types of partners, and the type of interactions of variables that explain the most variance in adult functioning.

This research is based on a retrospective study of the overall childhood sexual experiences of 501 women. Information was obtained regarding the sexual experiences the women had as children, including abusive experiences, and their partners, both relatives and nonrelatives. Instead of using yet another definition of incest and adding further to the confusion regarding definitions, this study discusses sexual experiences with relatives. Specific relatives are listed, and the types of sexual behaviors with each are discussed. Specific relatives included are parent, stepparent, brother, sister, male relative, and female relative. Types of behaviors included are kissing and hugging in a sexual way, exhibition, fondling, masturbation, oral sex, anal sex, attempted intercourse, and intercourse. In this way the reader knows exactly which relative and which behavior are being discussed, and much confusion regarding definition of incest is avoided. Information was also obtained to describe the present adult functioning of the 501 women subjects in the five areas of self-esteem, depression, marital satisfaction, sexual satisfaction, and family relations (see research questionnaire package in Appendix B).

## Methodology

The survey method was used in conducting this research. The survey is an appropriate method for studying the sexual behavior of children for three reasons. First, research findings confirm the notion that child and adolescent sexual experiences are widespread enough to be amenable to survey analysis. Second, although the sexual abuse of children and adolescents is now a recognized social problem and the reporting of incidents is mandated by law, the cases reported to agencies are believed to greatly underrepresent the actual incidence of sexual abuse. Thus, a survey provides a more reliable estimate of incidence rates and better descriptions than reported case material from agencies even with the limitations of retrospective date mentioned earlier. Third, a survey, especially when it is administered in groups, provides anonymity and ensures that no one will be able to recognize individuals who provide information that is both highly personal and sensitive. This level of anonymity is obviously not possible if individual case studies are used.

A major limitation of survey methods is lack of control. Subjects cannot be placed in a controlled environment where all factors other than sexual experiences are ruled out or controlled in contributing to consequences in adult life. To do so would mean that children would need to be observed in a controlled environment during sexual experiences and then maintained and observed in such an environment until they were adults, at which time consequences would be measured. Obviously, this methodology is not possible for this study.

However, other than control limitations, surveys introduce their own selection factors such as who chooses to volunteer. Surveys often force the respondent to describe complex experiences, responses, and interactions in terms of fixed response categories that may distort the meaning and impact of an experience.

In order to minimize these limitations, I made contact well in advance with any type of community, church, academic, or professional group that was willing to participate in the research. Information about the study was given with emphasis on the voluntary nature and anonymity of participation and the sensitive nature of the subject. Participants were given the opportunity to withdraw from the research at any time. The questionnaire package was structured in a way that minimized the problem of fixed response categorization of complex experiences, feelings, and interactions as much as possible. Response categories contained a full range of possibilities. For example, for the pleasure variable, the possible response range was *very unpleasant, unpleasant, neither pleasant nor unpleasant, pleasant,* and *very pleasant.* Some questions had an *other* category for additional responses. At the end of each of the 13 major questions in the questionnaire package, an opportunity was given for participants to write open-ended answers that more accurately explained the nature of their experiences (see consent form used in Appendix C).

In designing the study it was crucial that the sample be representative of the population and that the answers be valid and confidential/anonymous. Therefore, there were three primary considerations. First, the sample, which would not include respondents from social agencies such as clinical or offender populations. To do so would create a bias in the data, and the results could not be generalized to other populations. The second consideration was validity. The responses needed to be as truthful as possible. Using the survey method, administering the survey instrument in small groups, and giving specific instructions were intended to increase the validity. The last was the protection of subjects. The methods used should not embarrass or endanger the persons who participate in the study. Ensuring confidentiality of the data and anonymity of the participants and administering the survey questionnaire package in groups provided the needed protection.

This study attempted to avoid previous methodology problems as much as possible by using clear definitions of terms, specific measures, a large number of cases, and nonclinical, nonoffender populations.

As in all retrospective studies that relate early experiences to a person's current functioning, it is not possible to trace the current conditions in a direct causal line from the previous condition. However, the relationships of background variables to specific measures of adult functioning were explored, and then these relationships were held constant for other analyses. This was done in order to separate the relationships of child and adolescent sexual experiences from the relationships of background variables for adult functioning.

### Sample

The sample used for this study was from diverse populations in the southern portion of the United States. These populations contained enough diversity in regard to ethnicity, community size, age, and socioeconomic status that it was possible to represent a wide range of subgroups. In order to increase heterogeneity, the deliberate sampling model of Cook and Campbell (1979) was used. A series of convenience samples was taken from all regions of Georgia and northern Florida. Efforts were made to identify groups who provided a diversity in regard to the qualities previously mentioned. Contact in person or by phone was made with the groups to determine the feasibility of their participation.

TABLE 4.1
Number and Proportion of Respondents by Type of Group Sampled

| Group | Number | % of Sample |
|---|---|---|
| Undergraduate students | 174 | 35 |
| Graduate students | 79 | 16 |
| School teachers | 80 | 16 |
| Vocational training groups | 74 | 15 |
| Community groups | 35 | 7 |
| Professional groups | 36 | 5 |
| Church groups | 23 | 5 |
| Total | 501 | 100 |

Participating in the study were 501 women from Georgia (53%) and Florida (47%). They were drawn from various walks of life (see Table 4.1): undergraduate and graduate students, public school teachers, women in vocational-technical classes, community groups, church groups, and professional groups. Efforts were made to include a wide range of characteristics within each of the seven types of groups.

An example of a wide range of subgroups within each class is given by the target class defined as college students. The subgroups within this class were undergraduate students including upper and lower levels and graduate students through the doctoral level. The settings for these institutions of higher learning included urban, small-town, and rural areas. Some of the institutions had a predominantly White student body, whereas others had a predominantly Black student body. The graduate student subgroup, particularly, had a range of ages represented that provided information on the sexual experiences of women over a long period of time. Because many of the students were from other states, a larger geographic area was represented also.

Because more than 50% of the population now has some college experience (Fritz et al., 1981), it was reasonable that a substantial proportion of the sample had some college experience. Of the sample, 25% had completed 16 years of schooling. Approximately 85% of the sample had some type of training beyond 12 years of school. This training included cosmetology, business, licensed practical nursing, registered nursing, CETA training, and college experience.

The other groups represented in the sample had a wide range of characteristics also. The school teachers were from middle Georgia, of varying ages and ethnicity, and taught a variety of subjects in both elementary and high schools and in urban as well as rural settings. Additionally, the sample represented many types of vocational training. Community groups varied from new residents in an urban setting to singles groups. Professional groups were from both Florida and Georgia and represented many professional occupations. Church members were also from both states and came from fundamental, moderate, and liberal congregations. Although elderly women and women from lower socioeconomic backgrounds were included in the study, these two groups were underrepresented in the sample compared to the total U.S. population.

Most researchers who are interested in the sexual abuse of children have studied three populations: clinical populations (Briere & Runtz, 1988; Emslie & Rosenfeld, 1983; Forward & Buck, 1978; Kroth, 1979; Justice & Justice, 1979, Meiselman, 1978); offenders (De Francis, 1969; Jaffe, Dynneson, & Bensel, 1975); or undergraduate college students (Landis, 1956, Finkelhor, 1979; Fritz et al., 1981). The clinical and offender populations were studied primarily because abuse was known to be present. Undergraduate college students were studied primarily because of their availability. This study was deliberately designed to reach some groups other than these three populations. This study differs, therefore, from the Finkelhor, Fritz, and Landis studies because 31% of the students are graduate students (16% of the sample) and because about half of the sample is from nonuniversity settings. Additionally, it differs from the clinical and offender studies mentioned because no clinical or offender populations are included.

## Measures

A complex and lengthy questionnaire package was used to gather data. Three types of information were requested.

*Demographic Information.* This section requested information regarding age, education, income, marital status, ethnicity, number of children, present occupation, size of community in which respondents lived before age 14, and whether both parents worked when respondents were children.

*Measures of Adult Functioning (the Hudson Scales).* The second type of information requested concerned present adult functioning. Five standardized scales were used as dependent variables to measure the correlates of child and adolescent sexual experiences for present adult functioning (Hudson, 1982). The five scales were: (a) Index of Self-Esteem (ISE), measuring self-esteem problems; (b) Generalized Contentment Scale (GCS), measuring depression; (c) Index of Marital Satisfaction (IMS), measuring marital discord; (d) Index of Sexual Satisfaction (ISS), measuring sexual discord; and (e) Index of Family Relations (IFR), measuring intrafamilial stress. These scales are part of a larger Clinical Measurement Package (Hudson, 1982), and each has been found to be reliable and valid. Hudson reported that each scale has a coefficient alpha reliability of .90 or better. In order to check these assertions, the reliability for each of the five scales was examined by using the data obtained in this study. Coefficient alpha was computed and found to be .90 for ISE, .96 for IMS, .90 for GCS, .93 for ISS, and .93 for IFR scales. These findings are consistent with Hudson's and confirm the reliability of the measures. Methods used to establish validity for the scales are described by Hudson (1982).[1]

Hudson described each scale as having a clinical cutting score of 30. In other words, if a person scores above 30 on any of the scales, the person probably has a clinically significant problem in the area being measured, whereas persons who score below 30 are generally found to be free of such problems.

*Sexual Experiences.* The third type of requested information concerned the respondents' sexual experiences from birth through age 17. This section of the questionnaire package was specifically designed for this study and was the most complex. Information was requested for 13 different sexual behaviors ranging from kissing and hugging in a sexual way to intercourse. Some of the wording of questions in this section was adapted from Finkelhor's (1979) questionnaire. There were 14 questions asked about each of the 13 behaviors. These 14 questions concerned who initiated the behavior, the age discrepancy between the partner and the person, the frequency of each behavior with each type of partner, the short-term reaction to the experience (three questions), whether the experience was voluntary/forced (two questions), with whom and how often the experience had been discussed, who had been helpful in dealing with the experience, the long-range impact on the person's view of sex and their life in general, how the individual wished the incident had been handled, if the experience was perceived as abusive or harmful, whether others knew of the behavior, and, if so, if they should have done something about it. Each question was asked for each experience, reaction, or behavior during six different age spans: 0–6, 7–10, 11–14, 15, 16, and 17. The chart format gave the question, and on the same line had spaces to put the number of experiences under each age span. No reliability studies have been done on this part of the questionnaire package (see the questionnaire package in Appendix B).

### Procedure

As the researcher, I made personal contact with groups to arrange for the collection of data. This procedure was used because the return rate is higher than for mail surveys. The collection of data in groups also allowed me to clarify instructions and to ensure the anonymity of the participants. Data were collected

---

[1]For further data and a description of procedures used in establishing reliability and validity of the scales, see Hudson (1982) *The Clinical Measurement Package: A Field Manual.*

from 40 different groups ranging in size from 3 to 38 participants. Student groups from four state institutions of higher learning in northern Florida and middle and northern Georgia completed the questionnaire package. One institution was a large university in a metropolitan area, one was a large university in a small town, a third was a smaller college in an urban area with a predominantly Black population, and the fourth was a small college with graduate programs that was located in a small town in a rural area. Classes in which the questionnaire package was administered included statistics, research, anthropology, child development, social work, home and family life, sociology, home economics, psychology, women's studies, criminology, teacher education, and nursing. Courses ranged from introductory and upper-level courses to graduate courses at the doctoral level. Various community groups such as Newcomers groups and Parents Without Partners, church groups, professional groups, public school teachers, and women in vocational-technical classes were surveyed as shown in Table 4.1. All groups were contacted in advance, informed of the nature of the study, and requested to participate. Some groups, such as senior citizens, did not wish to give up their activity time to participate, and some church leaders did not consent to members' participation because of the sexual content of the study.

The procedure with each group was:

1. presentation of the research project, including the personal and sensitive nature of the study and the precautions taken to assure confidentiality and anonymity. Care was taken that neither individual nor particular group responses would be recognizable;

2. discussion of the contents of the study;

3. request for volunteers and signing of informed consent forms;

4. emphasis on voluntary participation, confidentiality, and anonymity; and

5. completion of the questionnaire with oral as well as with written instructions given for each section. Extreme care was taken in both the printed booklet and in the verbal instructions to avoid communicating any bias or value judgments regarding any type of sexual experience or no sexual experience.

Few women refused to participate. Most participants completed the questionnaire package in about 45 minutes. In some university classes, not enough time was allowed for the completion of the questionnaires, and the women took them home to complete. Of the questionnaires, 31 (6%) were not returned. Four women (.7%) started the questionnaire but did not complete it, and 3 women (.5%)

returned completely blank questionnaires. Thus, 38 questionnaires (7%) were lost or not completed.

## Background Characteristics of the Sample

The sample used for the data analysis consisted of 501 women. The mean, variance, and sample size are shown in Table 4.2 for selected background characteristics. The sample size varied because some women did not answer some of the questions.

The mean age of the sample was 28 ($SD$ = 9.59), and the age of the respondents ranged from 18 to 61 years. The mean number of years of school completed was 15. Three women finished from 3 to 7 years of school, 4 were high school dropouts, and 3 did not report the number of years of school completed. Over 90% of the women finished 12 years of school, and 25% completed 16 years of school. The mean income of $1,475 per month was below the median incomes of Florida and Georgia ($1,510 and $1,640 per month, respectively, in 1978 according to the Statistical Abstract of the United States (1980). Because approximately half the women were students, their reported income may not be an accurate portrayal of the socioeconomic status of their families.

Data regarding marital status and information concerning size and structure of families were obtained from each participant. Of the 501 women in the sample, 48% were single, 39% were married, and 9% were divorced. Of the remaining 4%, 4 were widowed, 9 were separated, 5 had *other* marital status, which presumably meant they were living with someone without being married, and 2 gave no answer. In regard to the number of times married, 49% had never been married, 45% had been married once, 6% had been married twice, and the remaining 2

TABLE 4.2
Mean, Variance, and Sample Size by Selected Background Characteristics

| Characteristics | Mean | Standard Deviation | Sample Size |
|---|---|---|---|
| Age | 28.1 | 9.59 | 500 |
| Years of school | 15.3 | 2.12 | 498 |
| Monthly income | $1,475 | 16.35 | 501 |
| Number of times married | 0.6 | 0.62 | 501 |
| Years with present spouse[a] | 7.7 | 7.33 | 290 |
| Number of children[b] | 2.1 | 1.25 | 200 |
| Number of persons in household | 2.1 | 1.75 | 498 |

Note:   The total number in the sample = 501.

   [a] Only women presently married.

   [b] Only women with children.

women had been married three times. The mean number of years with present spouse was 7.7 years, and the longest number of years with the current spouse or partner was 40. The majority of the women (60%) had no children, 16% had two children, and 14% had one child. The remaining 10% had from three to seven children. The mean number of children was 2.1.

The number of persons living in the household in addition to the respondent varied from 31% who had one other person in the household to 15% who had 4 to 12 other persons in the household. The norm was two persons. Of the remaining respondents, 21% had two other persons, and 18% had three other persons living in the household. Of the respondents, 15% lived alone.

Most women lived in towns (30%) or small cities (20%) while growing up. However, the sample included those who had grown up on farms (9%), tiny burgs (12%), and large cities (22%). Seven percent did not provide such information.

The ethnic composition of the sample was 63% White and 35% Black. The other 2% consisted of Hispanics (5), Orientals (1), and other (2). According to the 1980 census reports, Blacks comprised 14% of Florida's population and 7% of Georgia's population (Statistical Abstract of the United States, 1980). The average of the two states is 10.5% Black population. Although Black women made up only 35% of the sample, this proportion was well above the proportion of Blacks in the two states studied. The large number of Black women participants (174) contrasts with Finkelhor's (1979) New England study that had practically no Blacks in the sample.

TABLE 4.3
Number and Proportion of Women and Spouses in Differing Occupations

| Occupation | Women | | Spouses | |
|---|---|---|---|---|
| | Number | % | Number | % |
| Student | 253 | 51 | 37 | 7 |
| Professional | 154 | 31 | 81 | 16 |
| Service | 30 | 6 | 59 | 12 |
| Clerical | 30 | 6 | 7 | 1 |
| Homemaker | 17 | 3 | — | — |
| Unemployed | 7 | 1 | 9 | 2 |
| Sales | 5 | 1 | 30 | 6 |
| Production | 3 | 1 | 26 | 5 |
| Armed Forces | — | — | 11 | 2 |
| Administration | — | — | 8 | 2 |
| Agriculture | — | — | 8 | 2 |
| Not applicable | 2 | .004 | 225[a] | 45 |
| Total | 501 | 100 | 501 | 100 |

[a] Women were not married.

Occupations were categorized according to the *International Standard Classification of Occupations* (1969). The occupations of respondents and their spouses are given in Table 4.3. After students (51%), the occupation with the largest number of women was in the professional category (31%). These two categories of students and professionals made up 82% of the sample. The next highest categories were service and clerical, each of which made up 6% of the sample. Only 3% of the sample were homemakers, and 1% were in each of the categories of sales, production, and unemployed. The primary spouse occupation was professional (16%) with service (12%), student (7%), sales (6%), and production (5%) following. Only 2% or less of the spouse sample were in the remaining categories.

## CONCLUSION

This original research study was conducted in order to ascertain the nature of child and adolescent sexual experiences and to determine their consequences for adult functioning. The diverse sample of 501 women from the southern part of the United States was used in an effort to achieve heterogeneity in regard to ethnicity, age, socioeconomic background, and community size. However, the majority of the sample was middle class. The absence of clinical and offender populations in the sample made the findings more generalizable.

The three types of information requested in the rather complex questionnaire package were demographic information, information on present adult functioning consisting of five standardized scales that were used as dependent variables to measure the correlates of child and adolescent sexual experiences for present adult functioning, and specific and detailed information on the respondents' sexual experiences from birth through age 17. The last information was obtained through a questionnaire that was specifically formulated for this study.

The data for the study were collected in groups in order to ensure confidentiality and anonymity. Participation was voluntary, and there was great diversity in the type of groups sampled. The sample was 63% White, 35% Black, and 2% other. The ages ranged from 18 to 61 years, and about half were graduate and undergraduate students in various colleges and universities in the two states. The respondents lived in rural to urban communities, and the largest proportion, after students, were in professional occupations.

The extensive questionnaire package, deliberate sampling for heterogeneity on many levels, and the measures used to determine present adult functioning produced over 700 variables to be examined. This extensive data base produced findings that are presented in the following chapters.

# 5
## NATURE OF THE SEXUAL EXPERIENCES

In the effort to determine long-range consequences of child and adolescent sexual experiences, it is necessary to know the exact nature of those experiences. The importance of specificity cannot be over stressed. In this study, information was sought from each participant on the specific type of sexual experience in which she had participated and the circumstances surrounding the experience. The types of sexual behaviors that were studied ranged from kissing and hugging in a sexual way to intercourse. The study does not include sexual propositions.

Previous studies have found that the period of highest vulnerability of females to the occurrence of sexual abuse is below the age of 14 (Courtois, 1979; De Francis, 1969; Finkelhor, 1979; Gagnon, 1965; Landis, 1956; Meiselman, 1978). Kadushin and Martin (1980) reported that the average age of sexually abused children is between 11 and 14 years. For this reason the data from this study are analyzed by ages birth through 14 years of age (children) and by 15 through 17 years of age (adolescents). The data from these two groups are then used for comparative purposes.

## INCIDENCE

For the sample of 501 women, 55% of the women reported having at least one childhood sexual experience of some type, and 83% reported having at least one adolescent experience of some type. These figures compare to the 66% of women who had preadult sexual experiences as reported by Finkelhor (1979) whose study included propositioning experiences. The 278 women who had childhood sexual experiences and the 416 women who had adolescent sexual experiences were studied in order to determine if those sexual experiences had measurable consequences for their adult personal and social functioning. This means, however, that for the other part of the sample, sexual experiences had no bearing on adult functioning simply because there were no sexual experiences. The adult functioning of women with no sexual experiences is compared with the adult functioning of women who did have sexual experiences.

## TYPES OF SEXUAL EXPERIENCES

Tables 5.1 and 5.2 show the types of experiences women had as children and as adolescents by partner. The figures in these two tables mean that the specified behavior occurred with that specific partner one or more times for each woman reporting the experience. The figures never refer to how many times the behavior occurred with a particular partner. For example, in Table 5.1, kissing and hugging an unrelated male in a sexual way was reported by 127 women or 25% of the sample. This means that 127 women kissed and hugged an unrelated male one or more times.[1]

The sexual behavior most often reported by women when they were children and adolescents was kissing and hugging in a sexual way. As children, 37% engaged in sexual kissing and fondling, 35% had been shown the genitals of their partner, 23% displayed their own genitals, and 15% had their breasts fondled by their partner. Quite small percentages of the women participated in masturbation (5%) or intercourse (2%) at age 14 or younger. As adolescents, 77% of the women engaged in sexual kissing and fondling. Fifty-one percent had their breasts fondled by their partner, and 33% had been shown the genitals of their partner. Fewer experienced intercourse (27%), being masturbated by their partner (23%), or displayed their genitals (23%) to their partner. Smaller percentages participated in attempted intercourse (12%), oral sex (10%), and anal sex (2%). Percentages regarding fondling another person's breasts, anal sex, and attempted intercourse

---

[1]This is a very important point to remember throughout this chapter as the figures in the tables refer to number of women, not to number of experiences.

Table 5.1

Proportion of Women Reporting Type of Sexual Behavior by Partner as Children

| Partner | Types of Sexual Behavior[a] | | | | | | | No. of Women | |
| --- | --- | --- | --- | --- | --- | --- | --- | --- | --- |
| | Kiss & Hug | Show You Genitals | You Show Genitals | Partner Felt Breasts | You Masturbated | You Are Masturbated | Intercourse | N | % |
| *Had Experiences* | | | | | | | | | |
| | (n = 43) | (n = 81) | (n = 52) | (n = 18) | (n = 10) | (n = 11) | (n = 5) | | |
| *With Relatives* | 8.6% | 16.2% | 10.4% | 3.6% | 1.9% | 2.2% | 1.0% | 278[b] | 55 |
| Father | 1.8 | 1.2 | 0.4 | 0.4 | 0.4 | 0.2 | 0.2 | 120 | 24 |
| Stepfather | 0.6 | 0.2 | — | 0.4 | 0.4 | — | — | 16 | 3.2 |
| Mother | 0.4 | 0.2 | 0.2 | — | — | — | — | 5 | 1.0 |
| Stepmother | 0.2 | — | — | — | — | — | — | 4 | 0.8 |
| | — | — | — | — | — | — | — | 1 | 0.2 |
| Sister | 0.2 | 1.6 | 2.0 | 0.4 | — | — | — | 15 | 2.9 |
| Brother | 1.2 | 5.6 | 4.2 | 0.8 | 0.4 | 0.8 | 0.4 | 40 | 7.9 |
| Male relative | 4.9 | 7.4 | 3.6 | 1.0 | 0.4 | 0.8 | 0.4 | 60 | 11.9 |
| Female relative | 1.6 | 3.8 | 2.0 | 1.2 | 0.6 | 0.4 | — | 34 | 6.8 |
| | (n = 141) | (n = 102) | (n = 75) | (n = 52) | (n = 16) | (n = 22) | (n = 6) | | |
| *With Nonrelative* | 28.1 | 20.4 | 15.0 | 10.4 | 3.2 | 4.4 | 1.2 | 210 | 42 |
| Unrelated male | 25.4 | 16.4 | 10.6 | 7.2 | 2.4 | 3.2 | 1.2 | 184 | 36.5 |
| Unrelated female | 4.4 | 5.8 | 6.9 | 3.6 | 1.2 | 1.4 | — | 67 | 13.4 |
| Husband | 0.4 | 0.2 | 0.2 | — | — | — | — | 3 | 0.6 |
| Stranger | 1.2 | 1.2 | 0.2 | 0.6 | — | — | 0.2 | 14 | 2.8 |
| | | | | | | | | *No experiences* | |
| % of all women[b] | 37.1 | 35.1 | 22.9 | 15.2 | 4.9 | 1.8 | 1.8 | 223 | 45 |

[a] Oral sexual behaviors were omitted from this table because there was only one report of oral sex by you (on brother) and only two reports of oral sex on you (by brother and unrelated male).

[b] Twenty-three women with experiences did not give partner. There were 75 women who had sexual experiences with both relatives and nonrelatives. Because some women had multiple experiences, the numbers inside the various categories do not add up to the total category number.

as children were not included in this analysis because of the small numbers of times these experiences were reported. (There were 56 reported experiences with these behaviors: 36 of these experiences consisted of fondling another person's breasts, and they were usually reported by those who reported the fondling of the breasts by another person; anal sex behavior was reported by 9 women; and attempted intercourse was reported by 11 women.)

TABLE 5.2
Proportion of Women Reporting Type of Sexual Behavior by Partner
as Adolescents

| | Types of Sexual Behavior | | | | | |
|---|---|---|---|---|---|---|
| Partner | Kiss & Hug | Show You Genitals | You Show Genitals | You Felt Breasts | Partner Felt Breasts | You Mastur-bated |
| | (n = 17) | (n = 8) | (n = 9) | (n = 3) | (n = 6) | (n = 1) |
| Relatives | 3.0% | 1.6% | 1.8% | .6% | 1.2% | .2% |
| Father | .8 | .2 | .2 | 0 | 0 | 0 |
| Stepfather | .6 | .2 | 0 | 0 | .2 | 0 |
| Mother | .2 | .2 | .4 | .2 | 0 | 0 |
| Sister | .2 | 0 | 0 | 0 | 0 | 0 |
| Brother | .6 | 0 | .2 | 0 | .2 | 0 |
| Male relative | 3.2 | 1 | 1 | .6 | 1.4 | 0 |
| Female relative | 1.0 | .8 | .8 | 0 | .2 | 0 |
| | (n = 311) | (n = 123) | (n = 87) | (n = 15 | (n = 212) | (n = 75) |
| Nonrelatives | 62.1 | 24.6 | 17.4 | 3.0 | 42.3 | 15.0 |
| Male | 62.5 | 23.7 | 16.5 | 2.4 | 40.8 | 14.7 |
| Female | 1.6 | 1.0 | .8 | .6 | 1.8 | .4 |
| Husband | 1.8 | .8 | 1.0 | .4 | .6 | .2 |
| Stranger | 1.8 | 1.6 | .4 | 0 | .6 | .2 |
| | (n = 12) | (n = 4) | (n = 3) | (n = 1) | (n = 4) | (n = 0) |
| Both relatives & nonrelatives | 2.4 | .8 | .6 | .2 | .8 | 0 |
| | (n = 46) | (n = 28) | (n = 14) | (n = 3) | (n = 33) | (n = 8) |
| No partner given | 9 | 5.6 | 2.8 | .6 | 6.6 | 1.6 |
| % of all women | 77.0 | 33.0 | 23.0 | 4.4 | 51.0 | 17.0 |
| | (n = 115) | (n = 338) | (n = 388) | (n = 479) | (n = 246) | (n = 417) |
| No experiences | 23.0 | 67.0 | 77.0 | 95.6 | 49.0 | 83.0 |
| | 100.0 | 100.0 | 100.0 | 100.0 | 100.0 | 100.0 |

Note: No experiences were reported with stepmother. Numbers in parentheses refer to experiences with relatives only, with nonrelatives only, and with both relatives and nonrelatives. These three categories are unduplicated and are mutually exclusive for the totals. Proportions given for experiences with specific relatives and nonrelatives include those women who had experiences with both.

Table 5.2 (*continued*)

| You Are Masturbated | Oral Sex by You | Oral Sex on You | Anal Sex by You | Anal Sex on You | Attempted Intercourse | Intercourse | No. of Women | |
|---|---|---|---|---|---|---|---|---|
| | | | | | | | N | % |
| (n = 3) | (n = 1) | (n = 4) | (n = 1) | (n = 1) | (n = 3) | (n = 6) | 416 | 83.3 |
| .6% | .2% | .8% | .2% | .2% | .6% | 1.2% | 59 | 11.8 |
| 0 | .2 | .2 | 0 | 0 | 0 | 0 | 4 | .8 |
| .2 | 0 | 0 | 0 | 0 | 0 | .2 | 3 | .6 |
| 0 | 0 | 0 | 0 | 0 | 0 | 0 | 5 | 1.0 |
| 0 | 0 | 0 | 0 | 0 | 0 | 0 | 1 | .2 |
| 0 | 0 | 0 | 0 | 0 | 0 | 0 | 4 | .8 |
| .4 | 0 | .6 | .2 | .2 | .4 | 0 | 30 | 6.0 |
| .4 | 0 | .2 | 0 | 0 | .4 | 0 | 18 | 3.6 |
| (n = 89) | (n = 40) | (n = 40) | (n = 0) | (n = 9) | (n = 39) | (n = 109) | 371 | 74.5 |
| 17.8 | 8.0 | 8.0 | 0 | 1.8 | 7.8 | 21.8 | | |
| 18.1 | 7.8 | 8.0 | 0 | 0 | 7.8 | 21.5 | 362 | 72.7 |
| .4 | .6 | .2 | 0 | 0 | 0 | .2 | 20 | 4.0 |
| .2 | .2 | .2 | 0 | 0 | .2 | .8 | 9 | 1.8 |
| .4 | 0 | .2 | 0 | 0 | .6 | .8 | 21 | 4.2 |
| (n = 2) | (n = 1) | (n = 1) | (n = 0) | (n = 0) | (n = 1) | (n = 2) | 12 | 2.4 |
| .4 | .2 | .2 | 0 | 0 | .2 | .4 | 12 | 2.4 |
| (n = 20) | (n = 5) | (n = 7) | (n = 1) | (n = 2) | (n = 19) | (n = 19) | | |
| 4.0 | 1.0 | 1.4 | 0 | .4 | 3.8 | 3.8 | | |
| 23.0 | 9.4 | 10.4 | .2 | 2.4 | 12.4 | 27.2 | | 83.3 |
| (n = 387) | (n = 454) | (n = 449) | (n = 500) | (n = 489) | (n = 439) | (n = 365) | | (n = 85) |
| 77.0 | 90.6 | 89.6 | 99.8 | 97.6 | 87.6 | 72.8 | | 16.7 |
| 100.0 | 100.0 | 100.0 | 100.0 | 100.0 | 100.0 | 100.0 | 501 | 100.0 |

The partner most women had as children (37%) and as adolescents (73%) was an unrelated male. Next for children was an unrelated female (13%), and for adolescents it was a male relative (6%). Overall, 42% of women had sexual experiences with nonrelatives as children and 75% as adolescents, whereas 24% had sexual experiences with relatives as children and 12% as adolescents. Tables 5.1 and 5.2 show the type of behavior that was experienced with each partner.

Any time that sexual experiences with relatives are discussed, the term *incest* is likely to be mentioned. However, as previously discussed, there are varied definitions of this term. This study found that 24% of children and 12% of adolescents had sexual experiences with relatives. The incidence of incest found in this study varies tremendously according to the particular definition used. According to the dictionary definition of *incest* as "sexual intercourse between persons too closely related to marry legally" (*Webster's*, 1978), only sexual intercourse with parents and siblings would be included in many states. In this study, using the dictionary definition, only .6% of the sample had incestuous experiences. However, using Finkelhor's (1979) definition of *incest* as exhibition, fondling, petting, masturbation, oral–genital contact, and intercourse between any family members, the proportion of incestuous experiences in the sample jumps to 24%. This wide discrepancy underscores the caveat that researchers must be extremely careful to clearly define their use of the term *incest* when reporting the incidence of incest.

## WHO INITIATED THE EXPERIENCE

Respondents were asked the question, "How many times was this experience requested by you, your partner, or mutually?" The findings are presented in Table 5.3. For both children and adolescents, the majority of the women stated that the experience was initiated by the partner (42% and 71% respectively) one or more times, and then mutually (30% and 62%), followed by their own initiation (23% and 39%). Thus, although the majority of women were the recipients of sexual advances, others were active participants in their childhood sexual experiences, and this participation increased as they grew older. Indeed, if the number of women who initiated the experiences is combined with those who mutually initiated them with their partners, then the majority were active participants. Some women answered in more than one of these categories as they had various partners, and the experiences occurred more than once.

## EXPERIENCES BY BIRTH YEAR OF RESPONDENT

There is a widespread belief that much has changed in terms of premarital sexual behavior in the last 20 to 25 years (Reiss, 1966). Chilman (1978), in a review of

Table 5.3
Who Initiated the Experiences

| Age Group | You | Partner | Both |
|---|---|---|---|
|  | % | % | % |
| Children | 23 | 42 | 30 |
| Adolescents | 39 | 71 | 62 |

*Note:* Some women answered in more than one category.

research from the 1920s through the 1970s, concluded that the number of young people participating in nonmarital intercourse rose sharply during the mid- and late-1960s and on into the 1970s. Zelnik and Kanter (1977) found that between 1971 and 1976 a considerable increase had occurred in the prevalence of nonmarital intercourse among adolescents between 15 and 19 years of age. Zelnik and Kanter also found that the average age of first intercourse declined by about 4 months between the 1971 and 1976 studies. In cross-sectional surveys of 13- to 17-year-old students in 1970 and again in 1973, Vener and Stewart (1974) found an increase in the prevalence of eight levels of sexual behaviors from holding hands and kissing to intercourse. More recently the public's attention is focused on varied reports of the sexual abuse of children at very early ages that seems to indicate an increase in such experiences by children. This study looks at the various experiences women had as children and adolescents by birth year of respondent in order to determine if the prevalence is increasing or decreasing.

The findings of this study indicate that the previous findings of increased prevalence of sexual experiences and at earlier ages for adolescents are not a consistent pattern over time. Nor are the previous findings representative of the sexual behaviors of children 14 years of age and under. In fact, the opposite is true for children: Analysis by different age groups in the sample revealed a trend toward decreasing child sexual activity for the sample as a whole over the past 60 years. By comparison, the proportion of adolescents has remained more constant over the past 60 years. The graph in Fig. 5.1 shows the trend for both children and adolescents by birth year from 1915 to 1964. The present ages of women in the sample were broken down into 5-year intervals and presented in terms of birth-year cohorts. The ages of the respondents ranged from 18 to 66 years. The striking finding is that, except for an increase for the 1940–1949 birth-year cohorts, the trend is rather steadily toward a decrease in the proportion of children having sexual experiences over the past six decades. For the adolescents, the trend has been more consistent except for a decline for the 1930–1939 birth-year cohorts. These findings raise questions about the assertion that sexual experiences are beginning earlier and occurring more often.

A more detailed description of the breakdown by ages is given in Table 5.4 for women with childhood experiences and in Table 5.5 for women with adolescent experiences. This breakdown is by birth year and type of partner. As seen in the column showing the percentage of women with experience, the smallest proportion of women having childhood sexual experiences (46%) was born from 1960–1964. The largest proportion (74%) was born from 1915–1929. (Several 5-year intervals were combined because of the small number in this age group.) For adolescents, the smallest proportion of women (74%) was born from 1930–1939. The largest proportion (86%) was born from 1940–1944. It is interesting that the experiences for both children and adolescents dipped for the women born from

Table 5.5
Birth Year of Respondent by Type of Partner as Adolescents

| | Type of Partner | | | | | Women With Experiences | No Experiences[a] | Total Women |
| Birth Year | Parent Only | Other Relative Only | Non-relatives Only | Both Relatives and nonrelatives | Partner Not Given | | | |
|---|---|---|---|---|---|---|---|---|
| | % | % | % | % | % | % | % | % |
| 1915–1929[b] | — | — | 68 | — | 11 | 79 | 21 | 4 |
| 1930–1939[b] | — | — | 70 | 4 | — | 74 | 26 | 5 |
| 1940–1944 | — | — | 59 | 14 | 14 | 86 | 14 | 6 |
| 1945–1949 | 2 | 4 | 68 | 2 | 6 | 82 | 18 | 10 |
| 1950–1954 | 1 | 4 | 65 | 9 | 6 | 86 | 14 | 16 |
| 1955–1959 | — | — | 72 | 7 | 2 | 81 | 18 | 20 |
| 1960–1964 | 2 | 1 | 60 | 14 | 8 | 85 | 15 | 39 |
| Total | 1 | 1 | 65 | 10 | 6 | 83 | 17 | 100 |

[a]One woman who had no experiences did not give her age.
[b]Several 5-year age intervals were combined because of the small number in this age group.
$x^2(6, N = 500) = 3.11; p \geq .05$.

Other relatives are next (8% for children and 1% for adolescents), and parents are last (.8% for children and 1% for adolescents). The chi-square statistic for children, significant at the .01 level, shows that a systematic relationship does exist between the two variables of birth year and partner. This statistic is not significant for the adolescent group.

## CONCLUSION

The findings of the study concerning the nature of the sexual experiences that women had as children (ages 0–14) and as adolescents (ages 15–17) are presented in this chapter. It is found that 55% of the women had some type of sexual experience as children and 83% as adolescents. The sexual experience most often reported as both children and as adolescents is kissing and hugging in a sexual way. The partner that most women had as children and as adolescents is an unrelated male. Most women are active in initiating the experience both as children and as adolescents.

An issue that researchers must confront is their working definition of *incest*. Popular definitions include such behaviors as propositions and such partners as any relative. However, the dictionary definition of *incest* is confined to "sexual intercourse between persons too closely related to marry legally" (*Webster's*, 1978). When the broader definition is used, the incidence of incest soars and contributes to the present public hysteria that is sometimes unrelated to factual events.

A finding that challenges commonly held beliefs is that there is a definite trend toward decreasing childhood sexual activity as a whole over the past 60 years. For adolescents the pattern has remained more constant. Historically, a significant relationship exists between birth year and partner for women who had sexual experiences as children.

(1977) who reported that 63% of Black teen-agers and 31% of White teen-agers were sexually experienced in 1976. Even when examining the birth-year cohort group for those women in my study who were teen-agers in 1976 (Table 5.4, 1960–1964 birth-year group), the findings show the total proportion who had sexual experiences to be 86% for White teen-agers and 83% for Black teen-agers. Also, Reiss (1967) reported that Black high school students tend to be more sexually permissive than White students. More recent reports show few differences.

Although no significant ethnic differences are found when prevalence rates of Blacks are compared to rates for Whites, most studies have not examined the effects of sexual abuse by ethnicity (Peters et al., 1986). Of those that have, Browne and Finkelhor (1986) found in their review of the literature that, across the board, studies have consistently failed to find any Black–White differences in rates of sexual abuse. Wyatt's (1985) study, based on a community survey, and the related follow-up by Peters (1984) were specifically designed to look at possible Black–White differences and were remarkable in the similarities they found. Wyatt showed no overall differences in rates of abuse or types of abuse, and Peters found few differences in either risk factors or effects. The findings that significant

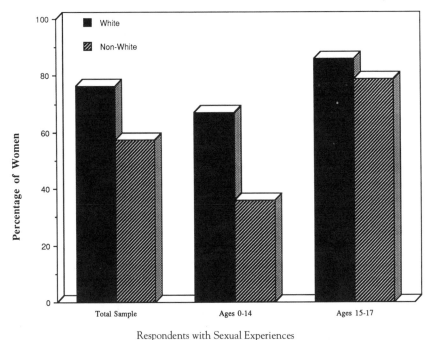

FIG. 6.1.   Sexual experiences by ethnicity and age groups.

differences in Black and White experiences do exist for this sample and that more White children and adolescents had sexual experiences than did Black children and adolescents are in sharp contrast to previous studies.

## SEXUAL BEHAVIORS

Differences in sexual behaviors by ethnicity are found to be highly significant for experiences that women had as children. Table 6.1 shows that significantly more Whites than Blacks experienced the sexual behaviors of kissing and hugging, partner shows you genitals, you show partner genitals, and partner felt your breasts. No Black women reported experiencing the remaining behaviors.

Table 6.2 shows the differences by ethnicity in the experiences that women had as adolescents. Additional behaviors of partner felt your breasts, anal sex by you, anal sex by partner, and attempted intercourse are included for adolescent experiences (relatively few women had these experiences as children). Differences by ethnicity are again significant. The proportion of White women experiencing

TABLE 6.1
Proportion of Women Who Reported Sexual Behavior by Ethnicity
as Children

| | Ethnicity of Respondent[a] | | | |
| Behavior | White (n = 316) % | Black (n = 182) % | Total Women (N = 498) % | $\chi^2$ |
|---|---|---|---|---|
| Had experiences[b] | 67 | 36 | 55 | 43.84[++] |
| Kiss and hug | 53 | 24 | 43 | 38.52[++] |
| Show you genitals | 58 | 19 | 44 | 71.78[++] |
| You show genitals | 44 | 8 | 31 | 65.50[++] |
| Felt breasts | 22 | 4 | 16 | 26.24[++] |
| You masturbated | 9 | — | 6 | — |
| You are masturbated | 10 | — | 7 | — |
| Oral sex by you | 2 | — | 1 | — |
| Oral sex on you | — | — | 0 | — |
| Intercourse | 4 | — | 2 | — |
| No experiences[c] | 33 | 64 | 45 | — |
| Total sample | 100 | 100 | 100 | 498 |

[a]Eight non-White respondents were included in the Black sample for purposes of analysis.
[b]Two women with experience did not report ethnicity.
[c]An additional woman with no experience did not report ethnicity.
[++]$p < .01$ ($df = 1$, $N = 498$ for each).

the total sample having one or more childhood or adolescent sexual experiences was 55% and 83% respectively, the proportions were 67% and 86% for the White sample alone. These proportions can be compared to Finkelhor's (1979) finding of 66% of primarily White college students who had sexual experiences before the age of 12. However, a difference is that Finkelhor included propositions as a sexual behavior. A second difference is that this study includes experiences through age 14. Further research on the child and adolescent experiences of Black women is needed to corroborate the findings of this study.

## EXPERIENCES WITH OLDER PARTNERS

Ethnic groups were also studied in relation to experiences with older partners. Table 6.5 shows that 17% of the White sample reported having partners as

TABLE 6.3
Proportion of Women Who Reported Sexual Partners by Ethnicity
as Children

| | Ethnicity of Respondent[a] | | | |
| | White (n = 211) % | Black[b] (n = 65) % | Total Women (N = 498) % | |
| Partner | | | | $x^2$ |
|---|---|---|---|---|
| Had experiences | 67 | 36 | 55[b] | 45.1[++] |
| With relative | 45 | 18 | 35 | |
| Father | 5 | 0.5 | 3 | |
| Stepfather | 2 | — | 1 | |
| Mother | 1 | 0.5 | 1 | |
| Sister | 3 | 3 | 3 | |
| Brother | 12 | 0.5 | 8 | 9.1[+] |
| Male relative | 13 | 11 | 12 | 12.5[++] |
| Female relative | 9 | 3 | 7 | |
| With nonrelatives | 70 | 25 | 53 | |
| Unrelated male | 45 | 21 | 36 | 6.5[+] |
| Unrelated female | 20 | 2 | 13 | 7.7[+] |
| Husband | 1 | — | 1 | |
| Stranger | 4 | 2 | 3 | |
| No experiences | 33 | 64 | 45[c] | |
| Total sample | 100 | 100 | 100 | |

[a]Eight non-White respondents were included in Black sample for purposes of analysis.
[b]Two women with experiences did not report ethnicity.
[c]An additional woman with no experiences did not report ethnicity.
[+]$p \leq .05$; [++]$p \leq .01$.

children who were at least 5 years older than they were, whereas only 5% of the Black sample reported having older partners. For experiences as adolescents, 23% of the White sample reported having older partners, whereas 15% of the Black sample reported such partners.

A hierarchical log linear analysis was conducted for children and adolescents in both ethnic groups who had older partners. The findings are that a significantly larger proportion (at the .01 level) of White children and adolescents had sexual experiences than did Black children and adolescents. There is also a significantly larger proportion of White women who had sexual experiences with older partners (at least 5 years older than they were) as children and adolescents than did their Black counterparts ($p \leq .05$). There is no significant difference in whether the women had sexual experiences with older partner as children or as adolescents. Therefore, if Finkelhor's definition of victimization as having a partner at least 5 years older is used, then children are not more victimized than are adolescents.

TABLE 6.4
Proportion of Women Who Reported Sexual Partners by Ethnicity
as Adolescents

| | Ethnicity of Respondent | | |
| | White (n = 316) (% = 63.5) | Black[a] (n = 182) (% = 36.5) | Total Women (N = 498) |
| Partner | % | % | % |
|---|---|---|---|
| Had experience | 86 | 79 | 83[b] |
| With relative | 11 | 14 | 12 |
| Father | 1 | 2 | 1 |
| Stepfather | 1 | 1 | 1 |
| Mother | 1 | 2 | 1 |
| Sister | 0 | 1 | .3 |
| Brother | .4 | 2 | 1 |
| Male relative | 8 | 8 | 8 |
| Female relative | 5 | 5 | 5 |
| With nonrelatives | 81 | 63 | 75 |
| Unrelated male | 94 | 95 | 95 |
| Unrelated female | 7 | 2 | 5 |
| Husband | 2 | 2 | 2 |
| Stranger | 6 | 5 | 6 |
| No experience | 14 | 21 | 17[c] |
| Total sample | 100 | 100 | 100 |

[a]Eight non-White respondents were included in the Black sample for purposes of analysis.
[b]Two women with experiences did not report ethnicity.
[c]An additional woman with no experiences did not report ethnicity.

TABLE 6.5
Proportion of Women Who Reported Sexual Experiences With Older
Partners by Ethnicity as Children and Adolescents

| | Ethnicity of Respondent | | | |
| | White (n = 316) | | Black (n = 182) | |
| Partner | Children % | Adolescents % | Children % | Adolescents % |
|---|---|---|---|---|
| Older partner | 17 | 23 | 5 | 15 |
| Other partner | 50 | 65 | 31 | 60 |
| Had experience | 67 | 88 | 36 | 75 |
| No experiences | 33 | 12 | 64 | 25 |

Total sample = 498

Ethnicity by age: $p \leq .01$.
Older partner by ethnicity: $p \leq .05$.

However, in the following chapters I present empirical evidence that undermines Finkelhor's victimization by age difference theory.

## CONCLUSION

Significant differences in child and adolescent sexual experiences by ethnicity are reported in this chapter. However, contrary to the popular notion that more Black children and adolescents have sexual experiences than do their White counterparts, the findings of this study are that this popular notion is more myth than reality. Almost twice the proportion of White women had sexual experiences as children than did the Black women. As adolescents, the total proportion was 7% more for White women than for Black women, with more White women experiencing all sexual behaviors except attempted and achieved intercourse.

Differences in sexual behaviors by White and Black women were found to be highly significant for experiences that women had as both children and as adolescents. For example, it was found that a larger proportion of White women participated in masturbation and oral–genital sex than did Black women but that more Black women participated in attempted and achieved intercourse as adolescents than did White women.

Differences in sexual partners for White and Black women were also found to be highly significant for women as children. For women as adolescents, there were no significant differences.

Sexual experiences with partners at least 5 years older were also investigated by age and ethnicity. A hierarchical log linear analysis shows that a significantly larger proportion of White women had sexual experiences with older partners as children and adolescents than did their Black counterparts. There was also a significantly larger proportion of White children and adolescents who had any type of sexual experiences than did Black children and adolescents. No significant difference was found in sexual experiences with older partners when women were children or adolescents.

These findings challenge many existing myths concerning the differences in sexual experiences of these two major ethnic groups. Empirical evidence from this and other studies is needed to confront notions built upon stereotypes and biases.

# 7

# CONDITIONS AND REACTIONS TO THE SEXUAL EXPERIENCES

In order to understand more fully the sexual experiences that women had as children and adolescents in terms of their subsequent long-range consequences, I asked respondents to give the conditions of and their reactions to the various types of sexual behaviors they had experienced with their partners. The rationale is that this type of specificity is important in delineating the variables that accompany and affect the sexual experiences.

## CONDITIONS

Information was gathered on various conditions that may have existed at the time of the sexual experience. These conditions were whether the experience was voluntary of forced, whether pressure was applied, whether the partner was 5 or more years older, the size of community in which they lived, and the type group in which they were sampled.

### Voluntary or Forced

When all partners (related and unrelated, old and young) and types of experiences (from kissing to intercourse) are considered as a group, a much larger proportion

## TABLE 7.1
### Conditions by Types of Sexual Behaviors of Women as Children

| | Types of Sexual Behavior | | | | | | | | | Totals | |
| Conditions | Kiss & Hug % | Show You Genitals % | You Show Genitals % | Felt Breasts % | You Masturbated % | You Are Masturbated % | Oral Sex by You % | Oral Sex on You % | Intercourse % | N | % |
|---|---|---|---|---|---|---|---|---|---|---|---|
| | (n = 186) | (n = 160) | (n = 108) | (n = 73) | (n = 24) | (n = 32) | (n = 7) | (n = 2) | (n = 12) | (N = 604) | |
| Participation | | | | | | | | | | | |
| Voluntary | 69 | 61 | 80 | 58 | 67 | 66 | 43 | 50 | 58 | 402 | 67 |
| Forced | 31 | 39 | 20 | 42 | 33 | 34 | 57 | 50 | 42 | 202 | 33 |
| Total | 100 | 100 | 100 | 100 | 100 | 100 | 100 | 100 | 100 | 604 | 100 |
| | (n = 85) | (n = 73) | (n = 40) | (n = 36) | (n = 19) | (n = 17) | (n = 6) | (n = 1) | (n = 8) | (N = 285) | |
| Pressure | | | | | | | | | | | |
| Subtle pressure | 61 | 62 | 73 | 56 | 74 | 82 | 33 | — | 38 | 179 | 63 |
| Verbal threats | 13 | 16 | 12 | 14 | 10 | 6 | 50 | 100 | 12 | 41 | 14 |
| Physical force | 26 | 22 | 15 | 22 | 16 | 12 | 17 | — | 50 | 62 | 22 |
| Use of a weapon | — | — | — | 8 | — | — | — | — | — | 3 | 1 |
| Total | 100 | 100 | 100 | 100 | 100 | 100 | 100 | 100 | 100 | 285 | 100 |

*Note:* The total number of reactions may exceed the number of women having sexual experiences (278) because some women had reactions to more than one type of experience. Numbers represent women, not experiences.

TABLE 7.2
Conditions by Types of Sexual Behaviors of Women as Adolescents

Types of Sexual Behavior

| Conditions | Kiss & Hug % | Show You Genitals % | You Show Genitals % | Felt Breasts % | You Masturbated % | You Are Masturbated % | Oral Sex by You % | Oral Sex on You % | Intercourse % | Totals N | Totals % |
|---|---|---|---|---|---|---|---|---|---|---|---|
| | (n = 415) | (n = 151) | (n = 106) | (n = 252) | (n = 81) | (n = 108) | (n = 46) | (n = 49) | (n = 127) | (N = 1,335) | |
| **Participation** | | | | | | | | | | | |
| Voluntary | 80 | 68 | 85 | 78 | 84 | 82 | 83 | 86 | 81 | 1,063 | 80 |
| Forced | 20 | 32 | 15 | 22 | 16 | 18 | 17 | 14 | 19 | 272 | 20 |
| Total | 100 | 100 | 100 | 100 | 100 | 100 | 100 | 100 | 100 | 1,335 | 100 |
| | (n = 157) | (n = 82) | (n = 53) | (n = 92) | (n = 37) | (n = 39) | (n = 20) | (n = 22) | (n = 72) | (N = 574) | |
| **Pressure** | | | | | | | | | | | |
| Subtle pressure | 68 | 74 | 70 | 73 | 94 | 80 | 80 | 86 | 71 | 424 | 74 |
| Verbal threats | 10 | 11 | 9 | 7 | 3 | 5 | 5 | 5 | 10 | 48 | 7 |
| Physical force | 20 | 12 | 17 | 18 | 3 | 15 | 15 | 9 | 16 | 91 | 17 |
| Use of a weapon | 2 | 2 | 4 | 2 | — | — | — | — | 3 | 11 | 2 |
| Total | 100 | 100 | 100 | 100 | 100 | 100 | 100 | 100 | 100 | 574 | 100 |

*Note:* The total number of reactions may exceed the number of women having sexual experiences (278) because some women had reactions to more than one type of experience. Numbers represent women, not experiences.

81

of the women were voluntary participants (67%) in their childhood sexual experiences than were forced participants (33%). The percentages are seen in Table 7.1. These percentages represent the total number of women who had experiences in each behavior and if they were voluntary or forced participants. It is important to note that the primary behaviors for women as children were kissing and hugging in a sexual way and exhibition. For women as adolescents, these same two behaviors plus fondling were primary. Very few women participated in the other behaviors as children as shown in Tables 7.1, 7.2, 7.3, 7.5, and 7.6.

Differences in numbers of women who voluntarily (as opposed to being forced) participated in kissing and hugging in a sexual way and you show genitals as children were especially large. The largest proportions of forced behavior were in the oral sex by you (57%) and the oral sex on you (50%) categories. These were the only two categories with larger proportions of forced behaviors. The number of women in both these categories were quite small, however (4 and 1 respectively).

For adolescents, the proportions of voluntary versus forced participation are shown in Table 7.2. Overall, the experiences that women had voluntarily (1,063) far outnumbered the forced experiences (272). These numbers represent the totals of the number of women who participated in the specific sexual behaviors. Many women participated in various sexual behaviors that contributed to the large numbers in the totals column. The totals do not represent the number of times women participated in each behavior. The voluntary proportions in each type of behavior also far exceed the forced proportions.

### Pressure

When asked about the use of pressure by partners to engage in sexual behaviors, by far the greatest proportion of women reported the use of subtle pressure both as children (63%) and as adolescents (74%). Physical force was next, again for both children (22%) and adolescents (17%). Verbal threats were reported by 14% as children and 7% as adolescents. The use of a weapon was reported by only 3 women as children (1%) and by 11 women as adolescents (2%).

### Older Partner

Finkelhor's (1979) definition of an abusive experience (as discussed earlier) was whether the partner was at least 5 years older than the child, thus violating a social norm. This study finds that 63 (23%) of the 278 women reporting sexual experiences as children had partners who were at least 5 years older than they were, and 99 (24%) of the 415 women reporting sexual experiences as adolescents had older partners. These figures are 13% and 20% of the sample of 501 compared to the finding by Finkelhor (1979) that 19% of his sample had partners 5 years or more older.

An analysis of the frequency of older partners by age groups as children reveals a trivial amount of explained variance (Pearson product-moment correlation = .05). An analysis of Black and White women who had older partners shows that 17% of the White sample had an older partner as children, and 5% of the Black sample had an older partner. For adolescents, there were 23% of the White sample who had older partners and 15% of the Black sample. These figures are shown in the chapter on ethnicity in Table 6.5. The results of a hierarchical multiple regression analysis, which shows the long-range correlates of having sexual experiences with older partners as children and adolescents, are presented in chapter 8.

## Community Size

The number of women reporting sexual experiences was analyzed by the size of community where the women lived as children. Table 7.3 gives the findings. Of women from farms, 55% had some type of sexual experience, 37% from rural nonfarm areas up to 5,000 population, 55% from 5,000 to 25,000 population, 63% from 25,000 to 100,000 population, 45% from 100,000 to 500,000 population, and 53% from larger areas [$X^2$ (5, N = 473) = 11.3, $p$ − .05]. The largest proportion of women who had experiences with relatives grew up on farms (34%). This figure is obtained by adding the number of women reporting experiences with relative and with both relatives and nonrelatives and dividing the sum by the totals of the size community. The largest proportion of those with father–daughter sexual experiences (4.3%) was from farm backgrounds. The largest proportion of step-father–stepdaughter sexual experiences (2.1%) also came from farm backgrounds. The chi-square statistic of community size and type partner or no partner was found to be significant. This means that community size and type of sexual partner women had as children are not independent but are related.

## Sample Groups

Respondents were sampled in seven types of groups: vocational training classes, undergraduate students, graduate students, school teachers, church groups, community groups, and professional groups. Professional groups (73%) and church groups (70%) reported the highest percentages of experiences as children, with community groups (66%), graduate students (60%), vocational training classes (55%), undergraduate students (41%), and public school teachers (40%) following [$X^2$ (6, N = 501) = 23.99, $p \leq$ .01.] The chi-square test of independence of type group and partner was significant at the .01 level as shown in Table 7.4.

TABLE 7.3

Number of Women With Sexual Experiences by Partner and Size of Community as Children

| Partner | Size of Community | | | | | | |
| --- | --- | --- | --- | --- | --- | --- | --- |
| | Farm | Up to 5,000 | 5,000–25,000 | 25,000–100,000 | 100,000–500,000 | Larger | Total Women |
| Women with sexual experiences | 26 (55%) | 22 (37%) | 83 (55%) | 64 (63%) | 23 (45%) | 33 (53%) | 251 (53%) |
| With relative | 7[a] | 4 | 17 | 12 | 1 | 4 | 45 |
| Father | 2 | 2 | 6 | 4 | 0 | 1 | 15 |
| Stepfather | 1 | 0 | 3 | 0 | 0 | 1 | 5 |
| Mother | 1 | 1 | 0 | 1 | 0 | 0 | 3 |
| Stepmother | 1 | 0 | 0 | 0 | 0 | 0 | 1 |
| Sister | 2 | 2 | 4 | 4 | 2 | 1 | 15 |
| Brother | 3 | 5 | 12 | 13 | 4 | 3 | 40 |
| Other male relative | 10 | 6 | 20 | 12 | 5 | 7 | 60 |
| Other female relative | 6 | 4 | 12 | 6 | 2 | 4 | 34 |
| With nonrelative | 10 | 10 | 42 | 34 | 14 | 22 | 132 |
| Unrelated male | 11 | 15 | 58 | 43 | 22 | 25 | 180 |
| Unrelated female | 9 | 7 | 24 | 13 | 3 | 8 | 64 |
| Husband | 2 | 0 | 0 | 0 | 0 | 1 | 3 |
| Stranger | 3 | 2 | 3 | 4 | 0 | 1 | 13 |
| With both relative and nonrelative | 9 | 8 | 24 | 18 | 8 | 7 | 74 |
| Women with no sexual experiences | 21 (45%) | 37 (63%) | 69 (45%) | 38 (37%) | 28 (55%) | 29 (47%) | 222 (47%) |
| Total | 47 | 59 | 152 | 102 | 51 | 62 | 473[b] |

[a] This figure means with relative only. For a true picture of how many women had experiences with specific relatives, the figures for with both relative and nonrelative must be considered.

[b] Twenty-three women did not give partner and 5 women did not give community size.

$X^2$ of community size (6 sizes plus size not given) and partner (relative, nonrelative, both relative and nonrelative, and no partner) = 33.87; $df$ = 18; $p$ = .0131.

$X^2$ of community size (6 sizes) and partner (relative, nonrelative, and both relative and nonrelative) = 7.96; $df$ = 10; $p$ = not significant.

TABLE 7.4
Number and Proportion of Sample From Various Groups by Type of Partner
as Children

| Group | Count Row % Column % Total % | No Experience | Relative | Nonrelative | Both[a] | Row Total |
|---|---|---|---|---|---|---|
| | | 33 | 9 | 21 | 11 | 74 |
| Vocational | | 44.6 | 12.2 | 28.4 | 14.9 | 14.8 |
| training classes | | 13.5 | 19.6 | 15.4 | 14.9 | |
| | | 6.6 | 1.8 | 4.2 | 2.2 | |
| | | 102 | 13 | 42 | 17 | 174 |
| Undergraduates | | 58.6 | 7.5 | 24.1 | 9.8 | 34.7 |
| | | 41.6 | 28.3 | 30.9 | 23.0 | |
| | | 20.4 | 2.6 | 8.4 | 3.4 | |
| | | 36 | 6 | 31 | 16 | 89 |
| Graduates | | 40.4 | 6.7 | 34.8 | 18.0 | 17.8 |
| | | 14.7 | 13.0 | 22.8 | 21.6 | |
| | | 7.2 | 1.2 | 6.2 | 3.2 | |
| | | 48 | 10 | 15 | 7 | 80 |
| School teachers | | 60.0 | 12.5 | 18.8 | 8.8 | 16.0 |
| | | 19.6 | 21.7 | 11.0 | 9.5 | |
| | | 9.6 | 2.0 | 3.0 | 1.4 | |
| | | 7 | 2 | 7 | 7 | 23 |
| Church groups | | 30.4 | 8.7 | 30.4 | 30.4 | 4.6 |
| | | 2.9 | 4.3 | 5.1 | 9.5 | |
| | | 1.4 | .4 | 1.4 | 1.4 | |
| | | 12 | 4 | 10 | 9 | 35 |
| Community groups | | 34.3 | 11.4 | 28.6 | 25.7 | 7.0 |
| | | 4.9 | 8.7 | 7.4 | 12.2 | |
| | | 2.4 | .8 | 2.0 | 1.8 | |
| | | 7 | 2 | 10 | 7 | 26 |
| Professional groups | | 26.9 | 7.7 | 38.5 | 26.9 | 5.2 |
| | | 2.9 | 4.3 | 7.4 | 9.5 | |
| | | 1.4 | .4 | 2.0 | 1.4 | |
| | | 245[b] | 46 | 136 | 74 | 501 |
| | Total | 48.9 | 9.2 | 27.1 | 14.8 | 100.0 |

[a] Both means sexual experiences with both relatives and nonrelatives.

[b] Twenty-three women who had sexual experiences did not give partner.

$X^2 (6, N = 501) = 23.99, p \leq .01.$

TABLE 7.5
Reactions of Women to Types of Sexual Behaviors as Children

Types of Sexual Behavior

| Reactions | Kiss & Hug % | Show You Genitals % | You Show Genitals % | Felt Breasts % | You Mastur- bated % | You Are Masturbated % | Oral Sex by You % | Oral Sex on You % | Intercourse % | Totals N | Totals % |
|---|---|---|---|---|---|---|---|---|---|---|---|
| Pleasure | (n = 249) | (n = 198) | (n = 134) | (n = 143) | (n = 29) | (n = 47) | (n = 8) | (n = 3) | (n = 15) | (N = 826) | |
| Very unpleasant | 11 | 19 | 8 | 8 | 17 | 11 | 25 | — | 27 | 103 | 13 |
| Unpleasant | 11 | 14 | 10 | 10 | 24 | 17 | 13 | — | 27 | 102 | 12 |
| Neither | 22 | 41 | 44 | 57 | 21 | 23 | 25 | 67 | 33 | 302 | 37 |
| Pleasant | 35 | 23 | 33 | 17 | 31 | 23 | 25 | 33 | 13 | 226 | 27 |
| Very pleasant | 21 | 3 | 5 | 8 | 7 | 26 | 12 | — | — | 93 | 11 |
| Total | 100 | 100 | 100 | 100 | 100 | 100 | 100 | 100 | 100 | 826 | 100 |
| Response | (n = 287) | (n = 226) | (n = 139) | (n = 103) | (n = 32) | (n = 54) | (n = 8) | (n = 3) | (n = 13) | (N = 865) | |
| Anger | 6 | 8 | 5 | 15 | 9 | 4 | 13 | — | 15 | 65 | 7 |
| Fear | 11 | 14 | 9 | 14 | 16 | 19 | 37 | — | 31 | 114 | 13 |
| Shock | 10 | 16 | 7 | 15 | 12 | 13 | 12 | — | 15 | 103 | 12 |
| Surprise | 19 | 18 | 14 | 17 | 16 | 20 | — | — | 8 | 149 | 17 |
| Interest | 33 | 39 | 50 | 26 | 41 | 24 | 25 | 67 | 31 | 316 | 37 |
| Enthusiasm | 21 | 5 | 15 | 13 | 6 | 20 | 13 | 33 | — | 118 | 14 |
| Total | 100 | 100 | 100 | 100 | 100 | 100 | 100 | 100 | 100 | 865 | 100 |
| Guilt | (n = 202) | (n = 188) | (n = 127) | (n = 77) | (n = 24) | (n = 40) | (n = 7) | (n = 2) | (n = 15) | (N = 682) | |
| Extremely guilty | 19 | 24 | 24 | 34 | 42 | 32 | 57 | 50 | 40 | 174 | 26 |
| Moderately guilty | 17 | 20 | 21 | 23 | 21 | 23 | 29 | — | 27 | 137 | 20 |
| A little guilty | 28 | 27 | 27 | 16 | 16 | 22 | — | — | 20 | 170 | 25 |
| Not guilty | 36 | 29 | 28 | 27 | 21 | 23 | 14 | 50 | 13 | 201 | 29 |
| Total | 100 | 100 | 100 | 100 | 100 | 100 | 100 | 100 | 100 | 682 | 100 |

Note: The total number of reactions may exceed the number of women having sexual experiences (278) because some women had reactions to more than one type of experience. Numbers represent women, not experiences.

## TABLE 7.6
### Reactions of Women to Types of Sexual Behaviors as Adolescents

Types of Sexual Behavior

| Reactions | Kiss & Hug % | Show You Genitals % | You Show Genitals % | Felt Breasts % | You Mastur-bated % | You Are Masturbated % | Oral Sex by You % | Oral Sex on You % | Intercourse % | Totals N | % |
|---|---|---|---|---|---|---|---|---|---|---|---|
| **Pleasure** | (n = 651) | (n = 220) | (n = 152) | (n = 321) | (n = 104) | (n = 149) | (n = 63) | (n = 77) | (n = 230) | (N = 1,967) | |
| Very unpleasant | 8 | 12 | 7 | 8 | 7 | 5 | 6 | 2 | 10 | 162 | 8 |
| Unpleasant | 10 | 12 | 7 | 7 | 5 | 7 | 14 | 8 | 15 | 194 | 10 |
| Neither | 17 | 28 | 23 | 16 | 33 | 16 | 35 | 26 | 21 | 398 | 20 |
| Pleasant | 35 | 31 | 38 | 39 | 35 | 34 | 29 | 31 | 30 | 680 | 35 |
| Very pleasant | 30 | 17 | 25 | 30 | 20 | 38 | 16 | 33 | 24 | 533 | 27 |
| Total | 100 | 100 | 100 | 100 | 100 | 100 | 100 | 100 | 100 | 1,967 | 100 |
| **Response** | (n = 673) | (n = 260) | (n = 156) | (n = 382) | (n = 110) | (n = 167) | (n = 63) | (n = 85) | (n = 224) | (N = 2,120) | |
| Anger | 7 | 4 | 5 | 8 | 3 | 3 | 6 | 1 | 5 | 116 | 6 |
| Fear | 7 | 14 | 10 | 6 | 6 | 7 | 6 | 7 | 15 | 189 | 9 |
| Shock | 7 | 11 | 4 | 8 | 7 | 8 | 5 | 10 | 6 | 156 | 7 |
| Surprise | 15 | 17 | 13 | 17 | 14 | 12 | 19 | 20 | 11 | 323 | 15 |
| Interest | 34 | 32 | 44 | 32 | 42 | 32 | 40 | 28 | 31 | 719 | 34 |
| Enthusiasm | 30 | 22 | 24 | 29 | 28 | 38 | 24 | 34 | 32 | 617 | 29 |
| Total | 100 | 100 | 100 | 100 | 100 | 100 | 100 | 100 | 100 | 2,120 | 100 |
| **Guilt** | (n = 482) | (n = 192) | (n = 141) | (n = 287) | (n = 104) | (n = 140) | (n = 50) | (n = 64) | (n = 189) | (N = 1,649) | |
| Extremely guilty | 12 | 18 | 14 | 12 | 9 | 8 | 10 | 11 | 19 | 215 | 13 |
| Moderately guilty | 13 | 20 | 20 | 17 | 20 | 15 | 12 | 13 | 19 | 271 | 16 |
| A little guilty | 30 | 34 | 33 | 33 | 32 | 41 | 36 | 34 | 32 | 542 | 33 |
| Not guilty | 45 | 28 | 33 | 38 | 39 | 36 | 42 | 42 | 30 | 621 | 38 |
| Total | 100 | 100 | 100 | 100 | 100 | 100 | 100 | 100 | 100 | 1,649 | 100 |

*Note:* The total number of reactions may exceed the number of women having sexual experiences (278) because some women had reactions to more than one type of experience. Numbers represent women, not experiences.

As seen in Table 7.4, the largest proportion of women who had sexual experiences had them with nonrelatives exclusively (27%), 15% had experiences with both relatives and nonrelatives, and 9% had experiences with relatives only. There were 60% of the public school teachers and 59% of the undergraduate students who reported no experiences. School teachers also showed the highest percentage of experiences with relatives (12.5%). The group reporting the highest percentage of sexual experiences with both relatives and nonrelatives were church groups (30.4%). When the percentage of women who reported experiences with relatives only are added to the percentage of women having sexual experiences with both relatives and nonrelatives, a grand total figure for women having experiences with relatives is obtained (120). Church groups again had the highest percentage (39%). The group reporting the largest percentage of experiences with nonrelatives only was the professional group (38.5%).

## REACTIONS

The reactions that women had to the sexual experiences as children and adolescents include pleasurable or not, responses from anger to enthusiasm, feelings of guilt or not, and considering them as harmful or abusive. The data concerning reactions to the sexual experiences are summarized in Table 7.5 as children and in Table 7.6 as adolescents. Also discussed here are the reactions to an older partner, with whom women talked about the sexual experiences, and whom they found to be most helpful in dealing with the experience.

## Pleasure

As seen in Table 7.5, 38% of the women found the experiences to be pleasant as children (total from combining the pleasant and very pleasant categories), 37% found them to be neither pleasant nor unpleasant, and 25% found the experiences to be unpleasant (total from combining the categories of unpleasant and very unpleasant). By combining the pleasant and very pleasant proportions and the unpleasant and very unpleasant proportions into the two variables of pleasurable and unpleasurable for all the sexual behaviors, the differences are clearer. Differences in the pleasurable and unpleasurable reactions were highest for intercourse (41% toward unpleasurable) and kiss and hug (34% toward pleasurable). Differences in proportions for the you show genitals (20%) and you are masturbated (21%) behaviors were also high and toward pleasurable. Other behaviors that had differences in proportion toward unpleasurable were you show genitals (7%), you masturbated (3%), and oral sex by you (1%). Again, note the small numbers of women who participated in certain behaviors as children.

The trend for the sexual experiences of women as children to be considered pleasurable is more pronounced for women as adolescents. The data for adolescents is shown in Table 7.6. By combining the categories into pleasurable and unpleasurable as done for children, the result is that 62% of the women found the experiences to be pleasant or very pleasant as adolescents, 20% found them to be neither pleasant nor unpleasant, and 18% found them to be unpleasant or very unpleasant. All of the reactions to specific behaviors were in the direction of pleasurable rather than unpleasurable reactions, and the differences in proportions ranged from 24% to 60%.

## Type of Response

Of the women, 68% had overall positive responses to the sexual experiences as children. This percentage was obtained by combining the three positive responses of surprise, interest, and enthusiasm as shown in Table 7.5. The most typical reaction to the sexual experiences by children was that of interest (37%). Negative reactions of anger, fear, or shock were experienced by 32% of the women as children. For specific behaviors, positive responses were dominant except for the oral sex and intercourse behaviors. Note the small number of women who participated in these behaviors as children.

For adolescents, 78% of the women had positive responses. Again the most typical reaction was interest (34%), and the negative reactions of anger, fear, or shock were experienced by 22% of the women, fewer by 10% than as children. Positive responses dominated for all behaviors.

## Guilt

Only 3% more women reported feeling not guilty at all about the sexual experiences as reported feeling extremely guilty as children. Fifty-four percent of the women had less guilty rather than more guilty overall reactions as seen in Table 7.6 by combining the four categories into two categories. However, in specific behaviors, women felt more guilty for a larger proportion of behaviors, especially toward behaviors that registered on the more intense end of the continuum. By far the largest proportions of women who felt more guilty as children were for the intercourse, oral sex by you, and you masturbated behaviors, in that order.

As adolescents, 71% of the women reported feeling less guilty than more guilty, whereas 29% reported feeling more guilty. Proportions for all behaviors were toward less guilty feelings by 24 to 56 percentage points. The highest proportions of more guilty feelings were for the behaviors of show you genitals and intercourse, both by 38% of the women.

Harmful or Abusive

The primary measures of long-term negative consequences are discussed and findings are reported in the following chapter. However, information obtained on experiences that women had that they themselves described as abusive or harmful are reported here.

*Harmful.* There were 78 women or 16% of the sample who reported that the sexual experiences they had as children were harmful, and they comprised 28% of the women who had any sexual experiences as children. The proportions of harmful experiences reported for the various behaviors were show you genitals, (31%), kissing and hugging (24%), you show genitals (15%), and fondling breasts (12%). The proportions for the remaining behaviors were 6% or less and were reported by few women. To summarize, 72% of the women who had sexual experiences as children felt that their child sexuality of predominantly kissing and hugging and exhibition behaviors was not harmful.

There were 105 women or 21% of the sample who reported that the sexual experiences they had as adolescents were harmful, which accounts for 25% of the women who had any sexual experiences as adolescents. The proportions of harmful experiences reported for the various behaviors were highest for kissing and hugging (7.4%), show you genitals (6%), intercourse (5.4%), and fondling your breasts (5%). The proportions for the remaining behaviors were less than 3%. These proportions were much lower for women having harmful sexual experiences as adolescents than they were as children. Also, 75% of the women who had sexual experiences as adolescents reported that their sexuality at that period of time was not harmful.

*Abusive.* There were 48 women or 10% of the sample who reported that they were sexually abused as children, which comprised 17% of the women who had any sexual experiences as children. The largest proportion of abusive experiences consisted of show you genitals (33%) compared to 23% for kissing and hugging in a sexual way and 16% for fondling breasts. The behaviors of you show genitals, you masturbated partner, and intercourse each comprised 7% of the experiences. The proportions of the remaining behaviors were 5% or less, and few women reported these behaviors.

As adolescents, there were 63 women or 13% of the sample who reported that they were sexually abused. They comprised 15% of the women who had any sexual experiences as adolescents. The largest proportion of abusive experiences consisted of kissing and hugging (5.6%), show you genitals (5%), fondling your breasts (2.4%), intercourse (1.6%), you are masturbated (1.4%), and attempted intercourse (1.2%). The proportions of the remaining behaviors were 1% or less.

Based on these figures for women as children, the incidence rates were 16% of the sample who reported having harmful experiences whereas 10% reported having abusive ones. However, of those women who had sexual experiences, 28% found them harmful, and 17% found them abusive. Therefore, 72% of the women felt their child sexuality was not harmful, and 83% felt it was not abusive. For women as adolescents, the incidence rates were 21% of the sample who reported having harmful experiences whereas 13% reported having abusive ones. However, of the women who had sexual experiences, 25% found them harmful, and 15% found them abusive. On the other hand, it can be deduced that 75% of the women felt their adolescent sexuality was not harmful, and 85% felt it was not abusive.

## Older Partners and Conditions and Reactions

Pearson product-moment correlations between the frequency of older partners and the frequency of different types of conditions and reactions that women experienced as children were conducted. In order to make these analyses more meaningful, data were weighted to reflect the degree of involvement in the sexual behavior. It would be improper to do a statistical analysis in which kissing and hugging were compared with equal weight to, for example, having intercourse. The sexual behaviors studied represented different degrees of intensity of sexual involvement. Six experts in the field of sexual behavior rated the thirteen behaviors (from kissing and hugging in a sexual way to intercourse) on a scale from 1 to 10 according to the degree of sexual involvement with a rating of 10 meaning the most intense involvement (see Appendix D for the rating scale). The expert ratings are shown in Table 7.7. In a human sexuality course, 37 social work students were also asked to do the same ratings. The mean rating of the students for each of the behaviors was exactly the same as the expert ratings for each behavior. These mean ratings of the students are also given in Table 7.7. As seen in the table, mean weights for each behavior are kissing and hugging = 2, exhibition = 3, breast fondling = 4, mutual masturbation = 6, oral sex = 8, anal sex = 8, attempted intercourse = 9, and intercourse = 10. These weights were used to scale the respondents' responses in relation to the behaviors in which they engaged.

New variables were also created for these analyses. Respondents were asked how much pleasure, guilt, and pressure were involved in their participation. Responses to these questions were on a continuum: For example, the continuum for pleasure was *very unpleasant, unpleasant, neither pleasant nor unpleasant, pleasant,* and *very pleasant.* In order to analyze these responses, new variables of pleasure, guilt, and pressure were created by thus ranking and weighting the reactions from 1 to 4 or 5 (depending on the number of variables in the category), with 5 meaning more pleasant, less guilty, and more pressure. To acquire a total pleasure score for

TABLE 7.7.
Ratings for Sexual Behaviors

| Behavior | Ratings | |
|---|---|---|
| | Experts | Students |
| Kissing and hugging | 2 | 2 |
| Exhibition | 3 | 3 |
| Breast fondling | 4 | 4 |
| Mutual masturbation | 6 | 6 |
| Oral sex | 8 | 8 |
| Anal sex | 8 | 8 |
| Attempted intercourse | 9 | 9 |
| Intercourse | 10 | 10 |

Note:  Ten represents the most intense involvement.

each respondent for all the behaviors, the new pleasure variable was also weighted according to the expert ratings for each behavior and totaled.

The findings of these analyses, using the weighted data and new variables, are shown in Table 7.8. Correlations between the frequency of older partners and the frequency of the conditions of voluntary, forced, and pressure and the reactions of pleasure, guilt, abusive, and harmful were conducted. The highest correlation was with voluntary and older partner (.49), with forced, abusive, and harmful next at .46 each. The lowest correlations was .09 for pleasure and older partner. These were all positive correlations that means that the frequency of older partners and the frequency of these reactions go up and down together. The squared correlations indicate the proportion of variance in the types of reactions that are associated with older partners. As seen in Table 7.8, the explained variance range from .24 to .008, that is, 24% of the variance in voluntary participation by the respondent is accounted for by older partners, to .8% for pleasure. These correlations are for children only.

TABLE 7.8
Correlations of Older Partner With Conditions and Reactions as Children

| Conditions and Reactions | $r$ | $r^2$ |
|---|---|---|
| Voluntary | .49 | .240 |
| Forced | .46 | .212 |
| Abusive | .46 | .212 |
| Harmful | .46 | .212 |
| Pressure | .42 | .176 |
| Guilt | .25 | .062 |
| Pleasure | .09 | .008 |

## Positive and Negative Effects

The women subjects who had sexual experiences as either children or adolescents were asked how they perceived the experience(s) in terms of long-range positive or negative views of sex and positive or negative effects on their lives.

Of the 448 women who had experiences, 28% retrospectively perceived the experiences as having both positive and negative effects on their lives, 27% perceived them as having primarily positive effects, and 6% perceived them as having primarily negative effects. Some women did not answer this question. These figures indicate that the long-range effects from self-reports by the women in the study are that their preadult sexual experiences are primarily positive.

In order to achieve more specificity regarding the women who answered this question, a specific analysis was done to obtain this information. Of the 448 women who had experiences and answered this particular question, 57% had experiences with nonrelatives, 13% had experiences with relatives other than parents or stepparents, and 3% had experiences with parents or stepparents. Of the experiences reported, 76% of the women had kissing and hugging and exhibition experiences, 56% had fondling and masturbation experiences, and 26% had oral or anal sex and attempted or completed intercourse. These findings reflect the answers from only this portion of the sample.

In the following chapter the findings of more sophisticated analyses are reported regarding long-range effects. These analyses utilize measures of adult functioning and specific sexual behaviors and partners in order to ascertain effects rather than simply to self-report.

## With Whom Respondents Talked

Of the 448 women, 151 (34%) had sexual experiences as either children or adolescents or both and talked about the experiences with someone. Table 7.9 shows with whom respondents chose to talk. The persons most women talked with were friends (19%), mother (11%), and sister (7%). Other relatives or adults were each talked to by 3% or less of the women. Persons considered to be helping professionals were talked to by only 3% of the women. These helping professionals were doctors, police, and agency staff. Only one woman talked to agency staff. This figure seems quite small when compared to the 55% to 83% of the sample who reported sexual experiences as children and adolescents respectively, the 12% to 24% of the sample who reported experiences with relatives, and the 10% to 13% of the sample who reported abusive experiences. However, it must be remembered that 67% to 80% of the women reported that the sexual experience was voluntary on their part, and the perceived need for help was obviously low.

TABLE 7.9
Number and Proportion of Respondents Who Talked With Others About the
Experience

| Person | Number[a] | %[b] |
|---|---|---|
| Talked with: | 151 | 34 |
| Friend | 85 | 19 |
| Mother | 47 | 11 |
| Sister | 29 | 7 |
| Other female adult | 11 | 3 |
| Father | 10 | 2 |
| Brother | 9 | 2 |
| Other male adult | 6 | 1 |
| Doctor | 5 | 1 |
| Police | 4 | 1 |
| Agency staff | 1 | 0.2 |
| Other | 5 | 1 |
| Talked with no one | 127 | 28 |
| Total | 448 | 100 |

[a] Total number of women who reported having sexual experiences as either children or adolescents or both is 448. Some women talked with more than one person.

[b] Percent of women reporting sexual experiences (448).

## Whom Respondents Found Helpful

Of those women who talked with someone, 52 (34%) found the person they talked with to be helpful. The persons that respondents found to be helpful in dealing with the sexual experiences are shown in Table 7.10. The largest number of women found friends (34%) and mother (27%) to be helpful. Other relatives (8%), father (6%), and helping professionals (9%) were reported as helpful. Social workers were found to be helpful by two women. An important finding here is that 34% of the women who had sexual experiences as children and adolescents talked with someone about them, and over one third (34%) of these women who talked with someone found them to be helpful. As most of the experiences were voluntary, pleasurable, and without guilt, one can assume that many women did not need help but wanted to talk about the experiences with someone. A second important finding is that all the women who talked with someone talked with a friend. Many also talked with others, but a friend was the one talked with consistently. However, it should be noted that there could have been many reasons for talking with someone about the experience other than the desire to seek help, such as simply sharing experiences, comparing experiences, bragging or otherwise attempting to integrate the experience into their own life context.

TABLE 7.10
Number and Proportion of Respondents Who Found Others to be Helpful

| Person | Number[a] | %[b] |
|---|---|---|
| Total Women | 52 | 34 |
| Friend(s) | 52 | 34 |
| Mother | 41 | 27 |
| Other relative | 12 | 8 |
| Father | 9 | 6 |
| Minister | 3 | 2 |
| Psychiatrist | 3 | 2 |
| Police | 3 | 2 |
| Social worker | 2 | 1 |
| Doctor | 2 | 1 |
| Psychologist | 1 | 1 |
| Other | 11 | 7 |

Note: Total number of women who talked with someone is 151.

[a] Number of women who found this person helpful is indicated. Some women found more than one person helpful.

[b] This is the percent of women who talked with someone (151).

## Help Wanted by Women

The women who participated in this study were asked what kind of help they would have liked to have had at the time the experience occurred, how they wish the situation had been handled, who knew about the experience, should the person(s) who knew have done something about it, and, if so, what should they have done. Although some of these questions seem redundant, they do provide various ways of obtaining the desired information. The portion of the sample who answered these subjective questions were described in the previous section on positive and negative effects.

Of the women who had experiences, 9% wanted someone with whom to talk, 7% wanted motherly advice, 6% wanted information, 5% wanted someone to intervene, and 4% wanted counseling. In regard to how they wished it had been handled, 6% wanted the partner reprimanded, 5% wanted more understanding, 3% wanted counseling, 2% wanted more information and wanted to discuss the experience with someone, 1% wanted counseling for the partner, and .4% wished their mother had not known about the experience.

The persons who the women thought knew about the experience(s) were parents (16%), friends, (11%), other family members (8%), the partner's friends (3%), neighbors and partner's family (2% each), and boyfriends or spouse (1%). When asked if these persons who knew about the experience(s) should have done something, women's responses were no (36%) and yes (11%). In response to the question of what the person who knew should have done about it, the answers were to talk about it with them (5%), to intervene (4%), to have the partner talk with them (.5%), to end the relationship (.2%), and to give information about sexuality (.2%).

The percentages of women answering questions on the type of help they wanted were rather small implying that few wanted help. From these findings and from the ones reported earlier in this chapter, it seems that the women wanted to talk about or share the experience with someone else more than they wanted help. This conclusion is re-enforced by the findings that most women found the experiences to have positive effects on their views of sex and on their lives in general and by the findings reported earlier that most of the experiences were voluntary, pleasant, and interesting.

## CONCLUSION

Conditions that existed at the time of the sexual experiences and the women's reactions to the experiences were explored in order to more fully understand their implications for long-range consequences. The conditions were whether the experience was voluntary or forced, whether pressure was applied, whether the partner was 5 or more years older, the size of community in which they lived as children, and the type group in which they were sampled.

Many more women were voluntary rather than forced participants as children. The proportions for kissing and hugging in a sexual way and you show genitals were especially high. For adolescents the larger percentages for all behaviors were voluntary rather than forced. For pressure, by far the greatest proportion reported the use of subtle pressure as both children and adolescents. However, the use of physical force, verbal threats, and weapons were reported by some women as children and as adolescents. Experiences with a partner at least 5 years older were reported by approximately 25% of the women both as children and as adolescents.

It was found that there does exist a significant relationship between community size and type of partner. The largest proportion of women who had experiences with relatives grew up on farms. More specifically, the largest proportion of those with father–daughter and with stepfather–daughter experiences were from farm backgrounds. These findings support the social isolation theory in relation to child sexual abuse that is that sexual abuse occurs more often in rural or other areas where families are isolated from other social contacts (Alexander, 1985; Finkelhor, 1979).

Respondents were from seven types of groups when sampled. When tested according to sample groups and type partner, the chi-square test of independence was highly significant. Professional groups and church groups reported the highest percentage of experiences as children.

The reactions explored were pleasure, type of response, guilt, harmful or abusive, reactions to older partner, with whom respondents talked, and whom they found to be helpful. As children many more women reported the experiences as pleasant than reported them as unpleasant especially for the behavior of kissing and hugging in a sexual way. The highest proportion of unpleasant reactions was for intercourse in which only 15 women participated as children and who reported this reaction. For women as adolescents all the specific behaviors were described as being more pleasant. The primary response of women to the experiences, both as children and as adolescents, was positive with interest being the most typical specific response. Larger proportions of women felt less guilty rather than more guilty about their sexual behaviors as both children and as adolescents. However, more felt guilty as children (46%) than as adolescents (29%). There were 72% of the women who reported their sexual experiences as children as not harmful and 75% as adolescents as not harmful. Also, 83% of women who had sexual experiences as children reported them as not abusive and 85% as not abusive as adolescents.

The weighted Pearson product-moment correlations between the frequency of older partners and the frequency of different types of conditions and reactions showed that the highest correlations were with voluntary reactions and older partners. That is, 24% of the variance for voluntary participation was accounted for by an older partner. For forced, abusive, and harmful, 21% of the variance was explained by an older partner in each one.

When asked if their sexual experiences had a positive or negative effect on their views of sex and on their lives, 28% of the 448 women who had such experiences perceived that the experiences had both positive and negative effects. There were 27% who reported the effects as primarily positive whereas 6% reported them as primarily negative.

Of the 448 women (89% of the sample) who had sexual experiences either as children (6% of the sample), as adolescents (32% of the sample), or as both (51% of the sample), over one third talked about the experience with someone, primarily friends, mother, or sister. Only 2% talked to any type of helping professional. There were 34% of those who talked with someone who found the person they talked with to be helpful. These persons were primarily friends and mother.

The type of help that most women who answered the questions wanted was someone to talk with, motherly advice, and information. Others wanted someone to intervene, to reprimand, and to counsel the partner. These percentages were, however, quite small. Parents and friends were the persons more women thought knew about the sexual experiences, and 36% of the women said that the person who knew should not have done anything about it as opposed to 11% who said they should have done something about it. Most women seemed to want someone to talk with more than they wanted help in the form of intervention or protection.

Findings reported in this chapter may seem unusual, especially to clinicians who work with survivors of abusive sexual experiences. However, there are crucial points that must be kept in mind when interpreting these findings. First, remember that no clinical or offender populations were sampled. Second, although all socioeconomic levels were sampled, the majority of the women were middle class. Third, the largest proportion of the sexual behaviors experienced were hugging and kissing and exhibition. Fourth, most of the women participated voluntarily, found the experiences to be pleasurable, and felt little guilt about them. For the minority who had different types of experiences with different partners, conditions, and reactions, the results were sometimes very different.

# 8

# CONSEQUENCES FOR ADULT FUNCTIONING

A primary purpose of this study is to determine whether sexual experiences during childhood and adolescence have long-term consequences for adult functioning. The measures of adult functioning used in this study consist of the five scales from Hudson's (1982) Clinical Measurement Package (CMP) that were discussed previously in the chapter on methodology (see Appendix B for the scales in the questionnaire package). These scales are valid and reliable indicators of problems with self-esteem (Index of Self-Esteem or ISE), depression (Generalized Contentment Scale or GCS), marital discord (Index of Marital Satisfaction or IMS), sexual discord (Index of Sexual Satisfaction or ISS), and intrafamilial stress (Index of Family Relations or IFR).

Each of the respondents was asked to complete each scale applicable to her present situation. For example, if a woman was presently unmarried, then she did not complete the Index of Marital Satisfaction, and if she was not presently relating to anyone sexually, she did not complete the Index of Sexual Satisfaction. However, the remaining three scales were applicable to all the women.

If a woman left blank more than five items on a scale, her responses to that scale were discarded from the analysis in order to reduce response bias (Hudson, 1982). The number of women completing each scale, as well as the mean and standard deviation for each scale, is presented in Table 8.1.

Each of the scales has a clinical cutting score of 30. If a person scores above 30 on any of them, it nearly always indicates that the person has a clinically

TABLE 8.1
Distribution of Scores on the Clinical Scales

| Statistic | Self-Esteem | Depression | Marital Satisfaction | Sexual Satisfaction | Family Relations |
|---|---|---|---|---|---|
| Mean | 25.6 | 23.2 | 21.2 | 17.8 | 13.9 |
| Standard deviation | 13.2 | 13.6 | 19.4 | 15.3 | 14.4 |
| Number | 497 | 497 | 259 | 383 | 486 |
| Percent < 30[a] | 67 | 72 | 74 | 80 | 89 |
| Highest score[b] | 71 | 74 | 89 | 80 | 91 |

Note:  The total number of women in the sample was 501.

[a] Scores above 30 indicate a clinically significant problem in the area measured.

[b] A score of 100 is the most pathological score.

significant problem in the area being measured, whereas a person who scores below 30 is generally found to be free of such problems (Hudson, 1982). As seen in Table 8.1, the mean for each of the scale scores is well below 30, and a majority of the scores are under 30. It must be emphasized again that no clinical populations were sampled. Therefore, it is expected that the majority of women in the sample are adequately functioning individuals.

## SCALE SCORES AND BACKGROUND VARIABLES

In order to determine the strength of the association between each of the scale scores and the continuous background variables, Pearson product-moment correlations were computed (see Table 8.2).

TABLE 8.2
Correlation of Clinical Scales With Background Variables

| Variables | Self-Esteem | Depression | Marital Satisfaction | Sexual Satisfaction | Family Relations |
|---|---|---|---|---|---|
| Age | −.066 | −.115[+] | −.020 | −.055 | .101 |
| Income | −.082 | −.024 | −.064 | −.163[++] | −.138[+] |
| School | −.107[+] | −.108[+] | −.022 | −.025 | −.139[+] |
| Number times married | .081 | .063 | .073 | .014 | .054 |
| Years with spouse | −.136[+] | −.070 | .241[++] | .210[++] | .028 |
| Number of children | .036 | −.012 | .103 | .098 | .013 |
| Number other persons in household | −.005 | .059 | .142[+] | .099 | −.074 |

Note:  Increasing scale scores indicate increasing severity of problems.

[+] $p < .05$; [++] $p < .01$.

The correlation coefficient shows the degree to which variation in one variable is associated with variation in another. The largest correlations are between the measures of marital and sexual satisfaction and the background variable of years with spouse. These correlations indicate a modest tendency for marital and sexual problems to increase with the number of years married. However, because the squared Pearson product-moment correlation describes the proportion of variance explained in such a relationship, the number of years married accounts for less than 6% of the variance in the marital or sexual discord scores. Although statistically significant, these relationships can only be regarded as trivial.

The next largest correlation (negative) is between income and sexual satisfaction, indicating that as income increases, sexual problems decrease. However, again this correlation is weak, and the amount of variance explained is small.

## SCALE SCORES AND SEXUAL EXPERIENCES

In order to measure the specific impact of child sexual experiences on adult functioning, several analyses of variance were conducted for each measure of adult functioning. Because, as children, these women had more experiences with relatives and because children are sometimes thought to be more vulnerable, these tests were done only for the reports of sex in childhood and did not include the sexual experiences of women as adolescents.

### Experiences With Relatives and Nonrelatives

The first set of analyses was conducted to determine whether variations in sexual experiences with parents, other relatives, nonrelatives, both relatives and non-relatives, or no sexual experiences are significantly related to scores on the five scales. The results of these analyses (see Table 8.3) suggest that in any of the five major dependent variables, by the time a woman reaches adulthood, the type of partner (if any) she had in her child sexual encounters is not significantly related to her functioning as assessed by the five scales used in the present investigation.

### Experiences With Older Partners

The second set of analyses of variance was conducted for each measure of adult functioning to determine if the age of the partner—older, younger, or no partner—accounts for a significant amount of variance in the scale scores. The partner was considered older if he or she was at least 5 years older than the woman at the time of the encounter.

TABLE 8.3

Analysis of Variance Summary Table for Scale Scores and Sexual Experiences With Relatives and Nonrelatives as Children

| Scale and Number | Mean Scores[a] | | | | | F Ratio | p | R | $R^2$ |
|---|---|---|---|---|---|---|---|---|---|
| | Parents | Other Relatives | Non-relative | Both Relatives & Nonrelatives | No Experiences | | | | |
| GCS | 21.0 | 18.48 | 24.17 | 22.01 | 23.75 | 1.80 | .13 | .116 | .014 |
| N | 4 | 42 | 134 | 74 | 220 | | | | |
| ISE | 26.75 | 21.31 | 27.23 | 25.78 | 25.61 | 1.61 | .17 | .116 | .014 |
| N | 4 | 42 | 135 | 74 | 219 | | | | |
| IMS | 25.00 | 22.14 | 19.41 | 19.02 | 22.15 | .36 | .84 | .077 | .006 |
| N | 2 | 29 | 66 | 43 | 108 | | | | |
| IFR | 13.50 | 12.05 | 14.05 | 15.63 | 13.23 | .54 | .71 | .07 | .005 |
| N | 4 | 42 | 133 | 73 | 211 | | | | |
| ISS | 18.33 | 18.03 | 17.80 | 19.07 | 16.99 | .21 | .93 | .048 | .002 |
| N | 3 | 37 | 104 | 57 | 166 | | | | |

[a] Higher scores indicate the presence of more problems in the area measured.

TABLE 8.4
Analysis of Variance Summary Table for Scale Scores and Sexual Experiences
With Older, Younger, and No Partner as Children

| Scale and Number | Mean Scores[1] | | | F Ratio | p | R | $R^2$ |
|---|---|---|---|---|---|---|---|
| | Older Partner | Younger Partner | No Experiences | | | | |
| ISS | 21.25 | 17.56 | 16.99 | 1.60 | .20 | .091 | .008 |
| N | 53 | 164 | 166 | | | | |
| IFR | 16.79 | 13.74 | 13.23 | 1.52 | .22 | .079 | .006 |
| N | 63 | 212 | 211 | | | | |
| GCS | 25.03 | 22.07 | 23.75 | 1.48 | .23 | .077 | .006 |
| N | 62 | 215 | 220 | | | | |
| ISE | 27.84 | 24.94 | 25.61 | 1.18 | .31 | .069 | .005 |
| N | 63 | 215 | 219 | | | | |
| IMS | 21.24 | 20.32 | 22.15 | .25 | .78 | .044 | .002 |
| N | 38 | 113 | 108 | | | | |

Note: Older partner is one who was at least five years older than the child. Younger partner is one who was less than five years older than the child.

[1] Higher scores indicate the presence of more problems in the area measured.

The results of these analyses (see Table 8.4) suggest that the relative age of her partner in her child sexual experiences is not significantly related to any of the measures of a woman's adult functioning. Although women who had older partners as children tended to score higher on all scales except the Index of Marital Satisfaction (higher scores mean more problems in the area being measured), none of the means for any scale reached the clinical cutting point of 30. Moreover, the variation of these experiences does not account for as much as 1% of the variance in any of the five major dependent variables.

## LONG-RANGE CONSEQUENCES

In order to examine the relationships between each outcome and a number of independent variables simultaneously, a five-step hierarchical multiple regression analysis was conducted for each of the five measures of adult functioning. First the regression model itself is elaborated, and then the findings are presented.

### The Regression Model Applied to Each Outcome

Data were weighted and new variables created as presented in the previous chapter. All independent or predictor variables were organized into sets and entered hierarchically by set into each of the five separate regression analyses, one for each measure of adult functioning.

The first set of independent variables was composed of all the socioeconomic, family, and other background variables. These measures were simultaneously entered first in each of the five analyses in order to eliminate, that is, control their effects. In this manner, some conclusions could be drawn about the independent effects of the sexual activity measures (entered later) once differences in socioeconomic, family, and background variables have been controlled for. Therefore, any effects found to be associated with sexual activity were not inflated by variation correctly attributable to differences in socioeconomic, family, and background variables.

The second set of independent variables consisted of weighted sexual activity scores with the various partners of nonrelative, relatives other than parents, parents, and both relatives and nonrelatives. These sexual partner variables were entered second in the analysis to find out how much of the scale score variance could be accounted for by sexual activity over and above that accounted for by the demographic variables. However, the four variables in this set were entered hierarchically in the order given above to determine how much of the scale score variance could be accounted for by each over and above that accounted for by the variables entered previously. For example, sexual activity with parents could account for only that variance over and above any other sexual activity with nonrelatives and with relatives other than parents.

The third set of independent variables represented conditions that existed at the time the sexual activity occurred. The condition variables at the time of the sexual activity, of necessity, followed the sexual activity set and was, therefore, the third set entered into the analysis. These variables represented the amount of pressure, voluntary participation, forced participation, and the presence of older partners (all weighted according to the ratings by experts). The variables in this set were all entered simultaneously as one block.

The fourth set of independent variables represented the reactions to the sexual activity in terms of pleasure, guilt, harm, and abuse (all weighted). These reactor variables logically followed the sexual activity and conditions sets and were entered as a block.

The fifth and final set of independent or predictor variables consisted of two-way interactions of the sexual partner variables with the conditions variables and the reaction variables. For example, such a two-way interaction could represent the situation where the partner was stepfather and the condition was physical force or where the partner was stepfather and the reaction was unpleasant, anger, and guilt. These interactions—the particular constellations of the encounter—could be significantly related to adult depression, low self-esteem, and poor marital, family, and sexual relations even after the main effects of the behavior, partner, condition, and reaction variables were taken into account. All interactions were entered as a single block.

### Findings

The first results summarize the explanatory power of the five blocks of independent variables: background, type of partner, conditions, reactions, and interac-

TABLE 8.5
Hierarchical Multiple Regression Analyses for Scale Scores and Sets
of Variables (Ages 0–14)

| Scales and Sets | R | $R^2$ | $R^2$ Change | $p <$ |
|---|---|---|---|---|
| IFR (N = 485) | | | | |
| Background variables | .377 | .142 | .142 | .001 |
| Sexual partners | .401 | .161 | .019 | .0005 |
| Conditions | .408 | .167 | .006 | .0005 |
| Reactions | .416 | .173 | .006 | .001 |
| Interaction | .487 | .237 | .064 | .0005 |
| GCS (N = 496) | | | | |
| Background variables | .372 | .138 | .138 | .001 |
| Sexual partners | .383 | .146 | .008 | .001 |
| Conditions | .386 | .149 | .003 | .003 |
| Reactions | .394 | .156 | .007 | .004 |
| Interactions | .479 | .229 | .073 | .001 |
| ISE (N = 496) | | | | |
| Background variables | .321 | .103 | .103 | .055 |
| Sexual partners | .329 | .108 | .005 | .068 |
| Conditions | .333 | .111 | .003 | .138 |
| Reactions | .338 | .114 | .003 | .209 |
| Interactions | .442 | .195 | .081 | .023 |
| IMS (N = 259) | | | | |
| Background variables | .455 | .207 | .207 | .028 |
| Sexual partners | .461 | .212 | .005 | .045 |
| Conditions | .477 | .228 | .016 | .062 |
| Reactions | .494 | .244 | .016 | .065 |
| Interactions | .607 | .368 | .124 | .019 |
| ISS (N = 382) | | | | |
| Background variables | .303 | .092 | .092 | .577 |
| Sexual partners | .304 | .092 | .001 | .684 |
| Conditions | .311 | .097 | .005 | .815 |
| Reactions | .350 | .122 | .025 | .587 |
| Interactions | .443 | .196 | .074 | .424 |

tions of these variables when used to predict the five adult functioning measures. Childhood and adolescent experiences are analyzed separately. Subsequently the specific variables within each set of predictor variables that are significantly related to adult functioning are explored.

TABLE 8.6
Hierarchical Multiple Regression Analyses for Scale Scores and Sets
of Variables (Ages 15–17)

| Scales and Sets | R | $R^2$ | $R^2$ Change | F | p < |
|---|---|---|---|---|---|
| IFR (N = 462) | | | | | |
| Background variables | .237 | .056 | .056 | 3.358 | .001 |
| Sexual partners | .249 | .062 | .006 | 2.707 | .002 |
| Conditions | .263 | .069 | .007 | 2.214 | .006 |
| Reactions | .294 | .086 | .017 | 2.193 | .003 |
| Interaction | .390 | .152 | .066 | 1.738 | .004 |
| GCS (N = 472) | | | | | |
| Background variables | .249 | .062 | .062 | 3.839 | .0005 |
| Sexual partners | .278 | .076 | .014 | 3.467 | .0005 |
| Conditions | .297 | .088 | .012 | 2.950 | .0005 |
| Reactions | .302 | .091 | .003 | 2.392 | .001 |
| Interactions | .413 | .171 | .080 | 2.051 | .0005 |
| ISE (N = 473) | | | | | |
| Background variables | .224 | .050 | .050 | 3.068 | .002 |
| Sexual partners | .250 | .062 | .012 | 2.784 | .002 |
| Conditions | .275 | .076 | .034 | 2.493 | .002 |
| Reactions | .282 | .080 | .004 | 2.059 | .006 |
| Interactions | .399 | .159 | .079 | 1.885 | .001 |
| IMS (N = 248) | | | | | |
| Background variables | .298 | .089 | .089 | 2.902 | .004 |
| Sexual partners | .305 | .093 | .004 | 2.198 | .015 |
| Conditions | .312 | .098 | .005 | 1.670 | .058 |
| Reactions | .343 | .117 | .010 | 1.595 | .059 |
| Interactions | .466 | .217 | .100 | 1.313 | .110 |
| ISS (N = 365) | | | | | |
| Background variables | .188 | .035 | .035 | 1.632 | .114 |
| Sexual partners | .193 | .037 | .002 | 1.242 | .258 |
| Conditions | .205 | .042 | .005 | 1.016 | .437 |
| Reactions | .242 | .059 | .017 | 1.130 | .319 |
| Interactions | .331 | .110 | .051 | 0.920 | .617 |

*Scales and Sets of Variables.* The results of the hierarchical multiple regression analyses for the measures of adult functioning and sets of variables are given in Table 8.5 for women as children and in Table 8.6 for women as adolescents.

The organization of both tables is the same. The first column lists the five measures of adult functioning with the five sets of predictor variables under each. The second column $(R)$ gives the correlations of the sets of predictors with a particular measure of adult functioning. The third column gives the squared correlations $(R^2)$ or the amount of variance in adult functioning that has been explained thus far by all the predictor variables. The fourth column $(R^2$ change) presents the amount of variance explained by each set, not the cumulative amount. The fifth column presents the statistical significance $(p)$ of each specific set of variables.

Findings for women as children are presented first. When looking at $R^2$ change for all five outcomes, the background variables, that is, the demographics of income, age, ethnicity, education, occupation, marital status, and community size surrounding the present adult circumstances of the women, are the most potent predictors of present adult functioning. They are significant and explain from 9% to 21% of the total variance. Although there are statistically significant main effects of the partners, conditions, and reactions variables, the second most influential and the only other consistent and substantively important factor in the analysis is the set of two-way interactions. The self-esteem and sexual satisfaction measures follow this pattern, although the probabilities do not reach statistical significance in all instances. The combined models explain a considerable percentage (20%–37%) of the variance in the scale scores.

When looking at $R^2$ change for all five outcomes in the adolescent analysis, the set of interactions is the most important single set of predictor variables, and the background (present circumstances) variables are the second.[1] Less variance (total) is explained (11%–21%) by these independent variables than is the case in the child analysis of the scale scores.

In order to visualize the differences in the analyses for women as children and as adolescents more vividly, the primary findings are listed together in Table 8.7.

---

[1]The differences in the amount of variance explained by the background variables for women as children and as adolescents are due to three factors: (a) differences in the size of community in which the women lived as children and as adolescents, (b) differences in whether both parents worked when the women were children or adolescents, and (c) some of the background variables that were not significant for women as children and the information that was the same for the women as adolescents were combined or omitted from the analyses conducted for women as adolescents. For example, neither the area of the southeast where the women lived nor the specific type of group from which the data were gathered was significant for women as children and, therefore, was omitted from the analyses for women as adolescents. Also, the categories of single and divorced were combined into a single category as neither was significant for the analysis for children.

TABLE 8.7
Hierarchical Multiple Regression Analyses for Scale Scores and Sets of
Variables: Comparison of Age Groups

| Scales and Significant Sets | 0–14 yrs. $p$ | $R^2$ Change | 15–17 yrs. $p$ | $R^2$ Change |
|---|---|---|---|---|
| IFR | (N = 485) | | (N = 462) | |
| Background variables | .001 | .142[a] | .001 | .056[a] |
| Sexual partners | .0005 | .019 | .002 | .007 |
| Conditions | .0005 | .006 | .006 | .007 |
| Reactions | .001 | .006 | .003 | .017 |
| Interactions | .005 | .064 | .004 | .066 |
| | | .095[b] | | .096[b] |
| | Total | .237 | Total | .152 |
| GCS | (N = 496) | | (N = 472) | |
| Background variables | .001 | .138[a] | .0005 | .062[a] |
| Sexual partners | .001 | .008 | .0005 | .014 |
| Conditions | .003 | .003 | .0006 | .012 |
| Reactions | .004 | .007 | .001 | .003 |
| Interactions | .001 | .073 | .0005 | .080 |
| | | .091[b] | | .109[b] |
| | Total | .229 | Total | .171 |
| ISE | (N = 496) | | (N = 473) | |
| Background variables | .— | .103[a] | .002 | .050[a] |
| Sexual partners | .— | .005 | .002 | .012 |
| Conditions | .— | .003 | .002 | .034 |
| Reactions | .— | .003 | .006 | .004 |
| Interactions | .023 | .081 | .001 | .079 |
| | | .092[b] | | .129[b] |
| | Total | .195 | Total | .179 |
| IMS | (N = 259) | | (N = 248) | |
| Background variables | .028 | .207[a] | .004 | .089[a] |
| Sexual partners | .045 | .005 | .015 | .004 |
| Conditions | .— | .016 | .— | .005 |
| Reactions | .— | .016 | .— | .010 |
| Interactions | .019 | .124 | .001 | .100 |
| | | .161[b] | | .119[b] |
| | Total | .368 | Total | .208 |
| ISS | (N = 382) | | (N = 365) | |
| Background variables | .— | .092[a] | .— | .035[a] |
| Sexual partners | .— | .001 | .— | .002 |
| Conditions | .— | .005 | .— | .005 |
| Reactions | .— | .025 | .— | .017 |
| Interactions | .— | .074 | .— | .051 |
| | | .015[b] | | .075[b] |
| | Total | .197 | Total | .110 |

[a] Variance explained by background variables.

[b] Total variance explained by other sets.

The significance levels and the explained variance ($R^2$ change in the table) for both age groups are listed side by side. Important findings are as follows: (a) Women who had early initiations seem to be more predictable in their scores; (b) the increased predictability is due to the increased association of their present circumstances with their scores over that evidenced by women who experienced sex as adolescents; (c) the interactions are about equally important for both sets of women; and (d) the isolated facts of who did it, how they did it, and how the woman felt about it at the time are not nearly so important as are the peculiar combinations of who did it and how and who did it and how the woman felt.

For the last two dependent variables, the Index of Marital Satisfaction and the Index of Sexual Satisfaction, one must remember that women who were not presently married or who did not presently have a sexual partner did not complete these scales. It could be that these women were having difficulty relating in these areas, but because they did not complete a scale, this difficulty can not be determined in these analyses.

One or more of the background (present circumstances) variables of income, age, occupation, education, community size, ethnicity, marital status, and number of times married scatter significant effects on all outcomes for both groups of women with the exception of sexual satisfaction in the group initiated as children. However, the interactions of who the sexual partner was with either conditions or reactions are significant for all five analyses for children and for all except marital satisfaction and sexual satisfaction for adolescents. Having parents as partners with the negative conditions of pressure or forced or the negative reactions of harmful, abusive, or guilt, is significant for four of the five measures of adult functioning for children and for family relations for adolescents. (See Appendix F for tables showing the specific variables in each set that are significant for a particular measure of adult functioning for both children and adolescents.)

## CONCLUSION

Analyses of the impacts of child and adolescent sexual experiences reveal some startling findings. It is found through analyses of variance that sexual experiences according to the type of partner women had as children, including relatives or nonrelatives and also older, younger, or no partners, are not significantly related to adult functioning. However, the relationship of adult functioning to sexual activity with various partners interacting with the conditions of and reactions to the sexual experiences explains more variance for all the measures of adult functioning than sexual partners, conditions, and reactions combined explain for each age group. This finding is considered to be one of the most important findings of the study and is discussed in the following chapter.

Notably missing from the background variables that are significant for adult functioning is the variable of mothers working when the women were children or adolescents. The findings from the regression analyses show that the variable of both parents working when the woman was up to 12 years of age or from 12 to 18 years of age explain less than .35% of the variance in any of the scale scores. Results are not statistically significant for any of the five measures of adult functioning. In other words, the long-range correlation for the child or adolescent of both parents working when the person was young is only trivial and inconsequential.

The findings of these analyses raise the issue of statistical significance versus substantive significance. Although many of the analyses are statistically significant for each age group, the largest amount of explained variance (12.4% for child sexual experiences) can only be described as minimal when the researcher's goal is to explain 100% of the variance. Thus a caveat is given to those who look at statistical significance only. It can be said, however, that these analyses lay a foundation upon which future research can be built. Perhaps the specific variables that proved significant in these analyses can be analyzed more closely in future studies.

# 9

# DISCUSSION AND IMPLICATIONS

Some of the findings that I have presented demand further discussion. The data challenge commonly held beliefs and have far-reaching implications for the helping professions and others who study human sexuality.

## DISCUSSION OF FINDINGS

This study of a primarily middle-class, nonclinical, and nonoffender sample balances the work by De Francis (1969) who studied a lower socioeconomic class, multiproblem, clinical, and offender sample. The study also corroborates in some ways (and challenges in others) the study of middle-class women by Gagnon (1965) and the study of undergraduates by Fritz et al. (1981) and Finkelhor (1979) in that it combines the two populations in one study. A difference, however, is the inclusion of graduate students (16% of the sample). The study of the sexual experiences of this group has not been reported in previous major works.

### Incidence Rates

The incidence rates of childhood sexual experiences (55% of the sample) and adolescent sexual experiences (83% of the sample) can be compared to those found by Finkelhor (1979) that were 66% for experiences while growing up. The 24% of the sample who had sexual experiences with relatives as children and 12%

as adolescents can also be compared with Finkelhor's total of 28%, although he included propositioning as a sexual experience and stepsiblings as partners and reported findings for both age groups together.

A finding of no small import in this study is that incest in middle-class families does not reach the alarming proportions that are currently reported in the media. In fact, the incidence rate varies from .6% to 24% in any one study depending on how the researcher defines incest. It seems that rather than the over-all incidence rate of incest increasing, it is the definition of incest that is expanding. Incest, as defined by *Webster's* (1978), has only a .6% incidence rate for children and 0% for adolescents in this study (intercourse was reported for only stepfather and male relatives by women as adolescents, and the rate only came to .02% with the dictionary definition), as opposed to Finkelhor's 28% incest rate using his expanded definition.

## Sexual Experiences

The types of behaviors most often reported in the present study are kissing and hugging in a sexual way and exhibition with both relatives and nonrelatives as children and kissing and hugging in a sexual way and fondling with unrelated male as adolescents. It is important to keep these primary behaviors in mind when looking at the implications for adult functioning. This finding of primary behaviors differs from De Francis' (1969) finding that rape occurred in more of the cases (40%). The disparity in these findings could be due to the differences in middle- and lower-class experiences, but De Francis' findings may also reflect both clinical and offender population characteristics.

*Ethnic Differences.* This study finds that significantly more White women had child and adolescent sexual experiences than did Black women. Because both populations are primarily middle class, one can only assume that previous popular beliefs that Black children and adolescents are more sexually active than are White children and adolescents are not grounded in reality and are not applicable to middle-class females.

Also in regard to ethnicity, findings show that a significantly larger proportion of White children and adolescents had older partners than did Black children and adolescents. However, across ethnicity there is not a significant difference in the proportion of children and adolescents who had partners at least 5 years older than themselves. In this study the significant differences found in the types of experiences and the identity of partners by ethnicity have additional implications. These differences need to be considered by professionals who counsel with these ethnic groups in order to increase understanding of cultural differences. Whereas most previous studies have been conducted with primarily White samples, there are no known comparable studies of Black populations with which to compare these findings. Need of further research on ethnic differences in preadult sexual experiences is indicated.

*Conditions and reactions.* It may come as a surprise to some that most women were voluntary participants in the sexual experience rather than forced. However, if one remembers that most of the behaviors were kissing and hugging and exhibition, this finding seems more plausible. The finding that most children and adolescents found the experiences pleasant rather than unpleasant fits well with the fact that they were voluntary and that the majority of the responses by both age groups were positive. Having an older partner involved voluntary participation primarily, but it also involved abuse, force, and harm.

On the negative side, some pressure was applied by partners although it was primarily subtle instead of threats, physical force, or use of a weapon. There were some substantive guilt reactions, and from 15% to 28% of the women who had sexual experiences as children or adolescents described their experiences as harmful or abusive.

For the 501 women in the study the primary reactions to the experiences were positive. Few studies have requested positive reactions, and most only report the negative ones, thus giving a distorted view of reality. Although negative reactions and conditions were reported in this study, they were in the minority.

*Historical Trends.* Another finding that challenges popular beliefs is that there is a definite trend toward decreasing child sexual activity as a whole over the past 60 years. The recent emphasis on human rights and heightened awareness of and sensitivity to child sexual abuse may be having some impact. The trend for adolescents has remained primarily constant over the past 60 years, despite the recent period of sexual freedom and the more recent conservative trend in relation to preadult sexuality.

## Influence of Background Variables for Adult Functioning

The findings of this study are consistent with De Francis' (1969) findings that adult functioning is related to both child sexual experiences and background or demographic characteristics. Generally, the background variables explain more of the variance in adult functioning than do the sexual experience variables. The analyses done in this study isolate specific background variables that were found to be significant for each of the five areas of adult functioning.

*Impact of Mother's Employment.* Significant in its absence from the primary background variables for adult functioning is the variable of mothers working when the women were below 13 years of age. The traditional social norm that "the mother's place is in the home" has long been a guilt producer for mothers who are either working out of economic necessity or personal preference. Contrary to these traditional views, whether or not both parents worked was found to be inconsequential for adult functioning. Therefore, despite persistent concerns over the effects of dual employment (more particularly, maternal employment) on the child, this study finds little evidence of appreciable effects, either positive or negative. These findings should be reassuring to families who have chosen, or who have had thrust upon them, the dual-employment type of family structure.

## Significance of Early Sexual Experiences for Adult Functioning

When the effects of background variables were controlled, the contributions of other variables concerning child and adolescent sexual experiences and their effects on adult functioning, over and above that accounted for by background variables, are seen. These findings are considered to be some of the most important of the study and have far-reaching implications. A striking finding, as reported earlier (Kilpatrick, 1986), is that adult functioning scores of women with child sexual experiences are not significantly different from those of women with no childhood sexual experiences. This is true even when analyzed across samples who had forced versus nonforced, pressured, guilt-producing experiences.

*Interactions.* Sexual experiences that are abusive, forced, guilt-producing, harmful, or pressured, interacting with the partner type, are significant for all measures of adult functioning except for sexual satisfaction. That is, the joint effect of abusive, harmful experiences of children that involved sexual behaviors that were forced, pressured, or guilt-producing, plus the identity of the partner, is highly correlated with adult functioning. These correlations are higher than the identity of the partner alone and are significantly related to intrafamilial stress, depression, marital discord, and self-esteem in the women as adults. For women as adolescents, a finding that stands out in contrast to the findings for women as children is that the identity of the partner, the conditions present at the time of the sexual experiences, the reactions to the experiences, and the interactions of all these are *all* significant at the .01 level for the measure of self-esteem, whereas only the interactions of all these are significant for women as children. This finding could be possibly a function of age and developmental differences, but it does provide strong evidence that adolescents may be more vulnerable to these factors that affect self-esteem than are children. Further research is certainly needed on this aspect.

Another finding that stands out is that for adolescents interactions of the identity of the partner with existing conditions and reactions to the experience was more influential than background variables for all measures except marital satisfaction. Background variables were more influential for all measures for children. This difference may be attributed to age and developmental aspects, but, again, this study provides strong evidence concerning the correlation of these specific types of experiences for women as adolescents for their future self-esteem, family relationships, sexual satisfaction, and depression. However, these findings should be further corroborated.

As with children, the interaction of the identity of the partner with the existing conditions and reactions to the experiences is significant across several measures of adult functioning. For women as adolescents, however, the prominent interactions are for parents as partners interacting with the variables of pressure, guilt, abusiveness, and pleasure. The findings show that more women had sexual experiences with parents and other relatives as children than as adolescents. However, this data indicates that adolescents who had such experiences with parents are as much or more at risk than are children. These findings pinpoint some of the risk factors or menaces inherent in these types of preadult sexual interactions.

*Relationship to Adult Sexual Satisfaction.* The finding that neither the relationship of child nor adolescent sexual experiences with adult sexual satisfaction is statistically significant needs to be clarified further. Women who did not have a current sexual partner did not complete this measure of adult functioning. For some women the absence of a partner may be due to a sexual problem, but because of the high proportion of college students coupled with the growing conservative trend in sexuality that could be due in part to political conservatism and AIDS, it cannot be assumed that absence of partners indicates problems. A different measure for sexual functioning and satisfaction may possibly have been more productive.

## AREAS OF CONCERN

The findings of this study pinpoint an issue of concern to researchers. This issue concerns the distinction between the actual harm done and the violation of social norms, mores, or political ideology. Within the definition of victimology currently employed by many researchers is the assumption that children, who have sexual experiences with or propositions from persons who are 5 or more years older than they, are automatically victimized, and harm is done.

The findings of this study repudiate such an assumption. Older partners are not found to be a significant factor in correlations with later adult functioning. Such simplistic linear assumptions must be seriously questioned. It is imperative that researchers not base their interpretations of data upon erroneous assumptions or moralistic beliefs. Furthermore, more attention must be given to the interactions of variables and multilevel causation in determining when harm has been done.

It is a matter of grave concern that the findings from this study may be misinterpreted to support the notion that aberrant childhood sexual experiences are not important or that offenders of societal norms should not be prosecuted. A major emphasis is, however, that reactions to undifferentiated events and experiences should be tempered and that one should not assume that harm has been done or make inappropriate assertions. Adherence to accepted scientific rules of evidence in interpreting observations, as presented in chapter 3, limits the drawing of inappropriate conclusions. An attempt should be made to separate the myths and the mores and to confirm the menaces in a humane and comprehensive approach.

Also, under no circumstances should the findings of this study be used as a sanction of child–adult sexual relationships. These relationships are violations of principles of informed consent. Unequal power relationships are also involved; sexual relationships with children and adolescents under these circumstances constitute *psychological*, if not physical, coercion and should be treated as such.

The findings of the analyses reported here raise the issue of statistical versus substantive significance. Although many of the sets in the analyses for both child and adolescent experiences are statistically significant, the squared multiple correlations are relatively small when the researcher's goal is to explain 100% of the variance. Therefore, a caveat is given to those who look at statistical significance only. Future research can build upon the substantively and statistically significant findings presented here.


## RECOMMENDATIONS

The following recommendations for clinicians and clinical researchers are made so that society can confront realistically the phenomenon of human sexuality.

*Move from Punishment to Treatment.*   It is vital that professionals be sensitive to sexual issues and comfortable in dealing with them without allowing their own emotions, biases, and morals to interfere with effective assessment and treatment. Many people assume harm when no harm has been done. However, when there is validated sexual trauma and abuse, failure to treat the victim is a far more serious societal deficiency than failure to punish the perpetrator (Kempe & Kempe,

1978). For too long the emphasis has been on punishing the perpetrator. Professionals such as social workers can take the lead in changing the emphasis to treatment of the child and family system as well as changing the social environment. Researchers have found that sexual trauma in children is responsive to social and clinical treatment, especially if treatment occurs as early as possible after the experience (Bender, 1954; Giarretto, Giarretto, & Sgroi, 1978; Rabinovitch, 1951).

*Do No Harm.* Clinicians point out that many times societal reactions to perceived abuse of children and adolescents are more harmful than the experience itself. Professionals must ensure that the results of detection, the investigation, and the agency program itself do not compound an already stressful situation. Immediate and long-range effects on children and adolescents must be contemplated when undertaking ameliorative actions, and efforts must be made to provide the least detrimental alternative. Some findings presented here help define the potentially harmful variables and their toxic interactions that most likely produce lasting negative effects.

*Break the Cycle of Violence.* Perhaps one of the most disturbing findings of research is that, in general, physical and sexual abuse is a learned behavior carried over from one generation to the next. Unless this cycle of violence is broken, abuse of children and adolescents will not be eliminated or reduced. Thus, professionals should design strategies and programs to work with the perpetrators, the victims, and other children who are part of an abusive family environment. Additionally, society needs to recognize the crucial roles that social and cultural factors play in abuse. The male dominance model or patriarchy, which some researchers assert is a contributing factor to child and wife abuse (Russell, 1986), needs to be replaced with more equitable and egalitarian family models by changing societal role expectations and by family life education.

*Assess Actual Harm Done and Build on Resiliency.* Belief in the resiliency of people is a cornerstone and basic tenet of social work and other human service professionals. Children and families can grow and change, and social functioning can be enhanced. Professionals must believe this tenet and integrate it into their practice. Although trauma may have occurred at the time of the abuse, long-range harmful effects may be ameliorated somewhat through such measures as talking with someone, treatment by professionals, or having positive life experiences that predominate over negative ones. As seen in this study, most women with preadult sexual experiences are well-functioning adults.

A study conducted by Saunders, Villeponteaux, Kilpatrick, and Veronen (1987) indicates that, as a group, child sexual abuse victims, upon discovery of the abuse by a social agency, do not show elevated signs of psychological distress. For the most part, the group of victims is functioning well psychologically. Attempts to describe a set of symptoms that all victims, or even most victims, exhibit appear to be futile. Therefore, the concept of a *child sexual abuse syndrome* that has commonly appeared in clinical literature is not supported scientifically, and the dangers of using the concept are substantial. For example, victims not exhibiting these symptoms may not be believed by their caretakers, social agencies, or the legal system. The challenge for the helping professionals is to assess accurately when actual harm has been done and then treat those cases appropriately.

*Document Effectiveness of Treatment.* Professionals who work with abuse victims have the responsibility to document change and effectiveness in the assessment and treatment process. Longitudinal studies on documented effectiveness are extremely helpful. Such documentation helps provide needed information regarding the most effective intervention procedures that ameliorate the long-term effects of the abusive experiences for all groups regardless of age or racial background.

*Study Family Environments, Ecological Factors, and Resource Factors.* De Francis found a strong correlation between family pathology and sexual experiences with relatives in lower-class families. Empirical research is needed to determine if a similarly strong correlation exists between family pathology and sexual experiences with relatives in middle- and upper-class families. Studies of the family environment using instruments such as the Moos Family Environment Scale (Moos & Moos, 1976) and more recent ones could be productive in showing the strength of correlations between different types of family environments and sexual abuse. Specific studies of family competence (Beavers & Hampson, 1990) and family interaction (Wampler, Halverson, Moore, & Walters, 1989) are now providing useful data on specific components of healthy and dysfunctional families.

Vander Mey and Neff (1987) found a high-to-moderate coincidence between adult–child incest and child emotional disturbance, behavior problems exhibited by the child, emotional neglect of the child by his or her parents, other sexual abuse suffered by the child, marital or other discord in the child's family, parental mental health problems, parental ignorance in the areas of child development, physical spouse abuse, alcoholism, physical health problems in the family, a parent who was abused as a child, unemployment, and money management problems. They cautioned the clinician and researcher to appreciate the fact that some of these correlates, especially in the case of victim characteristics, may be consequences of, rather than antecedents to, the sexual abuse. Other correlates may be the result of ecological and resource factors. They proposed an ecological model focused on neighborhood and subcultural definitions of appropriate responses to stressors (as opposed to Gelles', 1980, stress theory explanation for various types of family violence and deviance) and to the presence or absence of supportive experiences in one's family of origin, neighborhood support networks, self-esteem, and other factors pertaining to one's resources for coping. These factors are all avenues for further exploration.

*Study Children's Experiences Directly.*  In order to minimize problems associated with retrospective, verbally reported data as discussed earlier, it is necessary to work out acceptable methods of gathering explicit information from children and adolescents about their current and past sexual experiences. Such dialogues have been largely precluded by parental consent problems and by the undocumented though pervasive concern that children are substantially distressed by such dialogues. A study by Jones, Gruber, and Freeman (1983) raises questions about the basis of this problematic, albeit well-intended, concern. In their nonclinical sample of young adolescents (ages 13–17), less than 25% reported any degree of discomfort with interviews concerning sexual experiences. The precautions they took provide a preliminary basis for attenuating legitimate parental concerns about the effects of this kind of research on their children. In summary, these precautions are as follows:

1. careful attention to parental and participant informed consent;
2. assurance of absolute privacy and comfort of the youths during the interview;
3. confidentiality of the content and assurance that they would never be identified with the information;
4. judicious selection and intensive training of the interviewers; and
5. a structured interview format that begins with nonsensitive questions, progresses to questions concerning general sexual activity, and, only as required, to detailed questions about specific sexual assault experiences.

From the findings of Jones et al. (1983), one must recognize the possibility that professional and lay adults in society may have projected their own learned distress over explicit discussion of sexual material on the younger generation. Researchers must find other effective ways to minimize the actual distress experienced by young subjects of such research and expand the literature to include samples of children in general rather than samples of young victims exclusively.

*Conduct Replication and Cross-Cultural Studies.*  More studies on long-range effects of child and adolescent sexual experiences are needed. For example, if these studies were replicated in other geographic areas, if samples were comparable on race and socioeconomic class, and if data were gathered on the experiences of males, then there would certainly be more sufficient data. Replication studies with other cultures would also provide insights. Especially fruitful would be longitudinal studies that eliminate the problem of the validity of recall data and substantiate long-range effects.

Finally, findings from research may be refined substantially by incorporating multivariate analyses and by examining mediating and confounding variables. A focus on theory development and testing would be beneficial. With the accumulation of findings concerning child and adolescent sexual experiences and abuse, such as those presented here and by Wyatt and Powell (1988), research is now transcending description and is reaching a more sophisticated phase. This phase calls for clearer thinking, substantive explanatory models, adherence to scientific principles, and concern for the welfare of all involved. More than ever there is a need for open-mindedness and exploration as new ideas are being developed.

## LIMITATIONS

One limitation of this study is the proportion of college students in the sample (51%). However, only 35% of these were undergraduate students, an over-studied population generally. The remaining 16% were graduate students, an older and different population in many ways. An analysis shows that there are differences in these two groups. There are no previously known studies of child and adolescent sexual experiences of graduate students. The findings of this study make a unique contribution to the literature.

The fact that the sample is primarily middle class, as judged by the primary occupation, education, and income characteristics, is a limitation. The study does, however, corroborate to some extent previous studies of middle-class women. It also provides a contrast to previous studies on the sexual experiences of the lower socioeconomic class.

Because the sample utilized in this study is primarily a middle-class sample, the findings are not generalizable to lower-class populations. Further research that uses the methodology employed in this study and Hudson's (1982) *The Clinical Measurement Package* with lower socioeconomic groups is indicated.

Another limitation is that elderly women are underrepresented. The inclusion of more women in the 65 and over age group would have provided valuable information on the incidence, nature, and consequences of child sexual experiences over a half century ago. Thus, a more representative historical perspective would have been available. The nature of the study is an especially sensitive topic for this age group, however, and the additional difficulties of loss of sight, hearing, and mobility make this population less available.

A final limitation is related to the retrospective nature of the study. There is no way to check the accuracy of the information given. Partner's views are impossible to obtain. Longitudinal studies that gather data from children and adolescents and their partners either while experiences are occurring or after confirmed reports and then follow each over a number of years would be an especially helpful method for dealing with the limitations of using recall data.

In view of these limitations and the lack of definitive causal paths from specific variables to long-range consequences, the effects described in this study are considered correlational in nature. More definitive studies can be based on data presented here.

## CONCLUSION

The findings of this study on the long-range consequences of child and adolescent sexual experiences provide data that refute existing myths, delineate the factors of menaces in child and adolescent sexual experiences that have impact on adult functioning, and raise questions concerning the confusion of mores with actual harm done.

Myths that are challenged relate to incidence rates of incest, the impact of mother's employment, historical trends, ethnic differences, women's reactions to early sexual experiences, and long-range effects.

Specific factors or menaces from child and adolescent sexual experiences that correlate with adult dysfunctioning consist of no one factor but rather of interactions of various factors. These factors include the identity of the partner (whether a relative or close family member, not just older) and sexual behaviors that are abusive, forced, pressured, and guilt producing.

Questions regarding the confusion of mores with actual harm done are raised by the finding that older partners are not found to be a significant factor in correlations with later adult functioning. This finding challenges the linear assumption that all children are victimized by any type of sexual experience with a person who is 5 or more years older than they. One must guard against making assumptions that have no empirical bases and against buttressing existing mores that may be actually harmful to children and adolescents. Care must be taken that clinicians and researchers do no harm but build on the best available scientific evidence and practice wisdom.

# 10
# FUTURE DIRECTIONS IN TREATMENT

It is of great concern that some readers may come to the erroneous conclusion from the findings of this study that children and adolescents are not harmed by their sexual experiences. Although the findings do show that the majority of the sample did not demonstrate long-term harm from what could be interpreted as primarily exploratory experiences of kissing and hugging and exhibition, the findings do suggest that adult functioning for some was impaired by long-term harm from these child and/or adolescent sexual experiences. The findings do not deny the pain and turmoil of the many women who were harmed by unwanted, pressured, forced, abusive, and guilt-producing experiences in their early years. It is to these women who have been harmed that I address this final chapter.

## CURRENT TREATMENT PROGRAMS

Within a 5-year span, from 1976 to 1981, the number of treatment programs for child sexual abuse in the United States rose from 20 to 300 as reported by the National Center on Child Abuse and Neglect (MacFarlane & Brickley, 1982). Although the programs have many commonalities, they vary regarding their involvement with child protective service agencies and the court, their models of treatment, and their specific focus.

In a review of child sexual abuse treatment programs, Wodarski and Johnson (1988) described several of the prominent programs currently practiced in the United States. Most of these programs use court mandates for treatment of the offender and follow the general treatment process of individual, group, and then family therapy working toward the reunification of the family. Each, however, is considered to be effective and has its own way of viewing the family giving particular emphasis to various segments of the treatment process. The uniquenesses of each of these programs are discussed here.

One of the earlier programs is a community treatment model developed by Anderson and Shafer (1979). Their model is to establish an authoritative position with the family through the juvenile or criminal courts and to coordinate services through a treatment team. The model is oriented around the view of the sexually abusive family as having the psychiatric diagnosis of *character disordered*. Close supervision is stressed in order to avoid family members' manipulation of the system as well as to prevent their receiving confusing messages from the treatment team. This model advocates the removal of the victim or perpetrator from the home when necessary for protection.

A model developed by Boatman, Borkan, and Schetky (1981) views recurring themes or patterns found in a victim as consequences of abuse, such as a damaged or inadequate sense of self, problems with heterosexual relationships, guilt, anger, and sexuality, as important issues in treatment of the victim. The model uses a variety of treatment methods based on an analysis of several variables such as the child's age, developmental level, gender, diagnosis, and family situation. Individual psychotherapy is seen as a possibility for the treatment modality or in conjunction with family or group therapy. Group therapy is seen as helpful for the adolescent and preadolescent victim as it incorporates peer support. Family therapy is described as useful when the family structure is operational and only after individual issues have been addressed. Role clarification is recommended for the victim's substitute families such as foster homes, group homes, or family networks in appropriate cases.

The model described by Zefran et al. (1982) uses case management in the treatment of child sexual abuse in a juvenile court setting and emphasizes the importance of close cooperation between child protection service agencies, the court system, and treatment professionals. The assumptions are that these methods demonstrate that the child is believed and will be protected, and they help to gain admission of the abuse from the abuser. Primary attention is given to the victim within the context of treatment of the sexually abusing family. Treatment methods vary according to the family situation: (a) victim without family, (b) family without abuser, and (c) family together. In the victim without family situation, the victim is the only identified client. The focus of treatment is on helping the victim to deal with the abuse and with the reality that he or she may never be able to return home. The victim is seen in individual therapy and in victims support groups that are viewed as critical components in the treatment schedule for this type of situation.

In the family without abuser situation (i.e., the abuser has left home permanently), the treatment process begins with individual therapy and proceeds occasionally to placement in group therapy. In addition, casework services are offered to the nonabusing parent (usually the mother) through support groups or group therapy. The focus later shifts to the mother–daughter relationship.

In the situation where the family is together, the victim receives individual therapy, which continues throughout the treatment process. Mother–victim sessions are added later. Court sanctions are used to get the abuser into individual treatment where the treatment is aimed primarily at the abuser's responsibility for the abuse. Later on, abuser–child sessions begin and also abuser–spouse/partner sessions. The final phase of treatment is family therapy with the goals of having appropriate roles assumed by each family member and then reunification of the family.

Sgroi (1982) stressed the importance of an assessment of the family contribution to the abuse. One guideline is whether the abuse is extrafamily or intrafamily in nature. Treatment issues are differentiated by these two categories and also by whether the abuser is a parent, parent figure, or nonparent figure. Sgroi saw parental, sexually abusing families as being character disordered in their functioning and thought it unlikely that family treatment can effectively occur without an authoritative incentive such as the court system. In this model, individual therapy is established with family members first. Then family therapy is used in conjunction with a variety of treatment models such as individual therapy, dyads, couples, and groups for fathers, mothers, parents, or adolescents to provide peer support. Activity and play therapy are also used.

One of the foremost programs in the country and one that claims the lowest recitivism rate is the Child Sexual Abuse Treatment program established in Santa Clara County, California, by Henry Giarretto (1982a, 1982b). The treatment orientation is humanistic in nature, aiming at treatment of all members of the family, not at punishment. The goals are reuniting the family and preventing recurrence of the abuse, as well as helping family members deal with the problems that arise. The program is community based and incorporates the use of existing agencies including Child Protective Services and the criminal justice system. The staff of the program is comprised of professionals from officially responsible agencies in the community, volunteers (usually undergraduate and graduate students), and self-help groups including Parents United and Daughters and Sons United. In order for a case to be admitted to the program, the incident must be reported and the appropriate legal course pursued. The usual order of the various treatment methods is individual counseling, mother–daughter counseling, marital counseling, father–daughter counseling, and family counseling with group counseling throughout as is presented in more detail later.

An impressive program that combines a multilevel, multirespondent assessment protocol with an established protocol for treatment was developed by the Crime Victims Research and Treatment Center, Department of Psychiatry and Behavioral Sciences, Medical University of South Carolina (Saunders, McClure, & Murphy, 1987). Multiple family system levels are assessed based on the reports of multiple family members. Eight quantitative assessment instruments are completed by family members: Three are related to the whole family and are completed by the perpetrator, mother, victim, and siblings; five are related to the individual and are completed by the same family members. This assessment protocol is combined with a research component that has produced some pertinent findings. Foremost of these findings is that, for the most part, the group of victims is functioning well psychologically. The data suggest that the majority of victims do *not* have the type of symptoms commonly described in the child sexual abuse syndrome. This syndrome does not appear to be supported scientifically, and the authors stated there are substantial dangers in using the syndrome as the sole means of assessment.

The treatment protocol used by the Crime Victims Research and Treatment Center is a state-of-the-art program in child sexual abuse (Saunders & McClure, 1987). An appropriate progression of treatment is used: discovery and acknowledgment of child sexual abuse, engagement in treatment, individual family member focus (groups), clarification process, marital/sexual focus, parent–child relationship focus, structured visitation, family focus, family reunification, disengagement, and termination of treatment.

The components in the treatment program consist of masturbatory satiation and covert sensitization (for the offender), assertiveness training, social skills training, cognitive restructuring, sex education, fear reduction, anxiety reduction, stress inoculation training, marital therapy, sex therapy, parent education, and family therapy. Lockhart, Saunders, and Cleveland (1989) described these components in further detail, especially as they relate to adult male sexual offenders.

## A COMPOSITE TREATMENT MODEL

The composite treatment program model for the sexual abuse of children and adolescents in incestuous families that follows is taken from many of the programs described previously. The programs described by Saunders and McClure (1987), Lockhart et al. (1989), and Sturkie (1983) were especially helpful and were heavily utilized in developing this composite model. The primary parts of this

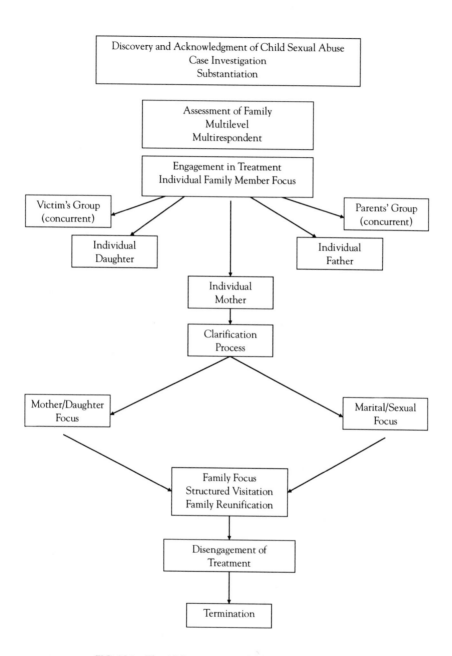

FIG. 10.1. The APC treatment model for incestuous families.

model are assessment, progression of treatment, and components of the treatment process. The model is therefore called the APC Model (see Fig. 10.1).

## The APC Model

*Assessment.* Any professional working with sexual abuse cases must first examine his or her own feelings about sexual abuse of children and adolescents, the offender, the nonoffending parent, and the victim. He or she must be aware of personal bias and provide controls for it. The discovery and acknowledgment of child sexual abuse that includes investigation and substantiation is the first step taken by the professional in specific cases. This investigation is generally conducted by state departments of family and children services. Referrals are usually made to other professionals for treatment. The professional utilizes a multilevel, multirespondent assessment protocol. These levels of assessment protocol include (a) interviews with multiple family members and others, (b) observation of family interactions and behaviors, and (c) quantitative assessment tools (including self-report measures and play or art therapy).

The multiple respondents include (a) individuals; (b) dyads; and (c) nuclear family, extended family, significant others, or other family groups such as siblings.

*Progression of Treatment.* The progression of treatment follows six basic steps as shown in Fig. 10.1.

1. Engagement in treatment: Family members begin the treatment process (usually mandated by the court in order to involve the offender).
2. Individual family member focus: This is usually the first treatment focus to deal with individual crises and issues. Family members meet in groups with other victims or parents.
     Victim's groups and parents' groups
     Individual family member focus
3. Clarification process: Interpersonal relationships are the focus, and restructuring and clarifying is the goal.
     Marital/sexual focus
     Parent–child relationship focus
4. Family focus: The purpose is to look at family interactions and work toward increasing family functionality.
     Structured visitation

Family reunification

5. Disengagement of treatment: This step solidifies the gains made and begins the preparation for termination.

6. Termination of treatment: The treatment process ends.

*Components in the Treatment Program.* The methods described in the treatment program of Lockhart et al. (1989) are used as needed and in the order necessary for any particular situation (due to lack of space these components are not listed in Fig. 10.1).

1. Crisis therapy: This method is utilized with the victim and family members, especially when the abuse is first detected.

2. Fear reduction: This is a behavioral treatment method used with the victim of sexual abuse to reduce fear.

3. Anxiety reduction: This is a behavioral treatment method used with the victim of sexual abuse to reduce anxiety.

4. Assertiveness training: This method is used with the victim, siblings, and nonoffending parents to increase appropriate assertiveness, that is, teaching the victim and siblings to say no or to tell someone.

5. Heterosocial skills training: The offender is taught appropriate ways of interacting with peers and appropriate sex partners.

6. Sex education: Although inadequate when used alone, sex education is particularly useful in conjunction with different types of skill-training treatment components.

7. Aversion therapy: The offender's deviant sexual behaviors or fantasies are paired with and/or immediately followed by the application of a highly physically aversive stimulus such as chemical agents that induce nausea, foul smells, or mild electric shock.

8. Covert sensitization: This method seeks to reduce deviant sexual arousal of the offender by repeatedly pairing sexually aberrant fantasies with highly aversive images that produce fear, anxiety, and distress.

9. Satiation therapy (masturbatory and verbal): This is a procedure used with the offender where a response is eliminated by repeatedly eliciting the response until the desire for the stimulus is eliminated. The offender may be required to verbalize his deviant sexual fantasies aloud for 30 minutes or longer without stopping while attempting to become sexually aroused until his repertoire is totally exhausted, or he may be required to go through a structured masturbatory satiation procedure. Satiation therapy has had

good results and is recommended as a standard treatment component for a sex offender.

10. Cognitive restructuring: This involves exposing and altering the offender's justifications of distorted cognitions for sexually deviant behaviors such as, "The child enjoyed it."

11. Pharmacotherapy (antiandrogen drug therapy): This antihormone drug treatment reduces testicular testosterone production and restrains sexual criminality in an offender.

12. Parenting skills classes: This is an adjunct to other treatment and is used as needed.

13. Marital therapy: This therapy focuses on the offending and nonoffending parents' relationship, including the sexual relationship, and usually occurs after individual treatment.

14. Family therapy: In incestuous families the interactions of all family members are taken into account in treatment. Functionality is restored, and a safe, nurturing environment is established.

Other supportive and concrete services are provided as needed.

The components in the treatment program are all possible treatment modalities. Although they generally follow an individual, dyad, and then family focus, it is not intended that the order in which they are listed is always the sequence to follow. Nor is the assumption to be made that all components are to be used with every situation. Professional judgment is needed to decide which specific components to use, when, and in what order.

In the concern for the treatment of sexual abuse as quickly as possible for children and adolescents, one must not lose sight of those adults who may still be suffering in their current lives the effects of such experiences as children and adolescents. Many helping professionals are still relatively unaware of potential effects in the adult clients they serve. Studies such as those presented in chapter 3 provide needed information to clinicians as they work with adult clients to recognize effects that may be indicative of such early trauma. Retrospective treatment for women incest victims/survivors is a relatively new treatment modality. Treatment is viewed as long term due to its reparative nature. General goals for retrospective incest therapy as given by Courtois and Sprei (1988) are: establishment of a therapeutic alliance; acknowledgment and acceptance of the occurrence of the abuse; exploration of issues of responsibility and complicity; breakdown of feelings of isolation; recognition, labeling, and expression of feelings; catharsis and grieving; cognitive restructuring of faulty beliefs; insight and behavioral change; education and information giving; and separation and individuation. Interventions and interpretations should be paced, with constant attention paid to the intense effect involved and the likely reaction to the material being elicited. The recommended minimum of 2 to 3 years of treatment is indicative of the serious repercussions suffered by some.


## PREVENTION

Although the treatment of those who have been harmed and who have caused the harm is essential, the prevention of sexual activities that are harmful to children and adolescents should also be a priority. The goals of primary prevention programs are to reduce the incidence of harmful sexual experiences, to influence the attitudes of the general public to make sexual abuse a less hidden and unrecognized problem, and to correct contradictory cultural beliefs about sexual abuse (Walker, 1988).

Prevention programs now exist in almost every part of the United States for children and adolescents from early preschool age through high school and in settings from day-care providers (Spungen, Jensen, Finkelstein, & Satinsky, 1989) to elementary schools (Paulk & Kilpatrick, 1990). However, as stated by Conte (1986), virtually no one in prevention activities believes that working with the weakest link in the abuse chain—children and adolescents—is the most efficient or desirable approach. Prevention should ideally focus on the perpetrator. However, the problems with this focus are rather obvious. Until the abuse occurs, the perpetrator is unknown. After the perpetrator is identified as a sexual abuser of children or adolescents, then prevention is impossible. Therefore, educational programs that teach children and adolescents how to protect themselves is the approach of most sexual abuse prevention programs.

Sexual abuse prevention usually involves teaching children and adolescents concepts and skills believed to be useful in preventing or escaping their own sexual victimization. Most prevention activities include the concepts of:

1. *body ownership* or the right to control access to one's own body;
2. *touch continuum* or the idea that there are a variety of ways to be touched and that not all kinds of touching need to be tolerated;
3. *secrets* or that secrets about touching should not be kept;
4. *intuition* or trusting one's own feelings to know that a touch is wrong or inappropriate and that someone should be told of its occurrence;
5. *saying no* or skill training in assertively saying no if someone touches them or asks to touch them on their private body parts; and
6. *telling* which encourages children and adolescents to tell if someone touches or tries to touch them on their private body parts.

Prevention programs such as these are often successful in identifying children who are currently being abused. This identification prevents further or prolonged abuse and is in itself a worthy activity.

Conte (1986) enumerated four typical errors to guard against in conducting educational programs to prevent sexual abuse:

1. using material designed for one age group with children of a different age group instead of more age-appropriate material;
2. spending too much time on relatively unimportant material, such as stranger abuse rather than abuse by someone the child knows which is usually the situation;
3. using scary stories, such as of child kidnappers, to get their attention rather than using more typical situations; and
4. communicating to students, subtly or not, that the trainer does not want to hear about any current abuse.

Many incidences of sexual abuse are reported by children during training sessions. Opportunities for such reports and treatment should be provided. Evaluations should be made of actual training classes, and students should be given pre- and post tests to determine if they are actually absorbing and can utilize the material being presented.

Although prevention programs exist in most parts of the United States, there is little research on the effectiveness of these efforts. There is available data that most students are able to learn prevention concepts and that there are differences by sex and race in how well they learn (Paulk & Kilpatrick, 1990). It is not known if prevention programs actually help students prevent their own abuse. More systematic studies of the abuse process are needed to identify new concepts or skills that might be useful in preventing more harm from being done.

On another level, society must ultimately evaluate its own contribution to the problem of harmful sexual experiences. Feminist theory has described the cultural and sex-role attitudes and assumptions that support sexual aggression against women and has exposed and challenged cultural myths about sexual aggression (Lockhart et al., 1989). Although myths still abound, feminist theory and advocacy have affected sex-offender treatment approaches significantly by enlarging the system that is viewed as dysfunctional. Sexual aggression tends now to be viewed as a problem involving not only the personal functioning of offenders but also cultural mechanisms guiding gender identity development, gender role interaction, and standards of gender behavior. Feminists explain our failure to develop a system to control incest as a result of the excess privilege accruing to men in our society and the inferior status of women: misbehaviors involving men as perpetrators and females as victims tend to remain underreported, underpunished, and unprevented (Brickman, 1984; Herman, 1981; Rush, 1980).

The prevalence of the concept of patriarchy must be examined. Patriarchy is simply considered as the power of individual men over women and children. Herman (1981) stated:

> Whereas male supremacy creates the social conditions that favor the development of father–daughter incest, the sexual division of labor creates the psychological conditions that lead to the same result. Male supremacy invests fathers with immense power over their children, especially their daughters. The sexual division of labor, in which women nurture children and men do not, produces fathers who are predisposed to use their powers exploitatively. The rearing of children by subordinate women insures the reproduction in each generation of the psychology of male supremacy. . . . The greater the domination of the father, and the more caretaking is relegated to the mother, the greater the likelihood of father–daughter incest. (pp. 62–63)

If we consider patriarchy as the pervasive and overarching context within which we are psychologically and behaviorally constructed, then a clinical account of incest or harmful sexual experience should work toward an interactional analysis of the construction of men and masculinity and women and femininity within a patriarchal culture (James & MacKinnon, 1990).

The place of the child in our society is crucial. As stated by Wodarski and Johnson (1988), those who are seen as subordinate objects or possessions to be controlled and manipulated for the comfort and enjoyment of the larger society are more prone to harmful experiences of various types. The rights of children and adolescents in our society remain at issue. Not only must children, adolescents, and adults be educated about the occurrence and effects of harmful sexual experiences and the means of prevention, but our society must begin to see the results of the "powerful use of the powerless" (Wodarski & Johnson, 1988, p. 169) mentality that is so prevalent and move to correct it. This type of broad social change is necessary before problems such as the prevention and treatment of harmful sexual experiences for all ages can be widely controlled.

## CONCLUSION

Although children are resilient and many transcend early traumatic experiences, it is imperative that effective treatment be provided for those who have been harmed by sexual experiences in childhood and adolescence. Based on programs that have demonstrated effectiveness, I have presented a composite treatment program model that can be adapted by others. Along with treatment, an emphasis must be given to prevention programs. Currently most of these focus on teaching children to protect themselves. A higher priority must be given to the elements in our society that contribute to the problem of harmful sexual experiences. Feminist theory has exposed and challenged many cultural myths about sexual aggression, expanded the system that is seen as dysfunctional in sex abuse to include society, and called for the critical examination of the concept and practice of patriarchy and the powerful use of the powerless. If the goal is to develop a "kinder, gentler nation," then the research findings and theory presented here contribute toward the "1,000 points of light" that will serve as a beacon toward achieving this end.

# APPENDIX A:
# ANALYSIS OF STUDIES

The studies in Appendix A support one of three hypotheses. The studies are analyzed by scientific criteria discussed in chapter 3 and are discussed in the order that they appear in Table 3.1 and according to the hypothesis to which they relate. The table at the end of the studies supporting each hypothesis shows the studies that met the scientific criteria at a sufficient level to say the findings contribute to our knowledge base. The primary findings are presented in chapter 3.

## Hypothesis 1: Child/Adolescent Sexual Experiences Inevitably Lead to Long-Term Harmful Effects

*Sloane and Karpinsky (1942).* The primary strength of this descriptive study of five adolescent incest cases is that the authors drew their conclusions from only adolescent cases. Hence differences can be compared with findings on effects of incest on preadolescents. There are, however, the sampling problems of no control group, a small number of cases, and the use of a clinical, lower-class population. The conclusion that "indulgence in incest in the postadolescent period leads to serious repercussions in the girl" (p. 673) is, therefore, questionable. The findings cannot be generalized and can, at best, serve as a working hypothesis for other studies. Other variables, such as background characteristics, should also be considered.

135

*Weinberg (1955).* Weinberg was one of the few researchers who adhered to the dictionary definition of incest. He studied 203 lower-class families in the Chicago area in which incest had occurred, primarily between fathers and daughters. These cases had all been reported to the courts. Although Weinberg used an offender population with no control group, he did study a large number of cases by structured interviews in the home. One can accept his evidence that childhood incest experiences in lower-class families where the perpetrator has been prosecuted lead to long-term harmful effects. Yet one must question how many of these harmful effects are due to the lower-class background or to the court procedure and incarceration of the family member.

*Greenland (1958).* Greenland analyzed seven letters written to an advice column in Great Britain regarding the writer's incestuous experiences during childhood and resulting present problems. The very small number of cases studied, lack of a control group, and the self-selected and nonrepresentative sample who wrote because of problems they were having lead to rejection of the evidence. His findings of harmful effects may be used as a working hypothesis for more definitive studies.

*Kubo (1959).* This Japanese study of 36 cases of incest from clinic or agency records and interviews defines terms specifically but contains the sampling problems of lack of a control group, a rather small number of cases, use of a clinical population, and the combining of age groups. Kubo was quite cautious and conservative when reporting effects, however. Although he saw strong negative behaviors such as crimes, misconduct, and mental disorders, he stated that "it cannot be concluded these . . . were directly attributable to incest" (p. 154). One can acknowledge the definite trend toward harmful effects but must realize these effects may have been caused by background variables.

*Vestergaard (1960).* This author studied 13 cases of parental incest in Copenhagen in which the fathers had been sentenced to prison. Vestergaard conducted interviews with women whose incestuous experiences took place more than 10 years previously. All the women felt the experiences were much worse than the court records showed. Although the definitions of terms are clear-cut, the problems of few cases, no control group, offender population, and combining age groups are present. Again, one must be cautious in interpreting the trend that is indicated by these data.

*Weiner (1962).* Weiner's study of five paternal incest cases in New York through psychotherapy with the fathers has the serious flaw of the perpetrator fathers being the only source of information on long-term effects on the daughters.

If the daughters had also been studied directly, this would have been a contribution to the literature because few studies have been done with both sexual partners. The other problems of extremely few cases, no control group, and offender population render these findings useless for purposes of generalization about long-range effects.

*Chaneles (1967).*[1] Chaneles studied 159 child victim cases as reported by public agencies in a 3-year project of the American Humane Association. Due to the clinical population, lack of control groups, and the preliminary conclusion by the author that "at present, we may only conjecture long-range effects" (p. 55), this evidence of a strong negative trend must be viewed with caution.

*Medlicott (1967).* This New Zealand study of 27 psychotherapy cases of reported parental incest compares the 17 actual incest cases with the 10 falsely alleged cases. In this sense there is a control group, but the nature of the evidence that permitted the judgment that the alleged cases were actually alleged is not described. No significance testing was reported, but the author did find rather large differences in some areas of sexual adjustment of the two groups. The small number of cases and clinical population do not provide conclusive support for the hypothesis, but a trend is indicated.

*De Francis (1969).* This study of 263 sex-offense cases reported by child protection agencies in New York and consisting primarily of lower-class families has no control group, but the sample is large, and both objective and subjective measures of consequences were obtained. His findings can not be generalized to nonclinical, middle- or upper-class populations, but the data suggest that child victims of reported sex crimes in lower-class families in large urban areas are likely to experience harmful effects.

*Katan (1973).* Katan psychoanalyzed six middle- to upper-class women who experienced oral, anal, or genital rape when they were 1 to 3 years of age. Again this is a small clinical study with no control group that makes generalizing to other populations impossible.

*Benward and Densen-Gerber (1975).* These authors studied 52 women in Odyssey House drug treatment centers who experienced incest as children. Of the 93 incestuous partners reported by the women, intercourse took place with only

---

[1]Upon close examination of the literature, I found that the Chaneles (1967) and De Francis (1969) studies were both funded under the Child Research Grant R-222, U.S. Children's Bureau. It is not known if these authors reported on some of the same cases. Therefore, both are included in this review.

34 (37%) of these. The other behaviors ranged from fondling to attempted seduction. Incestuous partners included steprelations, in-laws, and *quasi-family*. These definitional problems in a clinical setting cloud the study, which is admittedly an exploratory study of incest as a causative factor in antisocial behavior. The authors did use comparison groups that support their claim that "incest was a significant factor necessitating further study" (p. 339). This exploratory study should be viewed as such.

*Molnar and Cameron (1975).* Eighteen cases of parental incest in Canada were studied by these authors in psychotherapy interviews in a general hospital psychiatric unit. Behaviors described as incest were "a wider range of comportments which may or may not include intercourse" (p. 373). This study has the few cases, no controls, and clinical population configuration that is typical of many of the studies in this analysis. The author, of course, reported harmful effects because all the patients were there because they were having problems.

*James and Meyerding (1977).* Two studies of 228 prostitutes through questionnaires and interviews constitute this report. Through comparisons of their findings with findings of other studies of "normal" females, some interesting trends emerge that support the authors' conclusion that early sexual experiences and prostitution are related. The familiar configuration of a biased population and no control group is present.

*Meiselman (1978).* Meiselman studied 58 cases of incest that were seen at a Los Angeles psychiatric clinic. She used a control group that consisted of a random sample of 100 patient charts from the previous 5 years. Her definition of incest was clear and specific in regard to both behavior and partner. The primary problem with this study is the use of a clinical population for both the incest group and the control group. One does not know how these cases differ from a nonclinical population. One can, however, use the evidence from her findings regarding a clinical population that the occurrence of incest does predispose the individual to certain kinds of problems, such as difficult relationships with men or sexual maladjustment.

*Justice and Justice (1979).* These authors studied 112 incestuous families in Texas through a survey and therapy with selected cases. No control group was used for the clinical population studied. Conclusions regarding long-term consequences of incest were drawn from their review of the work of others regarding incest as much as from their own study. Therefore, their measures were more a summary of the literature than specific analyses of their own study. It is not possible to extract their own findings from the larger body of literature they discussed.

*Gross (1979).* Again this is a small clinical study (four cases of incest) without a control group. A unique feature of this study is that it studied hysterical seizures in adolescent girls and found incest in their backgrounds. As with all small descriptive studies, the findings of the study provide questions for further research.

*Tsai, Feldman-Summers, and Edgar (1979).* These authors compared a clinical group of 30 women who had been molested as children and were seeking therapy with a nonclinical group of 30 women who had been molested and also with a control group of 30 women who had not been molested. All of the women were secured through media advertisements, producing a potentially biased sample. Specific behaviors and partners were defined. Although no causal inferences can be made, these findings are certainly worthy of serious consideration. Noteworthy is that not all sexually molested children necessarily experience adult maladjustment and that a later age at cessation, stronger negative feelings, higher frequency, and longer duration of molestation are key variables in explaining adult maladjustment.

*Sedney and Brooks (1984).* This study is of 301 middle- to upper-class college women. Those having sexual experiences as children involving other people were compared to women with no such experiences. Definitions were clear, no clinical or offender populations were sampled, age groups were separated for purposes of some analyses, a primarily middle- to upper-class population was used, and there were specific measures of consequences. These features, together with the sizable number of women studied, make the findings that reports of childhood sexual experiences are frequently associated with symptoms of distress later in life acceptable. It must be remembered that this is a retrospective study of primarily middle-class women.

*Cleveland (1986).* Three women who had experienced incest with fathers were personally selected by the author from three different populations in order to study varied outcomes from a developmental perspective. One was from an offender population, one was from a clinical population, and one was referred by a friend. Definitions were clear, but the small number studied and the sampling method based on outcome with no control group make the findings interesting but not generalizable.

*Herman, Russell, and Trocki (1986).* A clinical sample of incest victims is compared with a community sample of incest victims in this San Francisco study of 205 women. No comparisons were made between pre- or postpubertal subjects as these two groups were collapsed in the chi-square analysis. A 4-point self-report scale was used to assess long-range effects. No efforts were made to control for background variables. The finding that victims who have experienced forceful or repeated, prolonged abuse or severe physical violation by much older men, especially fathers or stepfathers, are likely to report persistent difficulties in their adult lives must be seen as tentative due to the rather simplistic nature of the analysis.

*Bryer, Nelson, Miller, and Krol (1987).* Sixty-six women in a private psychiatric hospital were studied for physical and sexual abuse before they were 16 years of age. Women with no abuse were compared with women with physical abuse only, sexual abuse only, and both types of abuse. The obvious flaw in the design was that it included only a clinical sample. Definitions were clear and measures of consequences were specified. Various sophisticated analytic tools were utilized. These characteristics make the findings of a correlation between the severity of adult psychiatric symptoms and childhood physical and sexual abuse, and especially a combination of the two, of importance. An additional finding of no significant differences in symptoms between subjects who experienced incest and those who experienced other types of childhood sexual abuse is also an important one and needs to be further corroborated.

*Saunders, Villeponteaux, Kilpatrick, and Veronen (1987).* This retrospective study by Saunders et al. of childhood sexual assault victims is from a self-selected sample of 391 women who were part of a larger representative sample of 2,004 women. Structured interviews were conducted using a standardized instrument for assessing psychological functioning. A primary concern is whether or not the self-selected sample is representative of the larger sample on the sexual assault variable. The major finding is that victims of child sexual assault have a significantly greater risk for developing many psychiatric disorders, particularly anxiety disorders, than do nonvictims. Although the average age for the first assault is 11 years, the findings would have been more enlightening had childhood and adolescent assault been analyzed separately.

*Jackson, Calhoun, Amick, Maddever, and Habif (1990).* The question of using self-selected samples arises again in the study by Jackson et al. of young adult women who were recruited by newspaper and radio advertisements. One strength of the study is the identification of a sample consisting only of young adult women in order to assess adjustment after incest. They found that incest victims evidence poorer functioning with regard to sexuality, emotional response, social adjustment, and self-esteem than do nonvictims. Some important findings may have

TABLE A-1
Studies Supporting Hypothesis 1 by Scientific Criteria

| Author | N | Population | Clear Definition | Control Group | Age Group | SEC Group | Specific Measures |
|--------|---|-----------|------------------|---------------|-----------|-----------|-------------------|
| Weinberg | 203 | Offender | Yes | No | 15 av. | LC | Yes |
| De Francis | 263 | Clinical | Yes | No | 0–15 | LC | Yes |
| Meiselman | 58 | Clinical | Yes | Yes (Clinical) | 3–11 | LC-MC | Yes |
| Tsai et al. | 60 | Clinical/ Nonclinical | Yes | Yes (Nonclinical) | 6–12 | MC | Yes |
| Sedney & Brooks | 301 | Students | Yes | Yes | 9 av. | MC-UC | Yes |
| Herman et al. | 205 | Clinical | Yes | Yes | 0–18 | MC | Yes |
| Bryer et al. | 66 | Inpatients | Yes | Yes | | MC | Yes |
| Saunders et al. | 391 | Self-selected | Yes | Yes | | MC | Yes |
| Jackson et al. | 40 | Self-selected | Yes | Yes | 0–18 | UC | Yes |

been obscured by not separating those women who experienced incest as children and those who experienced incest as adolescents and by not using statistical controls for background characteristics.

## Hypothesis 2: Child/Adolescent Sexual Experiences Inevitably Lead to Long-Term Neutral Effects

*Rasmussen (1934).* This Norwegian study of 54 sexual assault cases selected from court records involving children from 9 to 13 years of age focuses on adult mental health and social adjustment. Victims were medically examined, and the offender convicted. There was no control group with this offender population. As mentioned previously, it is not known exactly what evidence led to Rasmussen's conclusion that 85% seemed none the worse for the experience. However, this early study provides much needed information on an offender population that has been used to compare results from other descriptive studies and shows a trend. It does not present conclusive evidence.

*Bender and Grugett (1952).* Social and psychiatric follow-up information was collected on 14 adults who as children, 11 and 16 years previously, had been referred for psychiatric attention by a children's court because of various and prolonged sexual experiences. The authors' conclusion that there exists no scientific proof of any resulting deleterious effects must be tempered by the knowledge that the small population studied was clinical and there was no control group.

*Landis (1956).* Of the 1,800 university students from middle- to upper-class backgrounds who completed questionnaires for this study, 500 were found to have had childhood experiences with adults. The author's conclusion that "the great majority of the victims seemed to have few permanently harmful effects from the experiences" (p. 108) can be accepted based on the clear definition of terms, large number of cases studied, use of a large control group, a nonclinical-nonoffender population, and acceptable measures of consequences. He did combine age groups (4–19 plus years), however, and his findings cannot be generalized to lower-class populations.

*Brunold (1964).* The information for Brunold's Netherlands study of 62 sexual assault cases from court records was gathered by personal and third person interviews at least 15 years after the offense. There was no control group, and an offender population was used. His conclusion that lasting "psychological" injury as a result of sexual assaults suffered in infancy is not very common can be questioned in two ways. First, he admittedly did not consider personality in his measures of consequences but based his conclusions on background, education, later occupation, and marital relationships, not psychological aspects. Second, his use of the term *infancy* is dubious because all his cases were from 5 to 15 years of age at the time of the offense.[2]

*Gagnon (1965).* Gagnon studied the 333 women who reported a sexual experience with an adult before age 13 in the Kinsey study by structured interviews. His use of a control group, large number of cases, clear definition of terms, and specific measures of consequences make his finding that "only 5% could be considered to have adult lives that had been severely damaged for whatever reason" (p. 188) acceptable. It must be remembered, however, that his population was primarily college-educated women, and it is a retrospective study.

*Lukianowicz (1972).* This is an Irish study of 55 incest cases with lower-class backgrounds found in a general hospital. Information was obtained by psychotherapy interviews. No control group was used. The finding that "the incestuous activities seemed to have been only a transitory, culturally permissible phase in the process of their normal psychosexual development, and as such did

---

[2]The inappropriate use of terms could be due to inaccurate translations from the original language.

not result in any bad effects" (p. 312) may need to be limited to this particular culture and to a lower-class, clinical population.

*Herman and Hirschman (1977)*. These authors studied 15 father–daughter incest cases where the victims were later seen in psychotherapy. Their use of the term *father–daughter* is misleading because three stepfathers, a grandfather, a brother-in-law, and an uncle were included. Herman and Hirschman observed that "nothing obvious distinguished them from the general population of women entering psychotherapy" and that "the severity of their complaints seemed to be related to the degree of family disorganization and deprivation in their histories rather than to the incest history per se" (p. 745). The familiar sampling trilogy of a few cases, no control groups, and a clinical population, plus the loose definition of terms and descriptive measures of consequences, makes these findings questionable. They can only discern a trend.

*Goodwin, Simms, and Bergman (1979)*. In a study similar to that of Gross (1979), Goodwin et al. described six cases in which adolescents developed hysterical seizures after parental incest. Two differences are that Gross' subjects experienced incest as adolescents whereas Goodwin et al.'s subjects experienced incest below the age of 10, and the seizures disappeared in Goodwin's subjects after psychotherapeutic exploration of the incestuous experience. This descriptive study raises questions for further investigation.

*Symonds, Mendoza, and Harrell (1981)*. These 109 cases of incest were self-identified in response to advertisements in newspapers and were studied by phone interviews. Respondents were middle class and, overwhelmingly, White males. This sampling bias, plus no control group and only descriptive measures of consequences, makes the authors' conclusions applicable only to white, middle-class, self-selected males in Los Angeles. A more sophisticated analysis of data would have been helpful.

*Nelson (1981)*. The findings of this exploratory, descriptive study on incest are based on survey data from 100 persons who responded to classified advertisements in periodicals. The majority were middle class, male, and from San Francisco and the Bay area. A high proportion were homosexuals, and ages at time of incest ranged from 3 to 50 years. The lack of a control group, a biased, self-selected sample, the combination of child and adult experiences, and the large number of homosexual males cause the findings to be questionable, although trends may be discerned.

*Finkelhor (1981).* Finkelhor used questionnaires to study 796 college students, 114 of which had sibling sexual experiences, in a predominantly White, middle-class sample. He used comparison groups and separated the sample by ages at time of the experience for purposes of analysis. He included *an invitation to do something sexual* as a sexual experience and also included stepsibling and half-siblings, which could skew his findings somewhat. He did not, however, use the value-laden term of *victimization* in relation to sibling sex as he did in relation to other older partners. Although he had three limited indicators of adult sexual behavior, his study is, admittedly, not well equipped to grapple with outcomes. He did move beyond the typical descriptive conclusions regarding outcome to statistical analyses, however. His finding that there is little reason to think that sibling sexual experiences are influential for adult sexual functioning should be considered as evidence.

*Fritz, Stoll, and Wagner (1981).* This study of 952 college students through questionnaires uses comparison groups and well-defined terms and separates the sexes for purposes of analysis of prepubescent sex play. A strength of this study is that some parametric statistical measures were used for measures of consequences. A limitation is that only adult sexual adjustment was studied. Fritz et al. found that 1.8% of all females have problems with adult sexual adjustment arising from prepubertal molestation and that molested males and females differ significantly in regard to long-term effects on sexual attitudes and relationships. This study meets the scientific criteria, and the findings should be considered.

*Emslie and Rosenfeld (1983).* These authors compared 7 incest cases with a control group of 19 cases, all of whom were hospitalized for psychiatric problems. Definitions were clear, and the use of a control group made possible the comparison of effects. No difference was reported. However, the small number of cases, use of a clinical population, the combining of age groups, and no specificity of socioeconomic class were given. No generalizations can be made from the finding.

*Kilpatrick (1986).* Kilpatrick used a deliberate sample in order to increase heterogeneity in her study of the childhood (0–14 years) sexual experiences of 501 predominantly middle-class women. Women with childhood sexual experiences were compared with those who had no such experiences. Her terms were well defined. A primary strength of this study is that the researcher utilized quite sophisticated analytic procedures, such as hierarchical multiple regression analyses, in order to determine long-term effects on five different measures of present adult functioning. With this type of procedure, factors such as background variables could be controlled. Her findings are that adult functioning of women who had childhood sexual experiences and those who had none do not differ

TABLE A-2
Studies Supporting Hypothesis 2 by Scientific Criteria

| Author | N | Population | Clear Definition | Control Group | Age Group | SEC Group | Specific Measures |
|--------|-----|-----------|-----------------|--------------|-----------|-----------|-------------------|
| Landis | 500 | Students | Yes | Yes | 4–19+ | MC-UC | Yes |
| Gagnon | 333 | Women | Yes | Yes | 0–13 | MC | Yes |
| Finkelhor | 796 | Students | Yes | Yes | 3–19 | MC-UC | Yes |
| Fritz et al. | 952 | Students | Yes | Yes | Prepubertal | MC | Yes |
| Kilpatrick | 501 | Women | Yes | Yes | 0–14 | MC | Yes |

significantly. However, sexual experiences that were abusive, forced, guilt-producing, harmful, or pressured interacting with the type partner (parents, other relative, nonrelative) are significant for all measures of adult functioning except for the sexual satisfaction scale. Her findings should be considered.

## Hypothesis 3: Child/Adolescent Sexual Experiences Inevitably Lead to Long-Term Beneficial Effects

*Bernard (1981)*. Bernard conducted a descriptive and biographical study of 30 pedophile cases with a convenience sample. The children were ages 7–15 years. The sampling method used presents primary problems. The researcher stated that the source of seven referrals was through professional and personal contacts. Three of these were from therapists, but he failed to state the source of the remaining 23 cases. The problems of lack of control group, small number of cases studied, combining age groups, and the use of clinical populations apply here as well as the probability of a biased, unrepresentative convenience sample. His evidence is not acceptable.

*Okami (1989)*. This is a self-selected sample composed of respondents to media advertisements throughout the United States and two foreign countries. The sample may be further biased due to the qualities of *at least in part, positive feeling* about the sexual contact with a person 5 years or more older. However, the full range of feelings were examined. In order to have had a *positive* experience the subject had to regard it as positive *both* at the time of occurrence and in retrospect. A *negative* experience could have been considered as such at *either* time. In the nonclinical sample, 67% of the experiences were given positive ratings, whereas 100% were given negative ratings by the clinical sample. Of the positive ratings, 82% were reported by males and 18% by females. This is one of the very few studies that allowed for positive responses to sexual experience as a child or adolescent.

TABLE A-3
Studies Supporting Hypothesis 3 by Scientific Criteria

| Author | N | Population | Clear Definition | Control Group | Age Group | SEC Group | Specific Measures |
|--------|---|------------|------------------|---------------|-----------|-----------|-------------------|
| Okami | 70 | Self-selected | Yes | Yes | 0–16 | MC | Yes |

# APPENDIX B:
# QUESTIONNAIRE PACKAGE

# THE FAMILY AND SEXUAL BEHAVIOR

# A RESEARCH PROJECT

Conducted By

Allie C. Kilpatrick

## SECTION I

Please complete the Background Information sheet and all other questions in Section I.

## BACKGROUND INFORMATION

Please complete each of the following items by placing your answer in the space provided in the right hand margin.

1. What is your present age?                                    _____

2. How many years of school have you completed?                _____

3. What is your total monthly family income?                   _____

4. What is your current marital status?                        _____

      1. Single        4. Widowed
      2. Married     5. Separated
      3. Divorced    6. Other

5. How many times have you been married?                       _____

6. How long (months or years, specify) have you been
   with your current spouse or partner?                        _____

7. What is your ethnic background?                             _____

      1. White       4. Hispanic (specify)
      2. Black      5. Other (specify)

8. How many children do you have?                              _____

9. What is the total number of persons living with
   you (other than yourself)?                                  _____

10. Please check the appropriate answer for each column.
    Did you live mostly in (pick the one you lived in
    longest for each age span)                Birth-12        13-18 years

      1. A Farm
      2. A town of under 5,000
      3. A town of between 5,000 & 25,000
      4. A town of between 25,000 & 100,000
      5. A town between 100,000 & 500,000
      6. A town larger than 500,000

11. Did both parents work while you were of age: Birth - 12____  13-18____

     1. Yes       2. No

12. What is your present occupation (state and briefly describe)?

_____

_____

13. What is your present spouse's or partner's occupation (describe)?

_____

_____

INDEX OF SELF-ESTEEM (ISE)

This questionnaire is designed to measure how you see yourself. It is not a test, so there are no right or wrong answers. Please answer each item as carefully and accurately as you can by placing a number by each one as follows:

1 Rarely or none of the time
2 A little of the time
3 Some of the time
4 A good part of the time
5 Most of all of the time

Please begin.

1. I feel that people would not like me if they really knew me well. ____

2. I feel that others get along much better than I do. ____

3. I feel that I am a beautiful person. ____

4. When I am with other people I feel they are glad I am with them. ____

5. I feel that people really like to talk with me. ____

6. I feel that I am a very competent person. ____

7. I think I make a good impression on others. ____

8. I feel that I need more self-confidence. ____

9. When I am with strangers I am very nervous. ____

10. I think that I am a dull person. ____

11. I feel ugly. ____

12. I feel that others have more fun than I do. ____

13. I feel that I bore people. ____

14. I think my friends find me interesting. ____

15. I think I have a good sense of humor. ____

16. I feel very self-conscious when I am with strangers. ____

17. I feel that if I could be more like other people I would have it made.____

18. I feel that people have a good time when they are with me. ____

19. I feel like a wallflower when I go out. ____

20. I feel I get pushed around more than others. ____

21. I think I am a rather nice person. ____

22. I feel that people really like me very much. ____

23. I feel that I am a likeable person. ____

24. I am afraid I will appear foolish to others. ____

25. My friends think very highly of me. ____

GENERALIZED CONTENTMENT SCALE (GCS)


This questionnaire is designed to measure the degree of contentment that you feel about your life and surroundings. It is not a test, so there are no right or wrong answers. Answer each item as carefully and accurately as you can by placing a number beside each one as follows:

    1  Rarely or none of the time
    2  A little of the time
    3  Some of the time
    4  Good part of the time
    5  Most or all of the time

Please begin.

1.  I feel powerless to do anything about my life.                        ____

2.  I feel blue.                                                          ____

3.  I am restless and can't keep still.                                   ____

4.  I have crying spells.                                                 ____

5.  It is easy for me to relax.                                           ____

6.  I have a hard time getting started on things that I need to do.       ____

7.  I do not sleep well at night.                                         ____

8.  When things get tough, I feel there is always someone I can turn to.  ____

9.  I feel that the future looks bright for me.                           ____

10. I feel downhearted.                                                   ____

11. I feel that I am needed.                                              ____

12. I feel that I am appreciated by others.                              ____

13. I enjoy being active and busy.                                       ____

14. I feel that others would be better off without me.                   ____

15. I enjoy being with other people.                                     ____

16. I feel it is easy for me to make decisions.                          ____

17. I feel downtrodden.                                                   ____

18. I am irritable.                                                       ____

19. I get upset easily.                                                   ____

20. I feel that I don't deserve to have a good time.                      ____

21. I have a full life.                                                   ____

22. I feel that people really care about me.                             ____

23. I have a great deal of fun.                                          ____

24. I feel great in the morning.                                         ____

25. I feel that my situation is hopeless.                                ____

INDEX OF MARITAL SATISFACTION (IMS)


This questionnaire is designed to measure the degree of satisfaction you have with your present marriage. It is not a test, so there are no right or wrong answers. Answer each item as carefully and as accurately as you can by placing a number beside each one as follows:

1  Rarely or none of the time
2  A little of the time
3  Some of the time
4  Good part of the time
5  Most or all of the time

Please begin.

1. I feel that my partner is affectionate enough. ____

2. I feel that my partner treats me badly. ____

3. I feel that my partner really cares for me. ____

4. I feel that I would not choose the same partner if I had it to do over again. ____

5. I feel that I can trust my partner. ____

6. I feel that our relationship is breaking up. ____

7. I feel that my partner doesn't understand me. ____

8. I feel that our relationship is a good one. ____

9. I feel that ours is a very happy relationship. ____

10. I feel that our life together is dull. ____

11. I feel that we have a lot of fun together. ____

12. I feel that my partner doesn't confide in me. ____

13. I feel that ours is a very close relationship. ____

14. I feel that I cannot rely on my partner. ____

15. I feel that we do not have enough interests in common. ____

16. I feel that we manage arguments and disagreements very well. ____

17. I feel that we do a good job of managing our finances. ____

18. I feel that I should never have married my partner. ____

19. I feel that my partner and I get along very well together. ____

20. I feel that our relationship is very stable. ____

21. I feel that my partner is pleased with me as a sex partner. ____

22. I feel that we should do more things together. ____

23. I feel that the future looks bright for our relationship. ____

24. I feel that our relationship is empty. ____

25. I feel there is no excitement in our relationship. ____

INDEX OF SEXUAL SATISFACTION (ISS)

This questionnaire is designed to measure the degree of satisfaction you have in the sexual relationship with your partner. It is not a test, so there are no right or wrong answers. Answer each item as carefully and accurately as you can by placing a number beside each one as follows:

1  Rarely or none of the time
2  A little of the time
3  Some of the time
4  Good part of the time
5  Most or all of the time

Please begin.

1. I feel that my partner enjoys our sex life. _____

2. My sex life is very exciting. _____

3. Sex is fun for my partner and me. _____

4. I feel that my partner sees little in me except for the sex I can give. _____

5. I feel that sex is dirty and disgusting. _____

6. My sex life is monotonous. _____

7. When we have sex it is too rushed and hurriedly completed. _____

8. I feel that my sex life is lacking in quality. _____

9. My partner is sexually very exciting. _____

10. I enjoy the sex techniques that my partner likes or uses. _____

11. I feel that my partner wants too much sex from me. _____

12. I think that sex is wonderful. _____

13. My partner dwells on sex too much. _____

14. I try to avoid sexual contact with my partner. _____

15. My partner is too rough or brutal when we have sex. _____

16. My partner is a wonderful sex mate _____

17. I feel that sex is a normal function of our relationship. _____

18. My partner does not want sex when I do. _____

19. I feel that our sex life really adds a lot to our relationship. _____

20. My partner seems to avoid sexual contact with me. _____

21. It is easy for me to get sexually excited by my partner. _____

22. I feel that my partner is sexually pleased with me. _____

23. My partner is very sensitive to my sexual needs and desires. _____

24. My partner does not satisfy me sexually. _____

25. I feel that my sex life is boring. _____

1,2,3,9,10,12,16,17,19,21,22,23

INDEX OF FAMILY RELATIONS (IFR)

This questionnaire is designed to measure the way you feel about your family as a whole. It is not a test, so there are no right or wrong answers. Answer each item as carefully and accurately as you can by placing a number before each one as follows:

1 Rarely or none of the time
2 A little of the time
3 Some of the time
4 A good part of the time
5 Most or all of the time

Please begin.

1. The members of my family really care about each other. ____

2. I think my family is terrific. ____

3. My family gets on my nerves. ____

4. I really enjoy my family. ____

5. I can really depend on my family. ____

6. I really do not care to be around my family. ____

7. I wish I was not part of this family. ____

8. I get along well with my family. ____

9. Members of my family argue too much. ____

10. There is no sense of closeness in my family. ____

11. I feel like a stranger in my family. ____

12. My family does not understand me. ____

13. There is too much hatred in my family. ____

14. Members of my family are really good to one another. ____

15. My family is well respected by those who know us. ____

16. There seems to be a lot of friction in my family. ____

17. There is a lot of love in my family. ____

18. Members of my family get along well together. ____

19. Life in my family is generally unpleasant. ____

20. My family is a great joy to me. ____

21. I feel proud of my family. ____

22. Other families seem to get along better than ours. ____

23. My family is a real source of comfort to me. ____

24. I feel left out of my family. ____

25. My family is an unhappy one. ____

## SECTION II

In this section you will be asked to remember various types of sexual experiences that you engaged in during childhood. The same questions will be asked for 13 different sexual experiences which range from kissing and hugging in a sexual way to intercourse. It is very important that you answer each question as carefully and as accurately as you can. If a question does not apply to you, leave it blank. If it does apply, be sure to answer all sections under this question.

Please note that the total numbers you give in each section must tally with the total numbers you gave in Section A under each age grouping (except for B,G,I and K). This is true for all 13 different sexual experiences.

## PLEASE WAIT FOR FURTHER INSTRUCTIONS
## BEFORE TURNING THIS PAGE

**PLEASE TURN THE PAGE AND CONTINUE**

## 1. HOW MANY TIMES DID YOU PARTICIPATE IN KISSING AND HUGGING IN A SEXUAL WAY WHEN YOU WERE OF

| | AGE | 0-6 | 7-10 | 11-14 | 15 | 16 | 17 |
|---|---|---|---|---|---|---|---|
| A. | How many times was this experience requested or initiated by | | | | | | |
| | 1. You | | | | | | |
| | 2. Your partner | | | | | | |
| | 3. Both mutually | | | | | | |
| B. | How many times was your partner as much as five years older than you? | | | | | | |
| C. | How many times did you do this with | | | | | | |
| | 1. Your father | | | | | | |
| | 2. Your stepfather | | | | | | |
| | 3. Your mother | | | | | | |
| | 4. Your stepmother | | | | | | |
| | 5. Your sister | | | | | | |
| | 6. Your brother | | | | | | |
| | 7. Another male relative | | | | | | |
| | 8. Another female relative | | | | | | |
| | 9 Unrelated male | | | | | | |
| | 10. Unrelated female | | | | | | |
| | 11. Husband | | | | | | |
| | 12 Stranger | | | | | | |
| D. | How many times was this experience | | | | | | |
| | 1. Very unpleasant | | | | | | |
| | 2 Unpleasant | | | | | | |
| | 3. Neither pleasant nor unpleasant | | | | | | |
| | 4. Pleasant | | | | | | |
| | 5. Very pleasant | | | | | | |
| E. | How many times was this experience | | | | | | |
| | 1. Voluntary on your part | | | | | | |
| | 2. Forced upon you | | | | | | |
| F. | How many times did you react with | | | | | | |
| | 1. Anger | | | | | | |
| | 2. Fear | | | | | | |
| | 3 Shock | | | | | | |
| | 4. Surprise | | | | | | |
| | 5. Interest | | | | | | |
| | 6. Enthusiasm | | | | | | |
| G. | How many times did you feel this experience was | | | | | | |
| | 1. Harmful | | | | | | |
| | 2. Abusive | | | | | | |
| H. | How many times did you feel | | | | | | |
| | 1. Extremely guilty | | | | | | |
| | 2. Moderately guilty | | | | | | |
| | 3. A little guilty | | | | | | |
| | 4. Not guilty at all | | | | | | |

| AGE | 0-6 | 7-10 | 11-14 | 15 | 16 | 17 |
|---|---|---|---|---|---|---|
| **I.** How many times did you engage in this experience because of | | | | | | |
| 1. Subtle pressure | | | | | | |
| 2. Verbal threats | | | | | | |
| 3. Physical force | | | | | | |
| 4. Use of a weapon | | | | | | |
| **J.** How many times did you talk about this experience with 1. No one | | | | | | |
| 2. Mother | | | | | | |
| 3. Father | | | | | | |
| 4. Brother | | | | | | |
| 5. Sister | | | | | | |
| 6. Other male adult | | | | | | |
| 7. Other female adult | | | | | | |
| 8. Friend (s) | | | | | | |
| 9. Doctor | | | | | | |
| 10. Police | | | | | | |
| 11. Agency (identify) | | | | | | |
| 12. Other | | | | | | |
| **K.** How many times did you find each of the following to be helpful in dealing with this experience 1. Father | | | | | | |
| 2. Mother | | | | | | |
| 3. Other relative | | | | | | |
| 4. Friend (s) | | | | | | |
| 5. Doctor | | | | | | |
| 6. Lawyer | | | | | | |
| 7. Nurse | | | | | | |
| 8. Teacher | | | | | | |
| 9. Police | | | | | | |
| 10. Social Worker | | | | | | |
| 11. Psychologist | | | | | | |
| 12. Psychiatrist | | | | | | |
| 13. Minister | | | | | | |
| 14. Other | | | | | | |

**L.** How many times did this experience produce for you a long range
  1. Positive view of sex
  2. Negative view of sex
  3. Positive effect on your life
  4. Negative effect on your life

**M.** If there were any of the times in which you engaged in this behavior and you felt the experience was abusive or harmful:
  1. Describe what kind of help you wish you could have received at the time:_____

  2. Describe how you wish the incident(s) had been handled:_____

**N.** If there were any of the times in which you engaged in this behavior and you thought someone else knew of the behavior without your telling them:
  1. Who do you think knew about this behavior?_____

  2. Do you think the person who knew about the sexual behavior should have done something about it?

  3. If you answered number 2 as yes, what do you think this person(s) should have done about the sexual behavior? _____

2. HOW MANY TIMES DID ANOTHER PERSON SHOW YOU HIS OR HER GENITALS WHEN YOU WERE OF

| AGE | 0-6 | 7-10 | 11-14 | 15 | 16 | 17 |
|---|---|---|---|---|---|---|
| A. How many times was this experience requested or initiated by | | | | | | |
| 1. You | | | | | | |
| 2. Your partner | | | | | | |
| 3. Both mutually | | | | | | |
| B. How many times was your partner as much as five years older than you? | | | | | | |
| C. How many times did you do this with | | | | | | |
| 1. Your father | | | | | | |
| 2. Your stepfather | | | | | | |
| 3. Your mother | | | | | | |
| 4. Your stepmother | | | | | | |
| 5. Your sister | | | | | | |
| 6. Your brother | | | | | | |
| 7. Another male relative | | | | | | |
| 8. Another female relative | | | | | | |
| 9. Unrelated male | | | | | | |
| 10. Unrelated female | | | | | | |
| 11. Husband | | | | | | |
| 12. Stranger | | | | | | |
| D. How many times was this experience | | | | | | |
| 1. Very unpleasant | | | | | | |
| 2. Unpleasant | | | | | | |
| 3. Neither pleasant nor unpleasant | | | | | | |
| 4. Pleasant | | | | | | |
| 5. Very pleasant | | | | | | |
| E. How many times was this experience | | | | | | |
| 1. Voluntary on your part | | | | | | |
| 2. Forced upon you | | | | | | |
| F. How many times did you react with | | | | | | |
| 1. Anger | | | | | | |
| 2. Fear | | | | | | |
| 3. Shock | | | | | | |
| 4. Surprise | | | | | | |
| 5. Interest | | | | | | |
| 6. Enthusiasm | | | | | | |
| G. How many times did you feel this experience was | | | | | | |
| 1. Harmful | | | | | | |
| 2. Abusive | | | | | | |
| H. How many times did you feel | | | | | | |
| 1. Extremely guilty | | | | | | |
| 2. Moderately guilty | | | | | | |
| 3. A little guilty | | | | | | |
| 4. Not guilty at all | | | | | | |

| AGE | 0-6 | 7-10 | 11-14 | 15 | 16 | 17 |
|---|---|---|---|---|---|---|
| **I.** How many times did you engage in this experience because of | | | | | | |
| 1. Subtle pressure | | | | | | |
| 2. Verbal threats | | | | | | |
| 3. Physical force | | | | | | |
| 4. Use of a weapon | | | | | | |
| **J.** How many times did you talk about this experience with 1. No one | | | | | | |
| 2. Mother | | | | | | |
| 3. Father | | | | | | |
| 4. Brother | | | | | | |
| 5. Sister | | | | | | |
| 6. Other male adult | | | | | | |
| 7. Other female adult | | | | | | |
| 8. Friend (s) | | | | | | |
| 9. Doctor | | | | | | |
| 10. Police | | | | | | |
| 11. Agency (identify) | | | | | | |
| 12. Other | | | | | | |
| **K.** How many times did you find each of the following to be helpful in dealing with this experience 1. Father | | | | | | |
| 2. Mother | | | | | | |
| 3. Other relative | | | | | | |
| 4. Friend (s) | | | | | | |
| 5. Doctor | | | | | | |
| 6. Lawyer | | | | | | |
| 7. Nurse | | | | | | |
| 8. Teacher | | | | | | |
| 9. Police | | | | | | |
| 10. Social Worker | | | | | | |
| 11. Psychologist | | | | | | |
| 12. Psychiatrist | | | | | | |
| 13. Minister | | | | | | |
| 14. Other | | | | | | |

**L.** How many times did this experience produce for you a long range
1. Positive view of sex
2. Negative view of sex
3. Positive effect on your life
4. Negative effect on your life

**M.** If there were any of the times in which you engaged in this behavior and you felt the experience was abusive or harmful:
1. Describe what kind of help you wish you could have received at the time: _____

_____

2. Describe how you wish the incident(s) had been handled: _____

_____

**N.** If there were any of the times in which you engaged in this behavior and you thought someone else knew of the behavior without your telling them:
1. Who do you think knew about this behavior? _____

2. Do you think the person who knew about the sexual behavior should have done something about it? _____

3. If you answered number 2 as yes, what do you think this person(s) should have done about the sexual behavior? _____

_____

**3. HOW MANY TIMES DID YOU SHOW ANOTHER PERSON YOUR GENITALS WHEN YOU WERE OF**

| AGE | 0-6 | 7-10 | 11-14 | 15 | 16 | 17 |
|---|---|---|---|---|---|---|
| **A.** How many times was this experience requested or initiated by | | | | | | |
| 1. You | | | | | | |
| 2. Your partner | | | | | | |
| 3. Both mutually | | | | | | |
| **B.** How many times was your partner as much as five years older than you? | | | | | | |
| **C.** How many times did you do this with 1. Your father | | | | | | |
| 2. Your stepfather | | | | | | |
| 3. Your mother | | | | | | |
| 4. Your stepmother | | | | | | |
| 5. Your sister | | | | | | |
| 6. Your brother | | | | | | |
| 7. Another male relative | | | | | | |
| 8. Another female relative | | | | | | |
| 9. Unrelated male | | | | | | |
| 10. Unrelated female | | | | | | |
| 11. Husband | | | | | | |
| 12. Stranger | | | | | | |
| **D.** How many times was this experience 1. Very unpleasant | | | | | | |
| 2. Unpleasant | | | | | | |
| 3. Neither pleasant nor unpleasant | | | | | | |
| 4. Pleasant | | | | | | |
| 5. Very pleasant | | | | | | |
| **E.** How many times was this experience 1. Voluntary on your part | | | | | | |
| 2. Forced upon you | | | | | | |
| **F.** How many times did you react with 1. Anger | | | | | | |
| 2. Fear | | | | | | |
| 3. Shock | | | | | | |
| 4. Surprise | | | | | | |
| 5. Interest | | | | | | |
| 6. Enthusiasm | | | | | | |
| **G.** How many times did you feel this experience was 1. Harmful | | | | | | |
| 2. Abusive | | | | | | |
| **H.** How many times did you feel 1. Extremely guilty | | | | | | |
| 2. Moderately guilty | | | | | | |
| 3. A little guilty | | | | | | |
| 4. Not guilty at all | | | | | | |

| AGE | 0-6 | 7-10 | 11-14 | 15 | 16 | 17 |
|---|---|---|---|---|---|---|
| **I.** How many times did you engage in this experience because of | | | | | | |
| 1. Subtle pressure | | | | | | |
| 2. Verbal threats | | | | | | |
| 3. Physical force | | | | | | |
| 4. Use of a weapon | | | | | | |
| **J.** How many times did you talk about this experience with | | | | | | |
| 1. No one | | | | | | |
| 2. Mother | | | | | | |
| 3. Father | | | | | | |
| 4. Brother | | | | | | |
| 5. Sister | | | | | | |
| 6. Other male adult | | | | | | |
| 7. Other female adult | | | | | | |
| 8. Friend (s) | | | | | | |
| 9. Doctor | | | | | | |
| 10. Police | | | | | | |
| 11. Agency (identify) | | | | | | |
| 12. Other | | | | | | |
| **K.** How many times did you find each of the following to be helpful in dealing with this experience | | | | | | |
| 1. Father | | | | | | |
| 2. Mother | | | | | | |
| 3. Other relative | | | | | | |
| 4. Friend (s) | | | | | | |
| 5. Doctor | | | | | | |
| 6. Lawyer | | | | | | |
| 7. Nurse | | | | | | |
| 8. Teacher | | | | | | |
| 9. Police | | | | | | |
| 10. Social Worker | | | | | | |
| 11. Psychologist | | | | | | |
| 12. Psychiatrist | | | | | | |
| 13. Minister | | | | | | |
| 14. Other | | | | | | |

**L.** How many times did this experience produce for you a long range
  1. Positive view of sex
  2. Negative view of sex
  3. Positive effect on your life
  4. Negative effect on your life

**M.** If there were any of the times in which you engaged in this behavior and you felt the experience was abusive or harmful:
  1. Describe what kind of help you wish you could have received at the time:_____

  2. Describe how you wish the incident(s) had been handled:_____

**N.** If there were any of the times in which you engaged in this behavior and you thought someone else knew of the behavior without your telling them:
  1. Who do you think knew about this behavior?_____

  2. Do you think the person who knew about the sexual behavior should have done something about it?

  3. If you answered number 2 as yes, what do you think this person(s) should have done about the sexual behavior? _____

**4.** HOW MANY TIMES DID YOU TOUCH OR FEEL ANOTHER PERSON'S BREASTS
WHEN YOU WERE OF

| AGE | 0-6 | 7-10 | 11-14 | 15 | 16 | 17 |
|---|---|---|---|---|---|---|
| **A.** How many times was this experience requested or initiated by 1. You | | | | | | |
| 2. Your partner | | | | | | |
| 3. Both mutually | | | | | | |
| **B.** How many times was your partner as much as five years older than you? | | | | | | |
| **C.** How many times did you do this with 1. Your father | | | | | | |
| 2. Your stepfather | | | | | | |
| 3. Your mother | | | | | | |
| 4. Your stepmother | | | | | | |
| 5. Your sister | | | | | | |
| 6. Your brother | | | | | | |
| 7. Another male relative | | | | | | |
| 8. Another female relative | | | | | | |
| 9. Unrelated male | | | | | | |
| 10. Unrelated female | | | | | | |
| 11. Husband | | | | | | |
| 12. Stranger | | | | | | |
| **D.** How many times was this experience 1. Very unpleasant | | | | | | |
| 2. Unpleasant | | | | | | |
| 3. Neither pleasant nor unpleasant | | | | | | |
| 4. Pleasant | | | | | | |
| 5. Very pleasant | | | | | | |
| **E.** How many times was this experience 1. Voluntary on your part | | | | | | |
| 2. Forced upon you | | | | | | |
| **F.** How many times did you react with 1. Anger | | | | | | |
| 2. Fear | | | | | | |
| 3. Shock | | | | | | |
| 4. Surprise | | | | | | |
| 5. Interest | | | | | | |
| 6. Enthusiasm | | | | | | |
| **G.** How many times did you feel this experience was 1. Harmful | | | | | | |
| 2. Abusive | | | | | | |
| **H.** How many times did you feel 1. Extremely guilty | | | | | | |
| 2. Moderately guilty | | | | | | |
| 3. A little guilty | | | | | | |
| 4. Not guilty at all | | | | | | |

| AGE | 0-6 | 7-10 | 11-14 | 15 | 16 | 17 |
|---|---|---|---|---|---|---|
| **I.** How many times did you engage in this experience because of | | | | | | |
| 1. Subtle pressure | | | | | | |
| 2. Verbal threats | | | | | | |
| 3. Physical force | | | | | | |
| 4. Use of a weapon | | | | | | |
| **J.** How many times did you talk about this experience with 1. No one | | | | | | |
| 2. Mother | | | | | | |
| 3. Father | | | | | | |
| 4. Brother | | | | | | |
| 5. Sister | | | | | | |
| 6. Other male adult | | | | | | |
| 7. Other female adult | | | | | | |
| 8. Friend (s) | | | | | | |
| 9. Doctor | | | | | | |
| 10. Police | | | | | | |
| 11. Agency (identify) | | | | | | |
| 12. Other | | | | | | |
| **K.** How many times did you find each of the following to be helpful in dealing with this experience 1. Father | | | | | | |
| 2. Mother | | | | | | |
| 3. Other relative | | | | | | |
| 4. Friend (s) | | | | | | |
| 5. Doctor | | | | | | |
| 6. Lawyer | | | | | | |
| 7. Nurse | | | | | | |
| 8. Teacher | | | | | | |
| 9. Police | | | | | | |
| 10. Social Worker | | | | | | |
| 11. Psychologist | | | | | | |
| 12. Psychiatrist | | | | | | |
| 13. Minister | | | | | | |
| 14. Other | | | | | | |

**L.** How many times did this experience produce for you a long range
1. Positive view of sex
2. Negative view of sex
3. Positive effect on your life
4. Negative effect on your life

**M.** If there were any of the times in which you engaged in this behavior and you felt the experience was abusive or harmful:
1. Describe what kind of help you wish you could have received at the time:_____

2. Describe how you wish the incident(s) had been handled:_____

**N.** If there were any of the times in which you engaged in this behavior and you thought someone else knew of the behavior without your telling them:
1. Who do you think knew about this behavior?_____

2. Do you think the person who knew about the sexual behavior should have done something about it?

3. If you answered number 2 as yes, what do you think this person(s) should have done about the sexual behavior?_____

**5. HOW MANY TIMES DID ANOTHER PERSON TOUCH OR FEEL YOUR BREASTS WHEN YOU WERE OF**

| AGE | 0-6 | 7-10 | 11-14 | 15 | 16 | 17 |
|---|---|---|---|---|---|---|
| **A.** How many times was this experience requested or initiated by | | | | | | |
| 1. You | | | | | | |
| 2. Your partner | | | | | | |
| 3. Both mutually | | | | | | |
| **B.** How many times was your partner as much as five years older than you? | | | | | | |
| **C.** How many times did you do this with | | | | | | |
| 1. Your father | | | | | | |
| 2. Your stepfather | | | | | | |
| 3. Your mother | | | | | | |
| 4. Your stepmother | | | | | | |
| 5. Your sister | | | | | | |
| 6. Your brother | | | | | | |
| 7. Another male relative | | | | | | |
| 8. Another female relative | | | | | | |
| 9. Unrelated male | | | | | | |
| 10. Unrelated female | | | | | | |
| 11. Husband | | | | | | |
| 12. Stranger | | | | | | |
| **D.** How many times was this experience | | | | | | |
| 1. Very unpleasant | | | | | | |
| 2. Unpleasant | | | | | | |
| 3. Neither pleasant nor unpleasant | | | | | | |
| 4. Pleasant | | | | | | |
| 5. Very pleasant | | | | | | |
| **E.** How many times was this experience | | | | | | |
| 1. Voluntary on your part | | | | | | |
| 2. Forced upon you | | | | | | |
| **F.** How many times did you react with | | | | | | |
| 1. Anger | | | | | | |
| 2. Fear | | | | | | |
| 3. Shock | | | | | | |
| 4. Surprise | | | | | | |
| 5. Interest | | | | | | |
| 6. Enthusiasm | | | | | | |
| **G.** How many times did you feel this experience was | | | | | | |
| 1. Harmful | | | | | | |
| 2. Abusive | | | | | | |
| **H.** How many times did you feel | | | | | | |
| 1. Extremely guilty | | | | | | |
| 2. Moderately guilty | | | | | | |
| 3. A little guilty | | | | | | |
| 4. Not guilty at all | | | | | | |

| AGE | 0-6 | 7-10 | 11-14 | 15 | 16 | 17 |
|---|---|---|---|---|---|---|
| **I.** How many times did you engage in this experience because of | | | | | | |
| 1. Subtle pressure | | | | | | |
| 2. Verbal threats | | | | | | |
| 3. Physical force | | | | | | |
| 4. Use of a weapon | | | | | | |
| **J.** How many times did you talk about this experience with 1. No one | | | | | | |
| 2. Mother | | | | | | |
| 3. Father | | | | | | |
| 4. Brother | | | | | | |
| 5. Sister | | | | | | |
| 6. Other male adult | | | | | | |
| 7. Other female adult | | | | | | |
| 8. Friend (s) | | | | | | |
| 9. Doctor | | | | | | |
| 10. Police | | | | | | |
| 11. Agency (identify) | | | | | | |
| 12. Other | | | | | | |
| **K.** How many times did you find each of the following to be helpful in dealing with this experience 1. Father | | | | | | |
| 2. Mother | | | | | | |
| 3. Other relative | | | | | | |
| 4. Friend (s) | | | | | | |
| 5. Doctor | | | | | | |
| 6. Lawyer | | | | | | |
| 7. Nurse | | | | | | |
| 8. Teacher | | | | | | |
| 9. Police | | | | | | |
| 10. Social Worker | | | | | | |
| 11. Psychologist | | | | | | |
| 12. Psychiatrist | | | | | | |
| 13. Minister | | | | | | |
| 14. Other | | | | | | |

**L.** How many times did this experience produce for you a long range
1. Positive view of sex
2. Negative view of sex
3. Positive effect on your life
4. Negative effect on your life

**M.** If there were any of the times in which you engaged in this behavior and you felt the experience was abusive or harmful:
1. Describe what kind of help you wish you could have received at the time:_____

2. Describe how you wish the incident(s) had been handled:_____

**N.** If there were any of the times in which you engaged in this behavior and you thought someone else knew of the behavior without your telling them:
1. Who do you think knew about this behavior?_____

2. Do you think the person who knew about the sexual behavior should have done something about it?

3. If you answered number 2 as yes, what do you think this person(s) should have done about the sexual behavior?_____

**6. HOW MANY TIMES DID YOU MASTURBATE ANOTHER PERSON'S GENITALS WHEN YOU WERE OF**

| AGE | 0-6 | 7-10 | 11-14 | 15 | 16 | 17 |
|---|---|---|---|---|---|---|
| **A.** How many times was this experience requested or initiated by<br>1. You | | | | | | |
| 2. Your partner | | | | | | |
| 3. Both mutually | | | | | | |
| **B.** How many times was your partner as much as five years older than you? | | | | | | |
| **C.** How many times did you do this with<br>1. Your father | | | | | | |
| 2. Your stepfather | | | | | | |
| 3. Your mother | | | | | | |
| 4. Your stepmother | | | | | | |
| 5. Your sister | | | | | | |
| 6. Your brother | | | | | | |
| 7. Another male relative | | | | | | |
| 8. Another female relative | | | | | | |
| 9. Unrelated male | | | | | | |
| 10. Unrelated female | | | | | | |
| 11. Husband | | | | | | |
| 12. Stranger | | | | | | |
| **D.** How many times was this experience<br>1. Very unpleasant | | | | | | |
| 2. Unpleasant | | | | | | |
| 3. Neither pleasant nor unpleasant | | | | | | |
| 4. Pleasant | | | | | | |
| 5. Very pleasant | | | | | | |
| **E.** How many times was this experience<br>1. Voluntary on your part | | | | | | |
| 2. Forced upon you | | | | | | |
| **F.** How many times did you react with<br>1. Anger | | | | | | |
| 2. Fear | | | | | | |
| 3. Shock | | | | | | |
| 4. Surprise | | | | | | |
| 5. Interest | | | | | | |
| 6. Enthusiasm | | | | | | |
| **G.** How many times did you feel this experience was<br>1. Harmful | | | | | | |
| 2. Abusive | | | | | | |
| **H.** How many times did you feel<br>1. Extremely guilty | | | | | | |
| 2. Moderately guilty | | | | | | |
| 3. A little guilty | | | | | | |
| 4. Not guilty at all | | | | | | |

| AGE | 0-6 | 7-10 | 11-14 | 15 | 16 | 17 |
|---|---|---|---|---|---|---|
| **I.** How many times did you engage in this experience because of | | | | | | |
| 1. Subtle pressure | | | | | | |
| 2. Verbal threats | | | | | | |
| 3. Physical force | | | | | | |
| 4. Use of a weapon | | | | | | |
| **J.** How many times did you talk about this experience with | | | | | | |
| 1. No one | | | | | | |
| 2. Mother | | | | | | |
| 3. Father | | | | | | |
| 4. Brother | | | | | | |
| 5. Sister | | | | | | |
| 6. Other male adult | | | | | | |
| 7. Other female adult | | | | | | |
| 8. Friend (s) | | | | | | |
| 9. Doctor | | | | | | |
| 10. Police | | | | | | |
| 11. Agency (identify) | | | | | | |
| 12. Other | | | | | | |
| **K.** How many times did you find each of the following to be helpful in dealing with this experience | | | | | | |
| 1. Father | | | | | | |
| 2. Mother | | | | | | |
| 3. Other relative | | | | | | |
| 4. Friend (s) | | | | | | |
| 5. Doctor | | | | | | |
| 6. Lawyer | | | | | | |
| 7. Nurse | | | | | | |
| 8. Teacher | | | | | | |
| 9. Police | | | | | | |
| 10. Social Worker | | | | | | |
| 11. Psychologist | | | | | | |
| 12. Psychiatrist | | | | | | |
| 13. Minister | | | | | | |
| 14. Other | | | | | | |

**L.** How many times did this experience produce for you a long range
1. Positive view of sex
2. Negative view of sex
3. Positive effect on your life
4. Negative effect on your life

**M.** If there were any of the times in which you engaged in this behavior and you felt the experience was abusive or harmful:
1. Describe what kind of help you wish you could have received at the time:_____


2. Describe how you wish the incident(s) had been handled:_____


**N.** If there were any of the times in which you engaged in this behavior and you thought someone else knew of the behavior without your telling them:
1. Who do you think knew about this behavior?_____

2. Do you think the person who knew about the sexual behavior should have done something about it?_____

3. If you answered number 2 as yes, what do you think this person(s) should have done about the sexual behavior? _____

**7. HOW MANY TIMES DID ANOTHER PERSON MASTURBATE YOUR GENITALS WHEN YOU WERE OF**

| AGE | 0-6 | 7-10 | 11-14 | 15 | 16 | 17 |
|---|---|---|---|---|---|---|
| **A.** How many times was this experience requested or initiated by | | | | | | |
| 1. You | | | | | | |
| 2. Your partner | | | | | | |
| 3. Both mutually | | | | | | |
| **B.** How many times was your partner as much as five years older than you? | | | | | | |
| **C.** How many times did you do this with | | | | | | |
| 1. Your father | | | | | | |
| 2. Your stepfather | | | | | | |
| 3. Your mother | | | | | | |
| 4. Your stepmother | | | | | | |
| 5. Your sister | | | | | | |
| 6. Your brother | | | | | | |
| 7. Another male relative | | | | | | |
| 8. Another female relative | | | | | | |
| 9. Unrelated male | | | | | | |
| 10. Unrelated female | | | | | | |
| 11. Husband | | | | | | |
| 12. Stranger | | | | | | |
| **D.** How many times was this experience | | | | | | |
| 1. Very unpleasant | | | | | | |
| 2. Unpleasant | | | | | | |
| 3. Neither pleasant nor unpleasant | | | | | | |
| 4. Pleasant | | | | | | |
| 5. Very pleasant | | | | | | |
| **E.** How many times was this experience | | | | | | |
| 1. Voluntary on your part | | | | | | |
| 2. Forced upon you | | | | | | |
| **F.** How many times did you react with | | | | | | |
| 1. Anger | | | | | | |
| 2. Fear | | | | | | |
| 3. Shock | | | | | | |
| 4. Surprise | | | | | | |
| 5. Interest | | | | | | |
| 6. Enthusiasm | | | | | | |
| **G.** How many times did you feel this experience was | | | | | | |
| 1. Harmful | | | | | | |
| 2. Abusive | | | | | | |
| **H.** How many times did you feel | | | | | | |
| 1. Extremely guilty | | | | | | |
| 2. Moderately guilty | | | | | | |
| 3. A little guilty | | | | | | |
| 4. Not guilty at all | | | | | | |

| AGE | 0-6 | 7-10 | 11-14 | 15 | 16 | 17 |
|---|---|---|---|---|---|---|
| **I.** How many times did you engage in this experience because of | | | | | | |
| 1. Subtle pressure | | | | | | |
| 2. Verbal threats | | | | | | |
| 3. Physical force | | | | | | |
| 4. Use of a weapon | | | | | | |
| **J.** How many times did you talk about this experience with 1. No one | | | | | | |
| 2. Mother | | | | | | |
| 3. Father | | | | | | |
| 4. Brother | | | | | | |
| 5. Sister | | | | | | |
| 6. Other male adult | | | | | | |
| 7. Other female adult | | | | | | |
| 8. Friend (s) | | | | | | |
| 9. Doctor | | | | | | |
| 10. Police | | | | | | |
| 11. Agency (identify) | | | | | | |
| 12. Other | | | | | | |
| **K.** How many times did you find each of the following to be helpful in dealing with this experience 1. Father | | | | | | |
| 2. Mother | | | | | | |
| 3. Other relative | | | | | | |
| 4. Friend (s) | | | | | | |
| 5. Doctor | | | | | | |
| 6. Lawyer | | | | | | |
| 7. Nurse | | | | | | |
| 8. Teacher | | | | | | |
| 9. Police | | | | | | |
| 10. Social Worker | | | | | | |
| 11. Psychologist | | | | | | |
| 12. Psychiatrist | | | | | | |
| 13. Minister | | | | | | |
| 14. Other | | | | | | |

**L.** How many times did this experience produce for you a long range

1. Positive view of sex

2. Negative view of sex

3. Positive effect on your life

4. Negative effect on your life

**M.** If there were any of the times in which you engaged in this behavior and you felt the experience was abusive or harmful:
1. Describe what kind of help you wish you could have received at the time:_____

2. Describe how you wish the incident(s) had been handled:_____

**N.** If there were any of the times in which you engaged in this behavior and you thought someone else knew of the behavior without your telling them:
1. Who do you think knew about this behavior?_____

2. Do you think the person who knew about the sexual behavior should have done something about it?

3. If you answered number 2 as yes, what do you think this person(s) should have done about the sexual behavior? _____

**8. HOW MANY TIMES DID YOU PERFORM ORAL SEX ON ANOTHER PERSON WHEN YOU WERE OF**

| AGE | 0-6 | 7-10 | 11-14 | 15 | 16 | 17 |
|---|---|---|---|---|---|---|
| **A.** How many times was this experience requested or initiated by | | | | | | |
| 1. You | | | | | | |
| 2. Your partner | | | | | | |
| 3. Both mutually | | | | | | |
| **B.** How many times was your partner as much as five years older than you? | | | | | | |
| **C.** How many times did you do this with | | | | | | |
| 1. Your father | | | | | | |
| 2. Your stepfather | | | | | | |
| 3. Your mother | | | | | | |
| 4. Your stepmother | | | | | | |
| 5. Your sister | | | | | | |
| 6. Your brother | | | | | | |
| 7. Another male relative | | | | | | |
| 8. Another female relative | | | | | | |
| 9. Unrelated male | | | | | | |
| 10. Unrelated female | | | | | | |
| 11. Husband | | | | | | |
| 12. Stranger | | | | | | |
| **D.** How many times was this experience | | | | | | |
| 1. Very unpleasant | | | | | | |
| 2. Unpleasant | | | | | | |
| 3. Neither pleasant nor unpleasant | | | | | | |
| 4. Pleasant | | | | | | |
| 5. Very pleasant | | | | | | |
| **E.** How many times was this experience | | | | | | |
| 1. Voluntary on your part | | | | | | |
| 2. Forced upon you | | | | | | |
| **F.** How many times did you react with | | | | | | |
| 1. Anger | | | | | | |
| 2. Fear | | | | | | |
| 3. Shock | | | | | | |
| 4. Surprise | | | | | | |
| 5. Interest | | | | | | |
| 6. Enthusiasm | | | | | | |
| **G.** How many times did you feel this experience was | | | | | | |
| 1. Harmful | | | | | | |
| 2. Abusive | | | | | | |
| **H.** How many times did you feel | | | | | | |
| 1. Extremely guilty | | | | | | |
| 2. Moderately guilty | | | | | | |
| 3. A little guilty | | | | | | |
| 4. Not guilty at all | | | | | | |

| AGE | 0-6 | 7-10 | 11-14 | 15 | 16 | 17 |
|---|---|---|---|---|---|---|
| **I.** How many times did you engage in this experience because of | | | | | | |
| 1. Subtle pressure | | | | | | |
| 2. Verbal threats | | | | | | |
| 3. Physical force | | | | | | |
| 4. Use of a weapon | | | | | | |
| **J.** How many times did you talk about this experience with 1. No one | | | | | | |
| 2. Mother | | | | | | |
| 3. Father | | | | | | |
| 4. Brother | | | | | | |
| 5. Sister | | | | | | |
| 6. Other male adult | | | | | | |
| 7. Other female adult | | | | | | |
| 8. Friend (s) | | | | | | |
| 9. Doctor | | | | | | |
| 10. Police | | | | | | |
| 11. Agency (identify) | | | | | | |
| 12. Other | | | | | | |
| **K.** How many times did you find each of the following to be helpful in dealing with this experience 1. Father | | | | | | |
| 2. Mother | | | | | | |
| 3. Other relative | | | | | | |
| 4. Friend (s) | | | | | | |
| 5. Doctor | | | | | | |
| 6. Lawyer | | | | | | |
| 7. Nurse | | | | | | |
| 8. Teacher | | | | | | |
| 9. Police | | | | | | |
| 10. Social Worker | | | | | | |
| 11. Psychologist | | | | | | |
| 12. Psychiatrist | | | | | | |
| 13. Minister | | | | | | |
| 14. Other | | | | | | |

**L.** How many times did this experience produce for you a long range
1. Positive view of sex
2. Negative view of sex
3. Positive effect on your life
4. Negative effect on your life

**M.** If there were any of the times in which you engaged in this behavior and you felt the experience was abusive or harmful:
1. Describe what kind of help you wish you could have received at the time:_____

2. Describe how you wish the incident(s) had been handled:_____

**N.** If there were any of the times in which you engaged in this behavior and you thought someone else knew of the behavior without your telling them:
1. Who do you think knew about this behavior?_____

2. Do you think the person who knew about the sexual behavior should have done something about it?

3. If you answered number 2 as yes, what do you think this person(s) should have done about the sexual behavior?_____

**9. HOW MANY TIMES DID ANOTHER PERSON PERFORM ORAL SEX ON YOU WHEN YOU WERE OF**

| AGE | 0-6 | 7-10 | 11-14 | 15 | 16 | 17 |
|---|---|---|---|---|---|---|
| A. How many times was this experience requested or initiated by |  |  |  |  |  |  |
| 1. You |  |  |  |  |  |  |
| 2. Your partner |  |  |  |  |  |  |
| 3. Both mutually |  |  |  |  |  |  |
| B. How many times was your partner as much as five years older than you? |  |  |  |  |  |  |
| C. How many times did you do this with |  |  |  |  |  |  |
| 1. Your father |  |  |  |  |  |  |
| 2. Your stepfather |  |  |  |  |  |  |
| 3. Your mother |  |  |  |  |  |  |
| 4. Your stepmother |  |  |  |  |  |  |
| 5. Your sister |  |  |  |  |  |  |
| 6. Your brother |  |  |  |  |  |  |
| 7. Another male relative |  |  |  |  |  |  |
| 8. Another female relative |  |  |  |  |  |  |
| 9. Unrelated male |  |  |  |  |  |  |
| 10. Unrelated female |  |  |  |  |  |  |
| 11. Husband |  |  |  |  |  |  |
| 12. Stranger |  |  |  |  |  |  |
| D. How many times was this experience |  |  |  |  |  |  |
| 1. Very unpleasant |  |  |  |  |  |  |
| 2. Unpleasant |  |  |  |  |  |  |
| 3. Neither pleasant nor unpleasant |  |  |  |  |  |  |
| 4. Pleasant |  |  |  |  |  |  |
| 5. Very pleasant |  |  |  |  |  |  |
| E. How many times was this experience |  |  |  |  |  |  |
| 1. Voluntary on your part |  |  |  |  |  |  |
| 2. Forced upon you |  |  |  |  |  |  |
| F. How many times did you react with |  |  |  |  |  |  |
| 1. Anger |  |  |  |  |  |  |
| 2. Fear |  |  |  |  |  |  |
| 3. Shock |  |  |  |  |  |  |
| 4. Surprise |  |  |  |  |  |  |
| 5. Interest |  |  |  |  |  |  |
| 6. Enthusiasm |  |  |  |  |  |  |
| G. How many times did you feel this experience was |  |  |  |  |  |  |
| 1. Harmful |  |  |  |  |  |  |
| 2. Abusive |  |  |  |  |  |  |
| H. How many times did you feel |  |  |  |  |  |  |
| 1. Extremely guilty |  |  |  |  |  |  |
| 2. Moderately guilty |  |  |  |  |  |  |
| 3. A little guilty |  |  |  |  |  |  |
| 4. Not guilty at all |  |  |  |  |  |  |

| AGE | 0-6 | 7-10 | 11-14 | 15 | 16 | 17 |
|---|---|---|---|---|---|---|
| **I.** How many times did you engage in this experience because of | | | | | | |
| 1. Subtle pressure | | | | | | |
| 2. Verbal threats | | | | | | |
| 3. Physical force | | | | | | |
| 4. Use of a weapon | | | | | | |
| **J.** How many times did you talk about this experience with | | | | | | |
| 1. No one | | | | | | |
| 2. Mother | | | | | | |
| 3. Father | | | | | | |
| 4. Brother | | | | | | |
| 5. Sister | | | | | | |
| 6. Other male adult | | | | | | |
| 7. Other female adult | | | | | | |
| 8. Friend (s) | | | | | | |
| 9. Doctor | | | | | | |
| 10. Police | | | | | | |
| 11. Agency (identify) | | | | | | |
| 12. Other | | | | | | |
| **K.** How many times did you find each of the following to be helpful in dealing with this experience | | | | | | |
| 1. Father | | | | | | |
| 2. Mother | | | | | | |
| 3. Other relative | | | | | | |
| 4. Friend (s) | | | | | | |
| 5. Doctor | | | | | | |
| 6. Lawyer | | | | | | |
| 7. Nurse | | | | | | |
| 8. Teacher | | | | | | |
| 9. Police | | | | | | |
| 10. Social Worker | | | | | | |
| 11. Psychologist | | | | | | |
| 12. Psychiatrist | | | | | | |
| 13. Minister | | | | | | |
| 14. Other | | | | | | |

**L.** How many times did this experience produce for you a long range

1. Positive view of sex ___
2. Negative view of sex ___
3. Positive effect on your life ___
4. Negative effect on your life ___

**M.** If there were any of the times in which you engaged in this behavior and you felt the experience was abusive or harmful:

1. Describe what kind of help you wish you could have received at the time:_____

2. Describe how you wish the incident(s) had been handled:_____

**N.** If there were any of the times in which you engaged in this behavior and you thought someone else knew of the behavior without your telling them:

1. Who do you think knew about this behavior?_____

2. Do you think the person who knew about the sexual behavior should have done something about it?

3. If you answered number 2 as yes, what do you think this person(s) should have done about the sexual behavior? _____

**10. HOW MANY TIMES DID YOU PERFORM ANAL SEX ON ANOTHER PERSON WHEN YOU WERE OF**

| AGE | 0-6 | 7-10 | 11-14 | 15 | 16 | 17 |
|---|---|---|---|---|---|---|
| **A.** How many times was this experience requested or initiated by<br>  1. You | | | | | | |
|   2. Your partner | | | | | | |
|   3. Both mutually | | | | | | |
| **B.** How many times was your partner as much as five years older than you? | | | | | | |
| **C.** How many times did you do this with<br>  1. Your father | | | | | | |
|   2. Your stepfather | | | | | | |
|   3. Your mother | | | | | | |
|   4. Your stepmother | | | | | | |
|   5. Your sister | | | | | | |
|   6. Your brother | | | | | | |
|   7. Another male relative | | | | | | |
|   8. Another female relative | | | | | | |
|   9. Unrelated male | | | | | | |
|   10. Unrelated female | | | | | | |
|   11. Husband | | | | | | |
|   12. Stranger | | | | | | |
| **D.** How many times was this experience<br>  1. Very unpleasant | | | | | | |
|   2. Unpleasant | | | | | | |
|   3. Neither pleasant nor unpleasant | | | | | | |
|   4. Pleasant | | | | | | |
|   5. Very pleasant | | | | | | |
| **E.** How many times was this experience<br>  1. Voluntary on your part | | | | | | |
|   2. Forced upon you | | | | | | |
| **F.** How many times did you react with<br>  1. Anger | | | | | | |
|   2. Fear | | | | | | |
|   3. Shock | | | | | | |
|   4. Surprise | | | | | | |
|   5. Interest | | | | | | |
|   6. Enthusiasm | | | | | | |
| **G.** How many times did you feel this experience was<br>  1. Harmful | | | | | | |
|   2. Abusive | | | | | | |
| **H.** How many times did you feel<br>  1. Extremely guilty | | | | | | |
|   2. Moderately guilty | | | | | | |
|   3. A little guilty | | | | | | |
|   4. Not guilty at all | | | | | | |

| AGE | 0-6 | 7-10 | 11-14 | 15 | 16 | 17 |
|---|---|---|---|---|---|---|
| **I.** How many times did you engage in this experience because of | | | | | | |
| 1. Subtle pressure | | | | | | |
| 2. Verbal threats | | | | | | |
| 3. Physical force | | | | | | |
| 4. Use of a weapon | | | | | | |
| **J.** How many times did you talk about this experience with | | | | | | |
| 1. No one | | | | | | |
| 2. Mother | | | | | | |
| 3. Father | | | | | | |
| 4. Brother | | | | | | |
| 5. Sister | | | | | | |
| 6. Other male adult | | | | | | |
| 7. Other female adult | | | | | | |
| 8. Friend (s) | | | | | | |
| 9. Doctor | | | | | | |
| 10. Police | | | | | | |
| 11. Agency (identify) | | | | | | |
| 12. Other | | | | | | |
| **K.** How many times did you find each of the following to be helpful in dealing with this experience | | | | | | |
| 1. Father | | | | | | |
| 2. Mother | | | | | | |
| 3. Other relative | | | | | | |
| 4. Friend (s) | | | | | | |
| 5. Doctor | | | | | | |
| 6. Lawyer | | | | | | |
| 7. Nurse | | | | | | |
| 8. Teacher | | | | | | |
| 9. Police | | | | | | |
| 10. Social Worker | | | | | | |
| 11. Psychologist | | | | | | |
| 12. Psychiatrist | | | | | | |
| 13. Minister | | | | | | |
| 14. Other | | | | | | |

**L.** How many times did this experience produce for you a long range
1. Positive view of sex _____
2. Negative view of sex _____
3. Positive effect on your life _____
4. Negative effect on your life _____

**M.** If there were any of the times in which you engaged in this behavior and you felt the experience was abusive or harmful:
1. Describe what kind of help you wish you could have received at the time:_____

2. Describe how you wish the incident(s) had been handled:_____

**N.** If there were any of the times in which you engaged in this behavior and you thought someone else knew of the behavior without your telling them:
1. Who do you think knew about this behavior?_____

2. Do you think the person who knew about the sexual behavior should have done something about it?_____

3. If you answered number 2 as yes, what do you think this person(s) should have done about the sexual behavior? _____

**11. HOW MANY TIMES DID ANOTHER PERSON PERFORM ANAL SEX ON YOU WHEN YOU WERE OF**

| AGE | 0-6 | 7-10 | 11-14 | 15 | 16 | 17 |
|---|---|---|---|---|---|---|
| **A.** How many times was this experience requested or initiated by | | | | | | |
| 1. You | | | | | | |
| 2. Your partner | | | | | | |
| 3. Both mutually | | | | | | |
| **B.** How many times was your partner as much as five years older than you? | | | | | | |
| **C.** How many times did you do this with 1. Your father | | | | | | |
| 2. Your stepfather | | | | | | |
| 3. Your mother | | | | | | |
| 4. Your stepmother | | | | | | |
| 5. Your sister | | | | | | |
| 6. Your brother | | | | | | |
| 7. Another male relative | | | | | | |
| 8. Another female relative | | | | | | |
| 9. Unrelated male | | | | | | |
| 10. Unrelated female | | | | | | |
| 11. Husband | | | | | | |
| 12. Stranger | | | | | | |
| **D.** How many times was this experience 1. Very unpleasant | | | | | | |
| 2. Unpleasant | | | | | | |
| 3. Neither pleasant nor unpleasant | | | | | | |
| 4. Pleasant | | | | | | |
| 5. Very pleasant | | | | | | |
| **E.** How many times was this experience 1. Voluntary on your part | | | | | | |
| 2. Forced upon you | | | | | | |
| **F.** How many times did you react with 1. Anger | | | | | | |
| 2. Fear | | | | | | |
| 3. Shock | | | | | | |
| 4. Surprise | | | | | | |
| 5. Interest | | | | | | |
| 6. Enthusiasm | | | | | | |
| **G.** How many times did you feel this experience was 1. Harmful | | | | | | |
| 2. Abusive | | | | | | |
| **H.** How many times did you feel 1. Extremely guilty | | | | | | |
| 2. Moderately guilty | | | | | | |
| 3. A little guilty | | | | | | |
| 4. Not guilty at all | | | | | | |

| AGE | 0-6 | 7-10 | 11-14 | 15 | 16 | 17 |
|---|---|---|---|---|---|---|
| **I.** How many times did you engage in this experience because of | | | | | | |
| 1. Subtle pressure | | | | | | |
| 2. Verbal threats | | | | | | |
| 3. Physical force | | | | | | |
| 4. Use of a weapon | | | | | | |
| **J.** How many times did you talk about this experience with | | | | | | |
| 1. No one | | | | | | |
| 2. Mother | | | | | | |
| 3. Father | | | | | | |
| 4. Brother | | | | | | |
| 5. Sister | | | | | | |
| 6. Other male adult | | | | | | |
| 7. Other female adult | | | | | | |
| 8. Friend (s) | | | | | | |
| 9. Doctor | | | | | | |
| 10. Police | | | | | | |
| 11. Agency (identify) | | | | | | |
| 12. Other | | | | | | |
| **K.** How many times did you find each of the following to be helpful in dealing with this experience | | | | | | |
| 1. Father | | | | | | |
| 2. Mother | | | | | | |
| 3. Other relative | | | | | | |
| 4. Friend (s) | | | | | | |
| 5. Doctor | | | | | | |
| 6. Lawyer | | | | | | |
| 7. Nurse | | | | | | |
| 8. Teacher | | | | | | |
| 9. Police | | | | | | |
| 10. Social Worker | | | | | | |
| 11. Psychologist | | | | | | |
| 12. Psychiatrist | | | | | | |
| 13. Minister | | | | | | |
| 14. Other | | | | | | |

**L.** How many times did this experience produce for you a long range
1. Positive view of sex
2. Negative view of sex
3. Positive effect on your life
4. Negative effect on your life

**M.** If there were any of the times in which you engaged in this behavior and you felt the experience was abusive or harmful:
1. Describe what kind of help you wish you could have received at the time:_____

2. Describe how you wish the incident(s) had been handled:_____

**N.** If there were any of the times in which you engaged in this behavior and you thought someone else knew of the behavior without your telling them:
1. Who do you think knew about this behavior?_____

2. Do you think the person who knew about the sexual behavior should have done something about it?

3. If you answered number 2 as yes, what do you think this person(s) should have done about the sexual behavior? _____

**12. HOW MANY TIMES DID YOU UNSUCCESSFULLY <u>ATTEMPT</u> INTERCOURSE WHEN YOU WERE OF**

| AGE | 0-6 | 7-10 | 11-14 | 15 | 16 | 17 |
|---|---|---|---|---|---|---|
| A. How many times was this experience requested or initiated by | | | | | | |
| 1. You | | | | | | |
| 2. Your partner | | | | | | |
| 3. Both mutually | | | | | | |
| B. How many times was your partner as much as five years older than you? | | | | | | |
| C. How many times did you do this with | | | | | | |
| 1. Your father | | | | | | |
| 2. Your stepfather | | | | | | |
| 3. Your mother | | | | | | |
| 4. Your stepmother | | | | | | |
| 5. Your sister | | | | | | |
| 6. Your brother | | | | | | |
| 7. Another male relative | | | | | | |
| 8. Another female relative | | | | | | |
| 9. Unrelated male | | | | | | |
| 10. Unrelated female | | | | | | |
| 11. Husband | | | | | | |
| 12. Stranger | | | | | | |
| D. How many times was this experience | | | | | | |
| 1. Very unpleasant | | | | | | |
| 2. Unpleasant | | | | | | |
| 3. Neither pleasant nor unpleasant | | | | | | |
| 4. Pleasant | | | | | | |
| 5. Very pleasant | | | | | | |
| E. How many times was this experience | | | | | | |
| 1. Voluntary on your part | | | | | | |
| 2. Forced upon you | | | | | | |
| F. How many times did you react with | | | | | | |
| 1. Anger | | | | | | |
| 2. Fear | | | | | | |
| 3. Shock | | | | | | |
| 4. Surprise | | | | | | |
| 5. Interest | | | | | | |
| 6. Enthusiasm | | | | | | |
| G. How many times did you feel this experience was | | | | | | |
| 1. Harmful | | | | | | |
| 2. Abusive | | | | | | |
| H. How many times did you feel | | | | | | |
| 1. Extremely guilty | | | | | | |
| 2. Moderately guilty | | | | | | |
| 3. A little guilty | | | | | | |
| 4. Not guilty at all | | | | | | |

| AGE | 0-6 | 7-10 | 11-14 | 15 | 16 | 17 |
|---|---|---|---|---|---|---|
| **I.** How many times did you engage in this experience because of | | | | | | |
| 1. Subtle pressure | | | | | | |
| 2. Verbal threats | | | | | | |
| 3. Physical force | | | | | | |
| 4. Use of a weapon | | | | | | |
| **J.** How many times did you talk about this experience with 1. No one | | | | | | |
| 2. Mother | | | | | | |
| 3. Father | | | | | | |
| 4. Brother | | | | | | |
| 5. Sister | | | | | | |
| 6. Other male adult | | | | | | |
| 7. Other female adult | | | | | | |
| 8. Friend (s) | | | | | | |
| 9. Doctor | | | | | | |
| 10. Police | | | | | | |
| 11. Agency (identify) | | | | | | |
| 12. Other | | | | | | |
| **K.** How many times did you find each of the following to be helpful in dealing with this experience 1. Father | | | | | | |
| 2. Mother | | | | | | |
| 3. Other relative | | | | | | |
| 4. Friend (s) | | | | | | |
| 5. Doctor | | | | | | |
| 6. Lawyer | | | | | | |
| 7. Nurse | | | | | | |
| 8. Teacher | | | | | | |
| 9. Police | | | | | | |
| 10. Social Worker | | | | | | |
| 11. Psychologist | | | | | | |
| 12. Psychiatrist | | | | | | |
| 13. Minister | | | | | | |
| 14. Other | | | | | | |

**L.** How many times did this experience produce for you a long range
1. Positive view of sex
2. Negative view of sex
3. Positive effect on your life
4. Negative effect on your life

**M.** If there were any of the times in which you engaged in this behavior and you felt the experience was abusive or harmful:
1. Describe what kind of help you wish you could have received at the time:_____


2. Describe how you wish the incident(s) had been handled:_____


**N.** If there were any of the times in which you engaged in this behavior and you thought someone else knew of the behavior without your telling them:
1. Who do you think knew about this behavior?_____

2. Do you think the person who knew about the sexual behavior should have done something about it?

3. If you answered number 2 as yes, what do you think this person(s) should have done about the sexual behavior?_____

**13.** HOW MANY TIMES DID YOU ENGAGE IN INTERCOURSE ( ACHIEVE PENETRATION OR WERE PENETRATED) WHEN YOU WERE OF

| AGE | 0-6 | 7-10 | 11-14 | 15 | 16 | 17 |
|---|---|---|---|---|---|---|
| **A.** How many times was this experience requested or initiated by | | | | | | |
|     1. You | | | | | | |
|     2. Your partner | | | | | | |
|     3. Both mutually | | | | | | |
| **B.** How many times was your partner as much as five years older than you? | | | | | | |
| **C.** How many times did you do this with | | | | | | |
|     1. Your father | | | | | | |
|     2. Your stepfather | | | | | | |
|     3. Your mother | | | | | | |
|     4. Your stepmother | | | | | | |
|     5. Your sister | | | | | | |
|     6. Your brother | | | | | | |
|     7. Another male relative | | | | | | |
|     8. Another female relative | | | | | | |
|     9. Unrelated male | | | | | | |
|     10. Unrelated female | | | | | | |
|     11. Husband | | | | | | |
|     12. Stranger | | | | | | |
| **D.** How many times was this experience | | | | | | |
|     1. Very unpleasant | | | | | | |
|     2. Unpleasant | | | | | | |
|     3. Neither pleasant nor unpleasant | | | | | | |
|     4. Pleasant | | | | | | |
|     5. Very pleasant | | | | | | |
| **E.** How many times was this experience | | | | | | |
|     1. Voluntary on your part | | | | | | |
|     2. Forced upon you | | | | | | |
| **F.** How many times did you react with | | | | | | |
|     1. Anger | | | | | | |
|     2. Fear | | | | | | |
|     3. Shock | | | | | | |
|     4. Surprise | | | | | | |
|     5. Interest | | | | | | |
|     6. Enthusiasm | | | | | | |
| **G.** How many times did you feel this experience was | | | | | | |
|     1. Harmful | | | | | | |
|     2. Abusive | | | | | | |
| **H.** How many times did you feel | | | | | | |
|     1. Extremely guilty | | | | | | |
|     2. Moderately guilty | | | | | | |
|     3. A little guilty | | | | | | |
|     4. Not guilty at all | | | | | | |

| AGE | 0-6 | 7-10 | 11-14 | 15 | 16 | 17 |
|---|---|---|---|---|---|---|
| **I.** How many times did you engage in this experience because of | | | | | | |
| 1. Subtle pressure | | | | | | |
| 2. Verbal threats | | | | | | |
| 3. Physical force | | | | | | |
| 4. Use of a weapon | | | | | | |
| **J.** How many times did you talk about this experience with 1. No one | | | | | | |
| 2. Mother | | | | | | |
| 3. Father | | | | | | |
| 4. Brother | | | | | | |
| 5. Sister | | | | | | |
| 6. Other male adult | | | | | | |
| 7. Other female adult | | | | | | |
| 8. Friend (s) | | | | | | |
| 9. Doctor | | | | | | |
| 10. Police | | | | | | |
| 11. Agency (identify) | | | | | | |
| 12. Other | | | | | | |
| **K.** How many times did you find each of the following to be helpful in dealing with this experience 1. Father | | | | | | |
| 2. Mother | | | | | | |
| 3. Other relative | | | | | | |
| 4. Friend (s) | | | | | | |
| 5. Doctor | | | | | | |
| 6. Lawyer | | | | | | |
| 7. Nurse | | | | | | |
| 8. Teacher | | | | | | |
| 9. Police | | | | | | |
| 10. Social Worker | | | | | | |
| 11. Psychologist | | | | | | |
| 12. Psychiatrist | | | | | | |
| 13. Minister | | | | | | |
| 14. Other | | | | | | |

**L.** How many times did this experience produce for you a long range
1. Positive view of sex
2. Negative view of sex
3. Positive effect on your life
4. Negative effect on your life

**M.** If there were any of the times in which you engaged in this behavior and you felt the experience was abusive or harmful:
1. Describe what kind of help you wish you could have received at the time:_____

2. Describe how you wish the incident(s) had been handled:_____

**N.** If there were any of the times in which you engaged in this behavior and you thought someone else knew of the behavior without your telling them:
1. Who do you think knew about this behavior?_____

2. Do you think the person who knew about the sexual behavior should have done something about it?

3. If you answered number 2 as yes, what do you think this person(s) should have done about the sexual behavior? _____

THANK YOU VERY MUCH FOR

YOUR PARTICIPATION IN THIS

RESEARCH PROJECT

# APPENDIX C:  CONSENT FORM

I freely and voluntarily and without undue inducement or any element of force, fraud, deceit, duress, or other form of constraint or coercion, consent to be a participant in the research project on the family and sexual behavior conducted by Allie C. Kilpatrick.

The procedures to be followed, the risks reasonably to be expected by my participation, and any benefits reasonably to be expected from my participation have been explained to me, and I understand them.

I understand that this consent may be withdrawn at any time without prejudice. I have been given the right to ask and have answered any inquiry concerning the above. Questions, if any, have been answered to my satisfaction. I have read and understand the above.

_____          _____
(Participant)                                             (Date)


_____
(Witness)

# APPENDIX D: SEXUAL INVOLVEMENT RATING SCALE

Please rate each of the following eight behaviors on a scale from 1 to 10 according to the degree of sexual involvement. Ten represents the most intense involvement. Place the number of the behavior at the appropriate point on the scale.

1. Hugging and kissing
2. Exhibition
3. Breast fondling
4. Mutual masturbation
5. Oral sex
6. Anal sex
7. Attempted intercourse
8. Intercourse

```
├─────────────────────────────────────────────────────────────┤
1      2      3      4      5      6      7      8      9      10
```

# APPENDIX E: SIGNIFICANT VARIABLES WITHIN SETS

TABLE E-1

Multiple Regression Analyses for Scale Score and Sets of Variables:
Significant Variables Within Sets (Ages 0–14)

| Scales, Sets, and Variables | F to Enter | p | $R^2$ Change |
|---|---|---|---|
| *IFR* | | | |
| Background variables | | | |
| Income | 11.009 | .001 | .028 |
| Married | 6.379 | .012 | .013 |
| Sexual partners | | | |
| Nonrelative | 6.738 | .010 | .013 |
| Interactions | | | |
| Other relative x pleasure | 5.712 | .017 | .0005 |
| Nonrelative x harmful | 3.902 | .049 | .003 |
| Other relative x voluntary | 7.150 | .008 | .006 |
| Other relative x abusive | 8.735 | .003 | .010 |
| Nonrelative x voluntary | 4.337 | .038 | .011 |
| *GCS* | | | |
| Background variables | | | |
| Production occupation | 10.212 | .001 | .025 |
| Community size | 12.769 | .0005 | .020 |
| Ethnicity | 5.287 | .022 | .011 |
| Number times married | 11.276 | .001 | .009 |
| Married | 4.778 | .029 | .009 |
| Sexual partners | | | |
| Other relative | 3.881 | .049 | .007 |
| Interactions | | | |
| Parents x pressure | 5.471 | .020 | .0005 |
| Parents x abusive | 8.483 | .004 | .015 |
| *ISS* | | | |
| Background variables | | | |
| Production occupation | 4.828 | .029 | .013 |
| Community size | 10.709 | .001 | .025 |
| Interactions | | | |
| Nonrelative x harmful | 5.081 | .025 | .005 |
| Other relative x abusive | 4.585 | .033 | .010 |
| Nonrelative x forced | 4.724 | .030 | .009 |
| Parents x abusive | 5.102 | .024 | .010 |

TABLE E-1 (Continued)

| Scales, Sets, and Variables | F to Enter | p | $R^2$ Change |
|---|---|---|---|
| IMS | | | |
| Background variables | | | |
| Agricultural occupation, spouse | 8.667 | .004 | .020 |
| Ethnicity | 8.273 | .004 | .032 |
| Married | 8.655 | .004 | .031 |
| Interactions | | | |
| Nonrelative x harmful | 9.938 | .002 | .016 |
| Parents x forced | 4.080 | .045 | .013 |
| ISS | | | |
| Reactions | | | |
| Pleasure | 4.011 | .046 | .016 |
| Interactions | | | |
| Parents x guilt | 4.178 | .031 | .0005 |
| Parents x pleasure | 4.333 | .038 | .067 |

TABLE E-2
Multiple Regression Analyses for Scale Scores and Sets of Variables:
Significant Variables Within Sets (Ages 15–17)

| Scales, Sets, and Variables | F to Enter | p | $R^2$ Change |
|---|---|---|---|
| IFR | | | |
| Background variables | | | |
| Age | 5.023 | .023 | .002 |
| Income | 11.820 | .001 | .030 |
| Education | 5.294 | .022 | .012 |
| Interactions | | | |
| Parents x pressure | 8.754 | .003 | .012 |
| Parents x guilt | 4.104 | .043 | .0001 |
| Parents x abusive | 10.636 | .001 | .007 |
| Parents x pleasure | 7.565 | .006 | .016 |
| GCS | | | |
| Background variables | | | |
| Community size | 6.622 | .010 | .008 |
| Education | 6.057 | .014 | .017 |
| Married | 6.985 | .008 | .014 |
| Sexual partners | | | |
| Other relative | 5.819 | .016 | .010 |
| Conditions | | | |
| Voluntary | 4.122 | .043 | .008 |
| Interactions | | | |
| Nonrelative x voluntary | 4.314 | .038 | .004 |
| ISS | | | |
| Background variables | | | |
| Community size | 9.067 | .003 | .023 |
| Education | 9.257 | .002 | .016 |
| Sexual partners | | | |
| Other relative | 3.901 | .049 | .006 |
| Conditions | | | |
| Voluntary | 5.441 | .020 | .011 |
| Interactions | | | |
| Nonrelative x voluntary | 5.304 | .022 | .007 |
| IMS | | | |
| Background variables | | | |
| Ethnicity | 5.955 | .015 | .046 |
| Married | 5.163 | .024 | .020 |
| Reactions | | | |
| Abusive | 4.349 | .038 | .017 |
| ISS | | | |
| Background variables | | | |
| Education | 4.358 | .038 | .011 |
| Reactions | | | |
| Abusive | 5.855 | .016 | .015 |

# REFERENCES

Achenbach, T. M., & Edelbrock, C. (1983). *Manual for the child behavior checklist*. Burlington: University of Vermont.

Alexander, P. (1985). A systems theory conceptualization of incest. *Family Process, 24*, 79–88.

American Humane Association. (1987). *Highlights of official child neglect and abuse reporting 1985*. Denver, CO: Author.

American Humane Association. (1988). *Highlights of official child neglect and abuse reporting 1986*. Denver, CO: Author.

American Humane Association. (1989). *Highlights of official child neglect and abuse reporting 1987*. Denver, CO: Author.

Anderson, L. M., & Shafer, G. (1979). The character disordered family: A community treatment model for family sexual abuse. *American Journal of Orthopsychiatry, 49*(3), 436–445.

Aries, P. (1962). *Centuries of childhood*. New York: Vantage.

Asher, S. J. (1988). The effects of childhood sexual abuse: A review of the issues and evidence. In L. E. Walker (Ed.), *Handbook on sexual abuse of children* (pp. 3–18). New York: Springer.

Ayrinhac, H. A. (1919). *Marriage legislation in the new code of canon law*. New York: Benzizner Brothers.

Bardill, D. R. (1977, Spring). Relational thinking and person abuse. *Social Work Metropolitan-Washington, 10*–12.

Beavers, W. R., & Hampson, R. B. (1990). *Successful families: Assessment and intervention*. New York: Norton.

Bell, A. (1968). *Black sexuality: Fact and fancy*. A paper presented to Focus: Black America Series, Indiana University, Bloomington, IN.

Bender, L. (1954). *A dynamic psychopathology of childhood*. Springfield, IL: Thomas.

Bender, L., & Blau, A. (1937). The reaction of children to sexual relations with adults. *American Journal of Orthopsychiatry, 7*, 500–518.

193

Bender, L., & Grugett, A. E., Jr. (1952). A follow-up report on children who had atypical sexual experiences. *American Journal of Orthopsychiatry, 22*, 825–837.

Benward, J., & Densen-Gerber, J. D. (1975). Incest as a causative factor in antisocial behavior: An exploratory study. *Contemporary Drug Problems, 4*, 323–340.

Berliner, L., & Stevens, D. (1982). Clinical issues in child sexual assault. *Journal of Social Work and Human Sexuality, 1*(1–2), 93–108.

Bernard, F. (1981). Pedophilia: A study of psychological consequences for the child. In L. L. Constantine & F. M. Martinson (Eds.), *Children and sex* (pp. 189–199). Boston: Little, Brown.

Boatman, B., Borkan, E. L., & Schetky, D. H. (1981). Treatment of child victims of incest. *The American Journal of Family Therapy, 9*(4), 43–51.

Bowlby, J. (1984). Violence in the family as a disorder of the attachment and caregiving systems. *American Journal of Psychoanalysis, 44*, 9–27.

Brickman, J. (1984). Feminist, nonsexist, and traditional models of therapy: Implications for working with incest. *Women and Therapy, 3*, 49–67.

Briere, J., & Runtz, M. (1988). Post sexual abuse trauma. In G. E. Wyatt & G. J. Powell (Eds.), *Lasting effects of child sexual abuse* (pp. 85–100). Newbury Park, CA: Sage.

Brooks, B. (1982). Familial influences in father–daughter incest. *Journal of Psychiatric Treatment and Evaluation, 4*, 117–124.

Browne, A., & Finkelhor, D. (1986). Impact of child sexual abuse: A review of the research. *Psychological Bulletin, 99*(1), 66–77.

Brownmiller, S. (1975). *Against our will: Men, women and rape.* New York: Simon & Schuster.

Brunold, H. (1964, January/February). Observations after sexual traumata suffered in childhood. *Excerpia Criminologica*, Lisse, The Netherlands: Swets & Fzitlinger, B.V.

Bryer, J. B., Nelson, B. A., Miller, J. B., & Krol, P. A. (1987). Childhood sexual and physical abuse as factors in adult psychiatric illness. *American Journal of Psychiatry, 144*(11), 1426–1430.

Burgess, A. W., Groth, A. N., Holmstrom, L. L., & Sgroi, S. M. (1978). *Sexual assault of children and adolescents.* Lexington, MA: Lexington Books.

Burgess, A. W., & Holstrom, L. L. (1974). *Rape! Victims of crisis.* New York: Brady.

Chaneles, S. (1967). Child victims of sexual offenses. *Federal Probation, 31*, 52–56.

Chilman, C. (1978). *Adolescent sexuality in a changing American society: Social and psychological perspectives* (NIH Publication No. 79–1426, Department of Health, Education and Welfare). Washington, DC: U.S. Government Printing Office.

Cleveland, D. (1986). *Incest: The story of three women.* Boston: Heath.

Comtors, C. (1979). The incest experience and its aftermath. *Victimology: An International Journal, 4*, 337–347.

Constantine, L. L., & Martinson, F. M. (Eds.). (1981). *children and sex.* Boston: Little, Brown.

Conte, J. R. (1986). *A look at child sexual abuse.* Washington, DC: National Committee for Prevention of Child Abuse.

Conte, J. R. (1987). Child sexual abuse. In A. Minahan (Ed.), *Encyclopedia of social work* (18th ed., Vol. 1, pp. 255–260). Silver Springs, MD: National Association of Social Workers.

Conte, J. R., & Berliner, L. (1981). Sexual abuse of children: Implications for practice. *Social Casework, 62*(10), 601–606.

Conte, J., Briere, J., & Sexton, D. (1989 August). *Mediators of long term symptomology in women molested as children.* Paper presented at the 93rd annual convention of the American Psychological Association, New Orleans, LA.

Cook, T. D., & Campbell, D. T. (1979). *Quasi-experimentation.* Chicago: Rand McNally.

Corwin, D. L. (1988). Early diagnosis of child sexual abuse: Diminishing the lasting effects. In G. E. Wyatt & G. J. Powell (Eds.), *Lasting effects of child sexual abuse* (pp. 251–269). Newbury Park, CA: Sage.

Courtois, C. (1979). The incest experience and its aftermath. *Victimology: An International Journal, 4,* 337–347.

Courtois, C. A., & Sprei, J. E. (1988). Retrospective incest therapy for women. In L. A. Walker (Ed.), *Handbook on sexual abuse of children* (pp. 270–308). New York: Springer.

De Francis, V. (1969). *Protecting the child victim of sex crimes committed by adults.* Denver, CO: Children's Division, American Humane Association.

deMause, L. (1974). *The history of childhood.* New York: Psychiatry Press.

Elwell, M. E. (1979, April). Sexually assaulted children and their families. *Social Casework,* pp. 227–235.

Elwin, V. (1939). *The Baiga.* New York: AMS.

Emslie, G. J., & Rosenfeld, A. (1983). Incest reported by children and adolescents hospitalized for severe psychiatric problems. *American Journal of Psychiatry, 140*(6), 708–711.

Fallow, K. C. (1987). Protective services for children. In A. Minahan (Ed.), *Encyclopedia of social work* (pp. 386–390). Silver Spring, MD: National Association of Social Workers.

Finkelhor, D. (1979). *Sexually victimized children.* New York: The Free Press.

Finkelhor, D. (1981). Sex between siblings: Sex play, incest, and aggression. In L. L. Constantine & F. M. Martinson (Eds.), *Children and sex* (pp. 129–150). Boston: Little, Brown.

Finkelhor, D. (1984). *Child sexual abuse: New theory and research.* New York: The Free Press.

Forward, S., & Buck, C. (1978). *Betrayal of innocence.* New York: Penguin Books.

Freud, S. (1954). Letters to Wilhelm Fleiss, Drafts and Notes: 1887–1902. In M. Bonaparte, A. Freud, & E. Kris (Eds.), *The origin of psychoanalysis.* New York: Basic Books.

Fritz, G. S., Stoll, D., & Wagner, N. N. (1981). A comparison of males and females who were sexually molested as children. *Journal of Sex and Marital Therapy, 1*(1), 54–60.

Fulton, J. (1883). *Laws of marriage.* London: Week, Gardner, Dalton.

Gagnon, J. H., & Simon, W. (1969, February). The child molester: Surprising advice for worried parents. *Redbook,* pp. 54–60.

Gagnon, J. H. (1965). Female child victims of sex offenses. *Social Problems, 13,* 176–192.

Gebhard, P. H., and others (1965). *Sex offenders: An analysis of types.* New York: Harper & Row.

Gelles, R. J. (1974). *The violent home: A study of physical aggression between husbands and wives.* Beverly Hills, CA: Sage.

Gelles, R. J. (1980). Violence in the family: A review of research in the seventies. *Journal of Marriage and Family, 42,* 873–885.

Gelles, R. K. (1978). Methods for studying sensitive family topics. *American Journal of Orthopsychiatry, 48*(3), 408–424.

Gelman, D. (1981, November 30). Finding the hidden Freud. *Newsweek,* pp. 64–70.

Giarretto, H. (1976). Humanistic treatment of father–daughter incest. In R. E. Helfer & C. H. Kempe (Eds.), *Child abuse and neglect: The family and community.* Cambridge, MA: Balinger.

Giarretto, H. (1982a). A comprehensive child sexual abuse treatment program. *Child Abuse and Neglect, 6,* 263–278.

Giarretto, H. (1982b). *Integrated treatment of child sexual abuse: A treatment and training manual.* Palo Alto, CA: Science and Behavior Books.

Giarretto, H., Giarretto, A., & Sgroi, S. M. (1978). Coordinated community treatment of incest. In A. W. Burgess, A. N. Growth, L. L. Holmstrom, & S. M. Sgroi (Eds.), *Sexual assault of children and adolescents* (pp. 231–240). Lexington, MA: Lexington Books.

Goodwin, J. (1982). *Sexual abuse: Incest victims and their families.* Boston: Wright/PSG.

Goodwin, J. (1988). Obstacles to policy making about incest: Some cautionary folk tales. In G. E. Wyatt & G. J. Powell (Eds.), *Lasting effects of child sexual abuse* (pp. 21–37). Newbury Park, CA: Sage.

Goodwin, J., Simms, M., & Bergman, R. (1979). Hysterical seizures: A sequel to incest. *American Journal of Orthopsychiatry, 49*(4), 698–703.

Greenland, C. (1958). Incest. *British Journal of Delinquency, 9*, 62–65.

Gross, M. (1979). Incestuous rape: A cause for hysterical seizures in four adolescent girls. *American Journal of Orthopsychiatry, 49*(4), 704–708.

Hale, M. (1847). *The history of the pleas of the crown.* Philadelphia: Robert H. Small.

Haugaard, J. J., & Reppucci, N. D. (1988). *The sexual abuse of children.* San Francisco: Jossey-Bass.

Herhold, S. (1982, March 20). Girl scout behind bars; won't testify. *The Union Recorder,* p. 12.

Herman, J. (1981). *Father–daughter incest.* Cambridge, MA: Harvard University.

Herman, J., & Hirschman, L. (1977). Father–daughter incest: A feminist theoretical perspective. *Signs: Journal of Women in Culture and Society, 2*(4), 735–756.

Herman, J., Russell, D., & Trocki, K. (1986). Long-term effects of incestuous abuse in childhood. *American Journal of Psychiatry, 143*(10), 1293–1296.

Hudson, W. W. (1982). *The clinical measurement package: A field manual.* Homewook, IL: The Dorsey Press.

International Labour Office. (1969). *International Standard Classification of Occupations.* Geneva: Author.

Jackson, J. L., Calhoun, K. S., Amick, A. E., Maddever, H. M., & Habif, V. L. (1990). Young adult women who experienced childhood intrafamilial sexual abuse: Subsequent adjustment. *Archives of Sexual Behavior, 19*, 211–221.

Jaffe, A. C., Dynneson, L., & Bensel, R. W. (1975). Sexual abuse of children: An epidemiologic study. *American Journal of Diseases of Children, 129*, 689–692.

James, J., & Meyerding, J. (1977). Early sexual experiences and prostitution. *American Journal of Psychiatry, 134*, 1381–1385.

James, K., & MacKinnon, L. (1990). The "incestuous family" revisited: A critical analysis of family therapy myths. *Journal of Marital and Family Therapy, 16*(1), 71–88.

Janeway, E. (1981). Incest: A rational look at the oldest taboo. *Ms Magazine, 109*, 61–64.

Johnson, M. S. (1983). Recognizing the incestuous family. *Journal of the National Medical Association, 75*(8), 757–776.

Jones, R. J., Gruber, K. J., & Freeman, M. N. (1983). Reactions of adolescents to being interviewed about their sexual assault experiences. *The Journal of Sex Research, 19*(2), 160–172.

Judge: 5-year-old victim "promiscuous." (1982, January 14). *The Atlanta Journal,* 9A.

Justice, B., & Justice, R. (1979). *The broken taboo.* New York: Human Sciences Press.

Kadushin, A., & Martin, J. A. (1988). *Child welfare services* (4th ed.). New York: Macmillan.

Katan, A. (1973). Children who were raped. *Psychoanalytic Study of the Child, 28*, 219.

Kaufman, I., Peck, A., & Tagiori, L. (1954). The family constellation and overt incestuous relations between father and daughter. *American Journal of Orthopsychiatry, 24*, 266–279.

Kempe, R. S., & Kempe, C. H. (1978). *Child abuse.* Cambridge, MA: Harvard University Press.

Kilpatrick, A. C. (1986). Some correlates of women's childhood sexual experiences: A retrospective study. *The Journal of Sex Research, 22*, 221–242.

Kilpatrick, A. C. (1987). Childhood sexual experiences: Problems and issues in studying long-range effects. *The Journal of Sex Research, 23*(2), 173–196.

Kilpatrick, A. C., & Lockhart, L. L. (in press). Studying sensitive family issues: Problems and possibilities for practitioners. *Families in Society.*

Kinsey, A. C., Pomeroy, W. B., & Martin, C. E. (1948). *Sexual behavior in the human male.* Philadelphia: Saunders.

Kinsey, A. C., Pomeroy, W. B., Martin, C. E., & Gebhard, P. H. (1953). *Sexual behavior in the human female.* Philadelphia: Saunders.

Kroth, J. A. (1979). *Child sexual abuse.* Springfield, IL: Thomas.

Kubo, S. (1959). Researches and studies on incest in Japan. *Hiroshima Journal of Medical Sciences*, 8(1), 99–159.

Landis, J. T. (1956). Experiences of 500 children with adult sexual deviation. *Psychiatric Quarterly*, 30, 91–109.

Lerman, H. (1988). The psychoanalytic legacy: From whence all come. In L. E. Walker (Ed.), *Handbook on sexual abuse of children* (pp. 37–52). New York: Springer.

Lewis, J. M., Beavers, W. R., Gossett, J. T., & Phillips, V. A. (1975). *No single thread: Psychological health in family systems*. New York: Brunner/Mazel.

Lockhart, L. L., Saunders, B. E., & Cleveland, P. (1989). Adult male sexual offenders: An overview of treatment techniques. In J. S. Wodarski & D. L. Whitaker (Eds.), *Treatment of sex offenders in social work and mental health settings* (pp. 1–32). New York: Haworth.

Lukianowicz, N. (1972). Incest. *British Journal of Psychiatry*, 120, 301–313.

MacFarlane, K., & Brickley, J. (1982). Treating child sexual abuse: An overview of current program models. *Journal of Social Work and Human Sexuality*, 1, 69–91.

Maimonides. (1972). *The book of women* (Book 4). New Haven, CT: Yale University Press.

Mann, E. M., & Gaynor, D. A. (1980). Emotional reactions and treatment of sexually abused children, adolescents, and their parents. In *Preventive child psychiatry in age of transitions, Vol. 6. The child in his family* (pp. 409–420). New York: Wiley.

Mary Ellen. (1878, April 10). *New York Times*, p. 8.

Masson, J. M. (Ed. & Trans.). (1985). *The complete letters of Sigmund Freud to Wilheim Fliess 1987–1904*. Cambridge, MA: Belknap Press of Harvard University Press.

McIntyre, K. (1981, November). Incest: A feminist analysis. *Social Work*, 26(6), 462–466.

McKerrow, W. D. (1973). Protecting the sexually abused child. *Proceedings of the Second National Symposium on Child Abuse* (pp. 38–44). Denver, CO: American Humane Association.

Medlicott, R. W. (1967). Parent–child incest. *Australia and New Zealand Journal of Psychiatry*, 1, 180–187.

Meiselman, K. C. (1978). *Incest: A psychological study of causes and effects and treatment recommendations*. San Francisco: Jossey-Bass.

Miner, L. (1966). Sexual molestation of children: A medicolegal problem. *Aeta Medinale Legalis et Socialis*, 19, 203–205.

Molnar, G., & Cameron, P. (1975). Incest syndromes: Observations in a general hospital psychiatric unit. *Canadian Psychiatric Association Journal*, 20, 373–377.

Moos, R. H., & Moos, B. S. (1976). Typology of family social environments. *Family Process*, 15(4), 357–371.

Murphy, S. M., Kilpatrick, D. G., Amick-McMullan, A. A., Veronen, L. J., Paduhowick, J., Best, C. L., Villeponteaux, L. A., & Saunders, B. E. (1988). Current psychological functioning of child sexual assault survivors: A community study. *Journal of Interpersonal Violence*, 3(1), 55–79.

National Center on Child Abuse and Neglect. (1978, January 23). *Federal Register*, Part 2, 3244.

National Center on Child Abuse and Neglect. (1980). *National Incidence Study* (NIS-1). Washington, DC: U. S. Department of Health and Human Services.

National Center on Child Abuse and Neglect. (1988). *National Incidence Study* (NIS-2). Washington, DC: U.S. Department of Health and Human Services.

Nelson, J. A. (1981). The impact of incest: Factors in self-evaluation. In L. L. Constantine & F. M. Martinson (Eds.), *Children and sex* (pp. 163–174). Boston: Little, Brown.

Newman, R. (1975). Masturbation, madness and the modern concept of childhood and adolescence. *Journal of Social History*, 8(3), 1–27.

New York Society for Prevention of Cruelty to Children. (1916). *Forty-second annual report*. New York: Author.

Nezikin, S. (Ed.). (1935). *The Babylonian talmud* (I. Epstein, Trans.). London: The Soncino Press.

Okami, P. (1988, November). *Child sexual abuse: A critical evaluation of new perspectives*. Paper presented at the meeting of the Society for the Scientific Study of Sex, San Francisco, CA.

Okami, P. (1989, November). *Confronting the unmentionable: A phenomenological investigation of non-abusive sexual abuse*. Paper presented at the meeting of the Society for the Scientific Study of Sex, Toronto, Ontario, Canada.

Olson, D. H., McCubbin, H. I., Barnes, H., Larson, A., Muxin, M., & Wilson, M. (1982). *Family inventories*. St. Paul: Family Social Sciences, University of Minnesota.

Olson, D. H., Sprenkle, D. H., & Russell, C. (1979, March). Circumplex model of marital and family systems. *Family Process, 18*(1), 3–28.

Pagelow M. D. (1981). *Women-battering: Victims and their experiences*. Beverly Hills, CA: Sage.

Paulk, L., & Kilpatrick, A. C. (1990). Prevention of child sexual abuse: A school based program evaluation. *Personnel Services* (ERIC #CG022566).

Peters, S. D. (1984). *The relationship between childhood sexual victimization and adult depression among Afro-American and white women*. Unpublished doctoral dissertation, University of California at Los Angeles, CA. (University Microfilms No. 84–28555)

Peters, S. D. (1988). Child sexual abuse and later psychological problems. In G. E. Wyatt & G. J. Powell (Eds.), *Lasting effects of child sexual abuse* (pp. 101–117). Beverly Hills, CA: Sage.

Peters, S. D., Wyatt, G. E., & Finkelhor, D. (1986). Prevalence. In D. Finkelhor (Ed.). *A source book on sexual child abuse* (pp. 75–93). Beverly Hills, CA: Sage.

Polansky, N. (1972). *Roots of futility*. San Francisco: Jossey-Bass.

Powell, G. J. (1988). Child sexual abuse research. In G. E. Wyatt & G. J. Powell (Eds.), *Lasting effects of child sexual abuse* (pp. 271–281). Beverly Hills, CA: Sage.

Rabinovitch, R. D. (1951). A study of sexually disturbed children. *Report of the Governor's Study Commission on the Deviated Criminal Sex Offender* (pp. 41–52). Lansing, MI.

Radzinowicz, L. (1948). *History of English criminal laws* (Vol. 1). New York: MacMillan.

Rasmussen, A. (1934). Die bedentung sexueller attenate auf kinder unter 14 jahren für die entwicklung von gister-Krank-heiten und charaktera normalien [The meaning of sexual attacks on children under 14 years of age for the development of mental illness and personality abnormalities]. *Acta Psychiatrica et Neurologica*, 351–434.

Reiss, I. L. (1966). The sexual renaissance: A summary and analysis. *Journal of Social Issues, 22*, 123–137.

Reiss, I. L. (1967). *The social context of premarital sexual permissiveness*. New York: Holt, Rinehart & Winston.

Renshaw, D. C. (1982). *Incest: Understanding and treatment*. Boston: Little, Brown.

Rogers, C. M., & Thomas J. N. (1984). Sexual victimization in the USA: Patterns and trends. *Clinical Proceedings, 40*(3/4), 211–221.

Rosenfeld, A. A. (1977). Sexual misuse and the family. *Victimology: An International Journal, 2*(2), 226–235.

Rush, F. (1980). *The best kept secret: Sexual abuse of children*. Englewood Cliffs, NJ: Prentice-Hall.

Russell, A. (1983). The incidence and prevalence of intrafamilial abuse of female children. *Child Abuse and Neglect, 7*(2), 133–146.

Russell, D. E. H. (1986). *The secret trauma: Incest in the lives of girls and women*. New York: Basic Books.

Saunders, B. E., & McClure, S. M. (1987, September). *Marital and family system functioning among incest families: Clinical and case management implications*. Paper presented at the 1987 annual program meeting of National Association of Social Workers, New Orleans, LA.

Saunders, B. E., McClure, S. M., & Murphy, S. M. (1987, July). *Structure, function, and symptoms in father–daughter sexual abuse families: A multilevel multirespondent empirical assessment*. Paper presented at the Family Violence Research Conference, Durham, NH.

Saunders, B. E., Villeponteaux, L. A., Kilpatrick, D. G., & Veronen, L. J. (1987, September). *Childhood sexual assault as a risk factor in mental health.* Paper presented at the 1987 annual program meeting of National Association of Social Workers, New Orleans, LA.

Schultz, L. G. (1973). The child sex victim: Social, psychological and legal perspectives. *Child Welfare, 52,* 148–149.

Schultz, L. G. (1980). The sexual abuse of children and minors: A short history of legal control efforts. In L. G. Schultz (Ed.), *The sexual victimology of youth* (pp. 3–17). Springfield, IL: Charles C. Thomas.

Sedney, M. A., & Brooks, B. (1984). Factors associated with a history of childhood sexual experience in a nonclinical female population. *Journal of the American Academy of Child Psychiatry, 23,* 215–218.

Sgroi, S. M. (1978). Child sexual assault: Some guidelines for investigation and assessment. In A. V. Burgess, A. N. Groth, L. L. Holmstrom, & S. M. Sgroi (Eds.), *Sexual assault of children and adolescents* (pp. 129–142). Lexington, MA: Heath.

Sgroi, S. M. (1982). *Handbook of clinical intervention in child sexual abuse.* Lexington, MA: Lexington Books.

Sloane, P., & Karpinski, E. (1942). Effects of incest on the participants. *American Journal of Orthopsychiatry, 12,* 666–673.

Spungen, C. A., Jensen, S. E., Finkelstein, N. W., & Satinsky, F. A. (1989). Child personal safety: Model program for prevention of child sexual abuse. *Social Work, 24*(2), 127–136.

Statistical Abstract of the United States. (1980). U.S. Department of Commerce, Bureau of the Census, Document No. C 3.134.

Straus, M. A., Gelles, R. J., & Steinmetz, S. K. (1980). *Behind closed doors: Violence in American families.* New York: Doubleday.

Sturkie, K. (1983). Structured group treatment of sexually abused children. *Health and Social Work, 8,* 29–308.

Summit, R., & Kryso, J. (1978). Sexual abuse of children: A clinical spectrum. *American Journal of Orthopsychiatry, 28*(2), 237–251.

Swift, C. (1978, January 11). *Sexual assault of children and adolescents.* From testimony prepared for the Subcommittee on Science and Technology of the United States House of Representatives, New York City.

Symonds, C. L., Mendoza, M. J., & Harrell, W. C. (1981). Forbidden sexual behavior among kin: A study of self-selected respondents. In L. L. Constantine & F. M. Martinson (Eds.), *Children and sex* (pp. 151–162). Boston: Little, Brown.

Thompson, S. (1955–1958). *Motif index of folk literature* (6 vols.). Bloomington, IN: University Press.

Tsai, M., Feldman-Summers, S., & Edgar, M. (1979). Childhood molestation: Differential impacts on psychosexual functioning. *Journal of Abnormal Psychology, 88,* 407–419.

U.S. Department of Commerce, Bureau of the Census. (1980). *Statistical Abstract of the United States* (Documents No. C3–134). Washington, DC: Author.

Vander Mey, B. J., & Neff, R. L. (1987). *Incest as child abuse.* New York: Praeger.

Vener, A. M., & Stewart, C. S., (1974). Adolescent sexual behavior in middle America revisited: 1970–1973. *Journal of Marriage and the Family, 36,* 728–735.

Vestergaard, E. (1960). Father–daughter incest. *Nord Tid. for Kriminalvid, 48,* 159.

Walker, L. E. (1988). *Handbook on sexual abuse of children: Assessment and treatment issues.* New York: Springer.

Wampler, K. S., Halverson, C. F., Moore, J. J., & Walters, L. H. (1989). The Georgia family Q-Sort: An observation measure of family functioning. *Family Process, 28,* 223–238.

Watkins, S. A. (1990). The Mary Ellen myth: Correcting child welfare history. *Social Work, 35*(6), 500–503.

*Webster's New World Dictionary of the American Language.* (1978). Second College Edition. Cleveland, OH: William Collins & World.

Weinberg, S. K. (1955). *Incest behavior.* New York: Citadel Press.

Weiner, I. B. (1962). Father–daughter incest: A clinical report. *Psychiatry Quarterly, 36,* 607–632.

Wilson, P. J. (1961). Incest: A case study. *Social and Economic Studies, 12,* 200–209.

Wodarski, J. S., & Johnson, S. R. (1988). Child sexual abuse: Contributing factors, effects, and relevant practice issues. *Family Therapy, 15*(2), 157–173.

Wyatt, G. E. (1985). The sexual abuse of Afro-American and White-American women in childhood. *Child Abuse and Neglect, 9,* 507–519.

Wyatt, G. E., & Powell, G. J. (Eds.). (1988). *Lasting effects of child sexual abuse.* Newbury Park, CA: Sage.

Zefran, J., Riley, H. F., Anderson, W. D., Curtis, J. H., Jackson, M., Kelly, P. H., McGury, E. T., & Suriano, M. K. (1982). Management and treatment of child sexual abuse cases in a juvenile court setting. *Journal of Social Work and Human Sexuality, 1,* 155–170.

Zelnik, M., & Kanter, J. (1977). Sexual and contraceptive experience of young unmarried women in the United States. *Family Planning Perspectives, 9,* 55–73.

# Author Index

# Subject Index